Ten Years of Federalism Reform in Germany

This book investigates the politics of federalism reform in Germany which has spanned over more than a decade. Different from reform attempts in other federal countries, the German reform was split up in three distinct steps: an adjustment of legislative powers between the federal and the state level, followed by the introduction of the 'debt brake', and, finally, the reform of fiscal equalization. Against the background of this sequential reform, this book not only discusses the effects of single reform steps, but also examines the results and inconsistencies of the overall reform process and reconsiders its cumulated effects. The contributions collected in this book cover a broad range of reform aspects, among them historical aspects, the role of party politics, changes in the legislative process, and the resurgence of joint decision-making. All chapters contribute to the theoretical framework which sheds a fresh view on the dynamics of federalism reforms. The chapters were originally published in a special issue of *Regional and Federal Studies*.

Nathalie Behnke leads the working group on Public Administration at the Department of Politics and Public Administration, University of Konstanz, Germany. In her research, she focuses on aspects of multi-level coordination, fiscal federalism and bureaucratic politics.

Sabine Kropp holds the chair for German Politics at the Otto Suhr Institute, Freie Universität Berlin, Germany. Her research interests cover various aspects of comparative federalism, governance and public administration.

Ten Years of Federalism Reform in Germany

Dynamics and Effects of Institutional Development

Edited by
Nathalie Behnke and Sabine Kropp

Routledge
Taylor & Francis Grou

LONDON AND NEW YORK

First published 2018 by Routledge

2 Park Square, Milton Park, Abingdon, Oxfordshire OX14 4RN
52 Vanderbilt Avenue, New York, NY 10017

Routledge is an imprint of the Taylor & Francis Group, an informa business

First issued in paperback 2019

British Library Cataloguing in Publication Data
A catalogue record for this book is available from the British Library

ISBN 13: 978-1-138-55057-5 (hbk)
ISBN 13: 978-0-367-89193-0 (pbk)

Typeset in Myriad Pro
by diacriTech, Chennai

Publisher's Note
The publisher accepts responsibility for any inconsistencies that may have arisen during the conversion of this book from journal articles to book chapters, namely the possible inclusion of journal terminology.

Disclaimer
Every effort has been made to contact copyright holders for their permission to reprint material in this book. The publishers would be grateful to hear from any copyright holder who is not here acknowledged and will undertake to rectify any errors or omissions in future editions of this book.

Contents

CONTENTS

Citation Information

The chapters in this book were originally published *Regional and Federal Studies*, volume 26, issue 5 (December 2016). When citing this material, please use the original page numbering for each article, as follows:

Chapter 1
Arraying institutional layers in federalism reforms: lessons from the German case
Nathalie Behnke and Sabine Kropp
Regional and Federal Studies, volume 26, issue 5 (December 2016) pp. 585–602

Chapter 2
The effects of federalism reform on the legislative process in Germany
Christian Stecker
Regional and Federal Studies, volume 26, issue 5 (December 2016) pp. 603–624

Chapter 3
The effect of reformed legislative competences on Länder *policy-making: determinants of fragmentation and uniformity*
Nicolai Dose and Iris Reus
Regional and Federal Studies, volume 26, issue 5 (December 2016) pp. 625–644

Chapter 4
The Role of Party and Coalition Politics in Federal Reform
Klaus Detterbeck
Regional and Federal Studies, volume 26, issue 5 (December 2016) pp. 645–666

Chapter 5
Marble cake dreaming of layer cake: the merits and pitfalls of disentanglement in German federalism reform
Sabine Kropp and Nathalie Behnke
Regional and Federal Studies, volume 26, issue 5 (December 2016) pp. 667–686

For any permission-related enquiries please visit:
http://www.tandfonline.com/page/help/permissions

Notes on Contributors

Nathalie Behnke is a Professor at the Department of Politics and Public Administration, Universität Konstanz, Germany.

Arthur Benz is a Professor at the Institute of Political Science, Technische Universität Darmstadt, Germany.

Klaus Detterbeck is based at the Institute of Political Science, Universität Göttingen, Germany.

Nicolai Dose is a Professor at the Institute for Political Science, Universität Duisburg-Essen, Germany.

Stefan Korioth is a Professor at the Faculty of Law, Ludwig Maximilian Universität München, Germany.

Sabine Kropp is a Professor at the Otto Suhr Institute, Freie Universität Berlin, Germany.

Astrid Lorenz is a Professor at the Institute of Political Science, Universität Leipzig, Germany.

Iris Reus is based at the Department of Social and Economic Sciences, Universität Bamberg, Germany.

Christian Stecker is based at the Mannheim Centre for European Social Research, Germany.

Arraying institutional layers in federalism reforms: lessons from the German case

Nathalie Behnke and Sabine Kropp

ABSTRACT
The introductory article to this Special Issue offers an analytical framework for investigating federal reforms. By looking through the lens of institutional theory, it provides an avenue for grasping the basic mechanisms which are at work in reform processes. It is argued that the German case which comprises three distinct reform steps stretching out over more than one decade represents an especially suitable example for understanding the general logics of federal reform. As a "prototype" of sequential, asynchronous reforms, it allows for generating theoretical insights beyond the findings of a single case study. The article reveals that layering, sequencing, and the linkage of different arenas are the most relevant aspects to be considered when examining federal reforms. Finally, it is established how the contributions to this Special Issue refer to the analytical categories worked out in this introduction.

1. The German federalism reform in comparative perspective

Germany, as one of the established federal democracies, is currently looking back to a decade of ongoing federalism reforms. Whereas the first constitutional reform finished in 2006 aimed at disentangling joint decision-making and effectively transferred a number of legislative responsibilities to the German *Länder*, the second reform stage finished in 2009 introduced the debt brake as a guarantor of the federal entities' fiscal responsibility and concomitantly established a stability council supervising their budgetary discipline. A major reform of the highly con-tested fiscal equalization scheme had initially been envisaged for the first stage, but was then shelved to the second and postponed again to some indefinite later time. Finally, since 2014, minister presidents and finance ministers of the *Länder* have been preparing proposals renegotiating the fiscal relations for a third step of federalism reform with a result still pending at the time of this writing. As a minimal solution, the *Bundestag* and *Bundesrat* can simply extend the validity of the current laws due to expire in 2019. There is a fair chance, however, for getting a reform law passed by parliament by the upcoming federal elections in 2017, which would then – albeit preliminarily – conclude a decade of stepwise federalism reform.

As a real-life laboratory of a long-term debate on reforming established federal institutions and norms, this process aroused considerable interest among federalism scholars. Similar to other federal reform processes in established federations[1] as well as in emerging or transforming federal structures,[2] the analysis of such continuing, sequential reforms helps to better grasp the inherent logic of federal reforms in general. The German case offers prolific evidence on the institutions that are being changed, the normative discourses employed to promote particular reform directions, and the role of different actors involved. Accordingly, research on the German reform process focuses on details of the issues at stake and their likely consequences. This includes for example the redistribution of legislative responsibilities in the first reform stage (Georgii and Borhanian, 2006; Höreth, 2007; Burkhart et al., 2008), a critical evaluation of the debt brake and concomitant provisions of administrative cooperation in the second phase (Baus, 2007; Feld, 2010; Kastrop et al., 2010), and controversial analyses of the principles and techniques stipulating how to distribute and redistribute public revenues among the federal units in the third reform step (Geißler et al., 2015). Other contributions are dedicated to actors and the normative arguments they employ to promote their preferred vision of the reform (Münch and Zinterer, 2000; Hrbek, 2003). A steadily growing strand of literature addresses the (more or less limited) dynamics of the reforms by offering particular explanations as to why such a big effort has resulted in such little change (Benz, 2005; Sturm, 2010; Schneider, 2013). Fritz W. Scharpf's notion of the joint decision trap (Scharpf, 1985, 2009; Auel, 2008; Benz, 2008) has probably been the explanation most frequently invoked when reasoning about the limited output and impact of the reform efforts (for a critique see Benz, 2005, 2008).

In spite of the numerous accounts on the issue, no encompassing analysis examining the complete sequence of reform steps has ever been offered so far. This research gap becomes all the more relevant, as it is particularly the long-term perspective which allows gaining a more precise understanding of the mechanisms that lie at the heart of developments of federal institutions and processes. Actually, federal dynamics has marked the cutting edge of comparative federalism scholarship in recent years (Gerber and Kollman, 2004; Benz and Broschek, 2013b; Bolleyer et al., 2014). One noteworthy insight stemming from comparative analyses of constitutional reforms in federal states is that change, continuity, and stability interact (Benz and Broschek, 2013a). The absence of change looks like stability only superficially, but it leads to stalemate and, ultimately, to the rupture of systems.

More precisely, the institutional complexity inherent in the federal architecture and the plurality of interests and positions involved make frequent adaptations necessary in order to sustain the stability of the system (Behnke and Benz, 2009). In addition to federal reforms, institutional, political, and jurisdictional safeguards help to balance centripetal and centrifugal dynamics (Bednar, 2009). Furthermore, mechanisms facilitating an ongoing dialogue between conflicting interests are an essential requisite for securing long-term federal stability without stalemate (Tully, 1995; Hueglin, 2000), a concept which Charles Taylor describes as "procedural liberalism" (Taylor, 1992).

In this context, we conceptualize federal reforms as formal and legally fixed provisions which respond to political, social, and economic dynamics by adapting and changing the institutional setting. Once enacted, however, they take on a life on their own: they affect other subsystems, trigger dynamics, and demand new institutional modifications. Germany is an especially illustrative case in point, since the reform was split up into three distinct stages. This particular dynamic becomes obvious in that decisions made in one round triggered new problems and created institutional tensions, to which actors responded with institutional adaptations and corrections in the next round of the reform. This piecemeal approach finally led to a meandering – not to say inconsistent – reform path, which, for its part, graphically illuminates the interdependence between institutional adaptation and stability. In this sense, a framework for analysing federal reforms must account for the mechanisms that maintain long-term stability through change or through adaptation of the differential features constituting the federal system.

This Special Issue contributes to gaining a deeper understanding of the outlined puzzle. By providing a common analytic framework for all contributions containing relevant variables for studying and explaining the initiation, development and consequences of long-term territorial reform processes, this introduction enables generalization beyond the German case and further advances our understanding of the mechanisms of federal reforms. Moreover, as the contributions assembled in this Special Issue study the reform process from different perspectives, a more complete picture of the federal dynamics caused by the sequential reforms is drawn. At the end of this introductory framework, it is briefly sketched how the contributions in this Special Issue echo the elements of this theoretical perspective in their analyses.

3

2. Understanding the dynamics of federal reforms – elements of an analytical framework

Federal systems are more frequently subject to constitutional reforms than their unitary counterparts (Lorenz, 2011). It is inherent in the nature of federal systems that they continually produce tensions and frictions which demand institutional adaptations (Benz and Broschek, 2013a). Hence, they are disposed to reform, although they are characterized by a high number of veto points which may lead to deadlock and stalemate.

While actors initiate change because of a rational motivation to solve problems or to improve their relative positions, the effects of those changes often produce unintended consequences and spill-overs as well as creating frictions or incompatibilities with other unchanged institutional layers, thus making adaptive reforms necessary to redress the frictions (Pierson, 2000b). Furthermore, rational motives may overlap with ideological ones, and ideas about the best world of federalism may change over time or with changing political majorities (Lieberman, 2002). The ensuing pattern is far from an unambiguous causal relationship between motive and result. The puzzle which calls for an explanation is thus not the fact that federal reforms are initiated and enacted at all, that is, not the fact of institutional change per se, but rather it is the sequential structure, the "layering" of reforms and the inconsistent or piecemeal approach to reforms over time. The framework developed here is meant to provide the ingredients for a systematic analysis of this inconsistent and stepwise reform path.

Even though institutionalist theories are sometimes said to explain stability better than change (Schmidt, 2008), the institutional perspective is useful in analysing federal reforms insofar as institutions substantially structure actors' role orientations, preferences, and interactions. Those actors are constrained by the existing institutions and produce outcomes which may themselves alter a given institutional framework. This account is very close to what Fritz W. Scharpf termed "actor-centred institutionalism" (ACI) (Mayntz and Scharpf, 1995; Scharpf, 1997). In our framework, however, we adhere to the broader institutionalist perspective (Hall and Taylor, 1996; Nee, 2005; Scott, 2014) which provides useful notions for investigating degrees, pace, and directions of change. This contribution upholds the focus on actors pursuing individual preferences as drivers and subjects of change that refers to Scharpf's ACI as well as Rational Choice Institutionalism in general (Shepsle, 2006). In addition, by focusing on the procedural nature of reforms which extend over a longer period of time and are marked by sequences, we employ the "historic" perspective distinctive of Historical Institutionalism (HI) (Mahoney et al., 2009). HI was traditionally more concerned with explaining the absence of change by notions such as path dependency (Pierson, 2000a) than by the extent or direction of change. In recent years, however, scholars of HI have developed a fine-tuned conceptual tool-kit to analyse processes of institutional changes stretching along longer time-spans (Orren and Skowronek, 1994; Lieberman, 2002; Pierson, 2004; Mahoney and Thelen, 2010; Broschek, 2011). The "multiple-orders approach" (Orren and Skowronek, 1994; Broschek, 2011) emphasizes the multi-dimensionality of complex institutional frameworks such as federal constitutions. Those different layers can embody incompatible logics, thus creating a mismatch and frictions as well as a permanent pressure for adjustment (Broschek, 2011: 540). Also, the role of ideas in shaping the content and direction of institutional change was conceptualized and integrated in the institutionalist framework (Lieberman, 2002). The solutions that actors envisage for perceived problems have been largely influenced by the visions or normative ideas they hold about the state of the world. Again, as such ideas are put into practice in federal reforms, this may produce discontinuities and incompatibilities that drive adaptive change (Lieberman, 2002: 698).

As regards the role of ideas in the institutional reform process, an important debate among institutionalist scholars revolves around the question whether the ideas guiding actors are endogenous or exogenous to the explanatory framework (Lieberman, 2002; Farrell and Héritier, 2007: 701): Should they be an integral part of the analysis or are they something of a residual explanatory variable resorted to when other explanations fail? In the sequential account to federal reforms, this is not an "either-or question". Rather, the extended time span of the process suggests that both will be the case. On the one hand, people change their opinions in reaction to outcomes they observe (in that case, ideas are endogenous to the process). On the other hand, external developments may support particular visions and thus contribute to changing majorities among advocates of a special vision or idea (exogenous, changing the decision situation for the actors).

Based on this broader institutionalist perspective, we further elaborate on the building blocks of analysis: the actors of reform; the role of ideas; the triggers and layers of reform causing particular reform dynamics; and the content, direction, and mode of reform in order to take into account not only the formal, but also the substantial aspects of change. In the final section of this introduction, we sketch how the contributions to this Special Issue make use of the analytical categories in building their explanations.

2.1. Actors of reform

All types of institutionalism acknowledge the crucial role of actors in triggering, negotiating, and enacting institutional changes. Actors need to perceive a necessity or opportunity for institutional change and they must have an incentive to enact change in a certain direction. Incentives may come from cost-benefit-calculations or from ideological persuasion (or both). In institutionalist analyses, actors are mostly treated as complex actors, in which internal processes of preference formation are neglected (Scharpf, 2000: 101–105). Relevant actors in federal reforms are executives (government and administration) as well as parliaments of federal entities holding a mix of interests. *Länder* governments, for example, pursue specific interests of their individual *Land*, of a group of *Länder* (e.g. Eastern vs. Western or rich vs. poor *Länder*) or of the entirety of *Länder* towards the federal level. Those interests that are tied to the status and structural properties of a territory intersect with party political interests of the governing coalitions. Parties are thus another group of relevant actors, because they usually set the electoral and legislative agenda. In comparative federalism studies, the relationship between party politics and territorial dynamics is an influential field of research. Parties, either statewide, nationalist, or regionalist, have been identified as the main drivers of territorial change (Meguid, 2005; Swenden and Maddens, 2009; Toubeau and Massetti, 2013). Sometimes, constitutional courts act as initiators or brokers of reforms. But also elites, citizens, and associations address specific demands to federal institutions (Erk, 2008). If their expectations do not match the functioning of given institutions, then dynamics can be triggered either from "below" or from "above".

While actors are the main drivers of institutional change, they are just as much affected by it. Institutional changes can alter actor constellations, attitudes, and behaviour of individual as well as organizational structures of collective actors. Federal reforms often generate new majorities and reshape actor constellations in addition to sculpting the internal structure of organizations. Having gained more rights of self-rule or shared rule, parliaments and executives of federal entities usually establish new committees or routines of information processing, of internal, horizontal, and vertical coordination. Parties need to adapt their internal organizations to the changing territorial power allocation. If social, political, and economic asymmetries increase, then parties need to grant their regional branches greater autonomy, thereby setting up processes which lead to the emergence of a more regionalized party system (Detterbeck, 2012). When parties recalibrate their internal structures to processes of regionalization, the result can be a perpetuated dynamic of decentralization (Hombrado, 2011; Petersohn et al., 2015) or at least a continued negotiation on how to balance unity and diversity (Hueglin, 2013). Like other European democracies, Germany has undergone such development of its party system, albeit to a smaller degree. Research has observed a growing diversification of the regional party systems which has generated multi-coloured *Länder* coalition governments. As a consequence, majorities often need to be negotiated in the *Bundesrat*, which makes joint decision-making less calculable for the federal government, but enhances flexibility by dissolving the logic of the formerly bipolar party competition (Kropp, 2010).

2.2. The role of ideas

While most actors in federal states may agree on the general virtues of a federal state architecture as opposed to the unitary state one, they still hold utterly distinct views on the basic ontological question: *e pluribus unum* – how much diversity or unity is desired and acceptable for the federal entity, and what does this diversity and unity refer to? Responses to this problem essentially shape the content and direction of reforms.

In multi-ethnic states, for example, the problem of balancing unity and diversity is most acute. It raises the questions as to which levels of individual vs. group rights are suitable for sustaining the stability of the federation, how federal units are adequately represented in federal processes, or which degree of autonomy they should possess (Gagnon and Tully, 2001; Choudhry, 2008). Even in largely homogenous societies, this tight relationship needs to be permanently calibrated. The German federal reform provides rich material for illustrating how challenging this task may become. Although the values of unity and equality are clearly placed over diversity and are reflected in various constitutional principles such as federal loyalty ("*Bundestreue*") or the equivalence of living conditions ("*Gleichwertigkeit der Lebensverhältnisse*"), the question of how to translate "equivalence" of living conditions into federal practice has recurrently been subject to conflict and redefinition.

If federations undergo piecemeal reforms, then prevalent normative ideas can be toned down or even replaced by alternative ones during the reform period. The German case perfectly illuminates the fact that the ideological underpinnings of proposals have changed several times. The first reform stage was dominated by the ideas of disentanglement, competition, autonomy, and dual federalism. An encompassing actor coalition of most parties, influential think tanks, and the federal as well as the governments of the donor *Länder* promoted those ideas. An ideological macro-trend – the neo-liberal market ideology promoting economic efficiency through competition and a withdrawal of the state – coincided with material interests of the donor *Länder*. The German unification had increased the number of recipient *Länder* from 5 to 11 and changed the political interests of the federal government which claimed more leeway in legislation (i.e. less influence of the *Bundesrat*) for enacting large-scale reforms. Some noteworthy adjudications of the federal constitutional court with their concomitant normative weight supported the shift towards disentanglement.

The second step, which in 2009 introduced the debt brake and the stability council, was deeply imprinted by the experience of the European economic, fiscal, and debt crisis. Hence, budgetary austerity and economic stability were broadly promoted as the leitmotiv of reform. The federal government was setting the pace, while the voices warning about the negative economic effects of strict austerity were being ignored. The ensuing German and

European "debt brakes" put additional pressure on the federal and the *Länder* governments. The restrictions put on the income side met increasing demands on the expense side, mainly due to the steadily increasing burden of social security expenses, but also because of the recent expansion of *Länder* tasks introduced by the first reform stage. The tightened financial leeway was, however, felt with differing intensity and contributed more to exacerbating the existing vertical and horizontal fiscal imbalance in Germany. The growing divide fuelled debates about which kind and degree of unity was to be pursued and generated disputes as to how the costs of unity should be distributed among the federal units. The second step thus heralded the third one which was designed to reassess the fiscal equalization scheme, which, in any case, became inevitable as the relevant fiscal laws will run out at the end of 2019. Currently, the idea of solidarity regains weight in the public debate, but it is far from being undisputed. Headed by Bavaria, a small but powerful coalition of the donor states strives for reducing the level and extent of fiscal equalization payments, arguing with the principles of autonomy and ability. At the same time, counter to the 2006 reform, some contested decisions which had implemented elements of dual federalism are being acknowledged as dysfunctional and were abrogated again.

2.3. Reform dynamics: triggers and layers

The interplay between actors and ideas helps to explain how, when, or under which circumstances federal reforms are triggered and unfold over time. Very generally, the existing institutional structure must be inefficient or dysfunctional to spark attempts at reform. However, the faulty working of an institution is not an objective matter of fact. It is not discovered by a calculation rule or undisputedly stated by a group of experts. Rather, actors judge the existing order as inadequate. This evaluation is permeated by beliefs and prevailing ideas and possibly influenced by diffusing institutional models which have gained interpretative authority.

It may happen, for example, that a group of actors holding a specific idea about the federal institutional structure gains more bargaining power and can thus press for reforms. They regard institutions as dysfunctional because the existing allocation of jurisdictions and responsibilities between federal units no longer mirrors their real power. Similarly, decision-making processes are considered as dysfunctional if they produce either abundant negotiation costs which result in deadlocks and delayed decisions due to the number of veto players involved (Buchanan and Tullock, 1962), or if they cause excessive external costs, involving decisions at the cost of minorities. Those perceptions are often caused by shifts of economic power, the socio-structural composition, and the political resources of groups.

In another scenario, external political developments contribute to a change in public opinion which brings together different groups of actors advocating a specific direction of change. The global financial crisis beginning in 2008, for instance, seriously undermined the legitimacy of neo-liberal ideas and gave notions like solidarity an – albeit limited – boost. Moreover, in European countries, the EU works as a constant source of institutional adaptation. Over the past decades all institutional and administrative settings have had to undergo encompassing processes (Börzel and Risse, 2003; Radaelli, 2003). External changes in the perception about the (dys-)functionality of the existing institutional structure may also be triggered by the incongruity of policy issues. As multi-level systems distribute power among different levels and territorial or non-territorial units (see for example McGarry and Moore, 2005), policy problems regularly intersect territorial or functional borders. When federal institutions impair the principle of congruity between those jurisdictions taking a decision and those which are affected by a decision (Benz and Sonnicksen, 2015; Kropp, 2015), reforms may aim at rescaling policies so that the boundaries of jurisdictions coincide better with their fiscal responsibilities and effects.

Finally, apart from questions of power of groups or external pressure for adaptation, existing institutions may be perceived to conflict with democracy because they blur accountability. Then, reforms may be triggered by different groups of actors, elites, the population, parties, or individual governments with the aim of restoring legitimacy by re-establishing more clear-cut accountabilities in the territorial structure. As federal systems provide strong veto points, they are reliant on consensus-building mechanisms and negotiations running through informal channels which make the formal institutions work. As such, federal institutions tend to obscure responsibilities and, consequently, are perceived as being opaque and prone to elite capture (Kropp, 2015). Due to the complex distribution of responsibilities, voters in federal systems often do not react to decisions at the level where they are made, but rather address demands and protest to the authorities of other jurisdictions. It may therefore become one of the major goals of reform to restore legitimacy by re-adapting decision-making structures to the boundaries of *demoi*. This sometimes implies such complex challenges as boundary shifting and authority migration (Gerber and Kollman, 2004).

Often, the changes achieved themselves become triggers for new rounds of negotiations, thus making the sequence of reform steps an important category for analysis. Different "layers" of a federal system can simultaneously or asynchronously be subject to just one or sometimes to even several changes. New rounds of reform are triggered if changes in institutions, power distributions, or actor constellations call for adapting other layers of the federal structure (Benz and Broschek, 2013a: 5ff.)[3] or if the changes result in tensions between formal and informal institutions. Later reforms can consequentially refine and reinforce erstwhile reforms; they can deviate from an already existing reform path, take up remaining topics or contradict them. Hence: timing, sequencing, layering, and the linkage of arenas prove to be the most relevant aspects to be considered when analysing reform processes (Braun, 2009; Benz and Sonnicksen, 2015). Analytically, however, it is sometimes hard to distinguish when one sequence ends and the next begins since reforms do not always consist of clear-cut, consistent phases.

Sequential reforms, as realized in the German case, are prone to generate meandering or even inconsistent reforms if its different stages are guided by divergent or perhaps conflicting principles, or if they modify different institutional layers which, again, trigger adaptive or restorative change in other layers. Vice versa, even though one reform sequence may suggest that it generates an encompassing change, an assessment of the whole reform can reveal that the federal institutional setting remains nonetheless on the established historical path. The German case thus offers deep and generalizable insights in the multi-directional and multi-layered effects of federalism reform.

2.4. Substance of reforms: content, direction, and extension

Federal reforms typically re-allocate power distributions and responsibilities for specific issues among various levels of government. Power and responsibilities comprise jurisdictions (legislative, executive, and judicial); financial resources and fiscal responsibilities (tax levying or tax varying powers and tax distribution); representation and modes of decision-making (such as quotas or reserved seats in parliament, veto rights or rights of co-decision, unanimity vs. majority rule, and the number and proportion of actors involved). Power distributions can shift horizontally, that is, from symmetry to asymmetry and vice versa, or vertically, that is, towards increasing centralization or decentralization. Still, the centralization–decentralization dimension cannot sufficiently capture degrees of change in self-rule or shared rule (Petersohn et al., 2015). While federal reforms may empower actors differentially, this may lead to new interest coalitions and trigger counter-movements in order to re-balance the power distribution.

In this sense, the duration, extent, and direction of results are also of relevance for the overall reform dynamic. In the German reform, we recurrently observe that formal reforms were later redressed either by superseding legislation, by adjudication of the constitutional court or by administrative practice. This shows that the distinction between *formal* and *informal* change is partially artificial, as processes of informal change often end in formal reforms and vice versa. Formal change is said to occur when it emerges as the result of institutionalized processes which alter norms at constitutional level, while informal change comes about by re-interpretations of existing norms, adaptation of routines or changes of norms at sub-constitutional and extra-legal level (Behnke and Benz, 2009; Benz and Colino, 2011; Lorenz, 2011), and is diagnosed when it takes place away from the surface of formal federalism reforms.

Similarly, the extent of reforms itself can explain further reform dynamics. Formal change often just leads to piecemeal adaptation due to the complexity of issues at stake. It is easier to evoke consensus among negotiation partners on single issues rather than on all encompassing reform packages. The failed constitutional convention in Austria is a good example for illuminating a reform process in which the complexity of interwoven topics could not be handled in the given time frame (Behnke, 2010). Such piecemeal approaches, on the other hand, trigger subsequent reforms, as due to the tight interrelation between policy issues, responsibilities, and resources, changes of one aspect of the federal structure usually spill over to others. A change in fiscal relations (e.g. tax allocation or equalization payments), for instance, cannot be neatly separated from the discussion about the allocation of and the financial responsibility for tasks. Reversing this argument, it can be assumed that connecting issues in reform debates offers opportunities for package deals and can thus contribute to avoiding deadlock.

3. Analysing federalism reform dynamics: insights from the contributions to this special issue

In highlighting different aspects of the ten years long federalism reform in Germany, the contributions to this Special Issue fill the analytic categories introduced in the preceding section with empirical evidence. Perspectives on the topic focus on historical (Benz) and immediate (Stecker) antecedents; they investigate the consequences and outcomes (Dose and Reus; Stecker; Korioth) and explore the sequences and layers of the process (Kropp and Behnke; Benz). Several contributions devote particular attention to the actors of the reform. Whereas Detterbeck examines the changing mode of the German federal party system, Stecker as well as Dose and Reus focus on the German *Länder*. Others investigate how ideas transformed into reform results, that is, which substantial answers were given to the basic question of how to balance unity and diversity (Stecker; Dose and Reus; Korioth). Finally, the contribution of Lorenz puts the German case in comparative perspective, thereby embedding the empirical findings into a broader context. In terms of the theoretical elements provided by this framework, the contributions present relevant findings and set the scene for a broader comparative perspective.

The role of different actors or actor coalitions and their interests in triggering reforms is analysed in all contributions. Main actors were the federal and *Länder* governments and parliaments (Stecker; Dose and Reus; Kropp and Behnke), the political parties (Detterbeck), the constitutional court (Korioth) as well as municipal umbrella organizations (Kropp and Behnke), think tanks, single experts, and societal pressure groups (Benz). Stecker elaborates on the significance of actor coalitions, showing that it was not the institutional provisions alone which caused the (dys-)functionality of an institution, but rather the strategic use actors make of it. Most prominent actors were the reform commissions during the first and second reforms. Composed of representatives of the federal and the *Länder* levels, of parliamentarians and the executive under the dual leadership of the two major parties, they mirrored almost exactly the cleavages of German federalism (Detterbeck) which formed an "octagon" consisting of East and West German *Länder*, of rich and poor ones, of federal and common *Länder* interests, and of party cleavages. At the third reform stage, in contrast, no commission was established. Instead, the negotiations on future fiscal relations have been conducted within the existing intergovernmental bodies mainly composed of either the minister presidents or the finance ministers. They proceed in a completely informal manner largely secluded from the public.

Most contributions identify *ideas* as the main *triggers* of reform. As noted above, those ideas considerably changed over the stages of the reform process, with the first reform stage being dominated by arguments highlighting the perceived dysfunctionality of existing federal institutions. Stecker highlights that the German federalism with its numerous veto points and, in particular, the strong legislative participation of the *Bundesrat* was identified as a basic cause for slow and incremental decision-making. Kropp and Behnke show how an informal coalition of the economically and financially powerful *Länder*, neo-liberal academics, and think tanks successfully challenged the ideational foundation of equivalent living conditions by advocating disentanglement and the model of dual federalism as a promising solution. Korioth elucidates how the Federal Constitutional Court changed its current ruling concerning financial solidarity towards more autonomy of the *Länder*. Regardless of lawyers' opinions which alerted decision-makers to the fragmentation of law and increasing asymmetries as consequences of the reform, the new distribution of legislative responsibilities allowed for greater variation in policy-making across the *Länder* due to a longer catalogue of exclusive legislative responsibilities or deviation rights from federal legislation. The effects of this paradigmatic shift on policy-making varieties are investigated by Dose and Reus who spell out the scope and consequences of the reform.

In the second and third reform steps, the triggering role of ideas was less explicitly pronounced than in the first. While the relevant political and societal actors at all levels of government made use of a similar rhetoric, the reform content and direction marked a move away from the competitive and dual federalism ideal of the first reform step. Accordingly, Korioth points out that the second reform step, which led to the establishment of the debt brake and the stability council, was guided by the model of fiscal austerity. His article reveals that the *Länder* no longer pursued the goal of autonomy, but were rather willing to accept increased involvement and control of the federal government in exchange for financial support. Finally, in the third reform step aimed at reforming fiscal relations in the federal system, the article of Kropp and Behnke reveals how the basic ideas of federalism partially returned to the notion of solidarity and joint responsibility.

Responding to the shifting models guiding the reform sequences, actors reversed the *content and direction* of reform from one stage to the next. Stecker analyses the reform of legislative competences by looking into changes of shared rule in the *Bundesrat*. Indeed, the number of approval laws in the *Bundesrat* decreased. Accordingly, as Dose and Reus show, policy fragmentation in fields of devolved legislative responsibilities increased slightly. The second reform step, in contrast, strengthened the federal government by establishing the stability council and the debt brake. From the perspective of constitutional law, Korioth illustrates how the debt brake and the stability council question the *Länder's* exclusive jurisdictions. In terms of administrative procedures and joint tasks, this led to a remarkable re-entanglement, partly reversing the initiatives of the first reform step (Kropp and Behnke). The third stage is aimed exclusively at unwinding fiscal entanglements, readjusting the tax distribution, and simplifying the equalization scheme. Whether this will lead to more centralization or to a decentralization of fiscal jurisdictions is to date still an open question. While no final compromise has been struck yet, first agreements among the *Länder* show a unanimous tendency towards a "verticalization" of fiscal transfers. That is, the *Länder* are willing to trade in a part of their (anyway strongly limited) fiscal autonomy in exchange for receiving greater and more reliable financial support from the federal level – a solution which would clearly work in favour of centralization.

The contributions come to divergent assessments of the *extent* of change. In its strictest terms, the reform package of 2006 was the most comprehensive constitutional reform since the adoption of the Basic Law in 1949. In substance, though, it did not effectively alter the substance of intertwined federalism. Even though a limited number of responsibilities were disentangled and transferred to the state or the federal level (Dose and Reus), the reform did not extensively move the federal system towards the pole of dual federalism, something which Benz criticizes in his contribution. Similarly, Korioth blames the second step as mainly symbolic politics and questions its effectivity in limiting new deficits.

In several contributions, a long-term perspective of constitutional reform is taken (Kropp and Behnke; Lorenz; Benz) which pays particular attention to aspects of timing, sequence, and layering. Kropp and Behnke explain the zig-zag pattern of the stepwise reform across the three stages – from disentanglement to re-entanglement – by pointing out that initially one layer of the federal system – the allocation of responsibilities – had been changed, but was not accompanied by a concomitant transfer of fiscal duties. This generated an institutional incongruity which in itself called for subsequent reforms to remedy the inconsistencies. In her comparative analysis, Lorenz argues that frequency and scope of reforms depend on a country's constitutional culture, something which can be attributed to the tradition of shared rule federations on the one hand and dual federations on the other hand. Shared rule federations are shaped by a collaborative interaction style, and actors prefer explicit constitutional agreements. Both characteristics facilitate frequent amendments. As Germany is categorized as a shared rule federation, the relative frequency of constitutional reforms as well as the cooperative interaction mode is consistent with her argument. Taking on the perspective of HI, Benz maintains that the German reform process can best be understood from a long-term perspective. According to his analysis, the insufficient reform result is owed to path dependent institutions, particularly to contradicting developments of visions and institutions, some of which worked in favour of unity and some of which were in favour of diversity. Benz highlights that these contradictions have for centuries called for mechanisms appropriate to overcome tensions; they have given rise to the practice of negotiation and governing by consensus and thus have strengthened inter-administrative relations.

The contributions assembled in this Special Issue provide some generalizable features of federalism reform which can be fruitful for further comparative research. The German case is a striking – not to say extreme (Gerring, 2008) – case representing a sequential, asynchronous reform attempt. As such, it reveals that layering, sequencing, and the linkage of different arenas are the most relevant aspects when federations undergo institutional reforms. It exemplarily demonstrates that reforms confined to one institutional layer trigger dynamics in others and that synchronous changes in various layers interact, sometimes producing unintended outcomes. All these elements play a role in other reform processes as well, albeit in various combinations and to different degrees. Considering this inherent logic of federalism reforms, it becomes evident why many of them need to be readjusted after a while, be it formally or by applying informal adaptations. As institutionalized attempts which respond to existing change and set up new developments, federal reforms usually represent just one chapter in a long-term horizon of federal dynamics.

Notes

1. Examples are the long-lasting constitutional reform debate in Canada (Russell, 2004) or the constitutional reforms in Switzerland (1987–2004) and in Austria (2002–2005) with varying success (Freiburghaus, 2002; Bußjäger, 2004; Braun, 2009; Behnke, 2010).
2. Examples are the devolution policy in the UK (Bradbury and Mitchell, 2005; Jeffery, 2009; Keating and McEwen, 2005; Mitchell, 2009) or the series of

constitutional reforms in Belgium (Poirier, 2002; Hooghe, 2003; Swenden et al., 2006; De Winter and Baudewyns, 2009; Deschouwer, 2009).

3. Benz and Broschek (2013a: 8) distinguish four federal layers, which they call "societal", "institutional", "normative/ ideational", and "constellation of actors". Those factors are all contained in our analytic framework as well, either as triggers for change or as elements of change. Therefore, we can directly build on their very useful notion of "layers".

Acknowledgements

We would like to thank the two reviewers for their thoughtful comments on this paper.

Disclosure statement

No potential conflict of interest was reported by the authors.

References

Auel, K. (2008), Still no exit from the joint decision trap: the German federal reform(s), *German Politics*, Vol.17, No.4, pp.424–439.

Baus, R. (ed) (2008), *Föderalismusreform II: Weichenstellungen für eine Neuordnung der Finanbeziehungen im deutschen Bundesstaat*. Baden-Baden: Nomos.

Bednar, J. (2009), *The Robust Federation. Principles of Design*. Cambridge: Cambridge University Press.

Behnke, N. (2010), Föderalismusreform in Deutschland, der Schweiz und Österreich, in J. v. Blumenthal and S. Bröchler (eds), *Föderalismusreform in Deutschland. Bilanz und Perspektiven im internationalen Vergleich* (pp.37–58). Wiesbaden: VS-Verlag.

Behnke, N. and Benz, A. (2009), The politics of constitutional change between reform and evolution, *Publius: The Journal of Federalism*, Vol.39, No.2, pp.213–240.

Benz, A. (2005), Kein Ausweg aus der Politikverflechtung? – Warum die Bundesstaatskommission scheiterte, aber nicht scheitern musste, *Politische Vierteljahresschrift*, Vol.46, No.2, pp.204–214.

Benz, A. (2008), From joint decision traps to over-regulated federalism: adverse effects of a successful constitutional reform, *German Politics*, Vol.17, No.4, pp.440–456.

Benz, A. and Broschek, J. (2013a), Introduction, in A. Benz and J. Broschek (eds), *Federal Dynamics: Continuity, Change and Varieties of Federalism*, pp.i.E. Oxford: Oxford University Press.

Benz, A. and Broschek, J. (eds) (2013b), *Federal Dynamics*. Oxford: Oxford University Press.

Benz, A. and Colino, C. (2011), Constitutional change in federations – a framework for analysis, *Regional & Federal Studies*, Vol.21, No.4–5, pp. 381–406.

Benz, A. and Sonnicksen, J. (2015), Federalism and democracy – compatible or at odds with one, in C. Fraenkel-Haeberle, S. Kropp, F. Palermo and K.-P. Sommermann (eds), *Citizen Participation in Multi-Level Democracies*. Leiden: Brill Nijhoff.

Bolleyer, N., et al. (2014), A theoretical perspective on multi-level systems in Europe: constitutional power and partisan conflict, *Comparative European Politics*, Vol.12, No.4, pp.367–383.

Börzel, T.A. and Risse, T. (2003), Conceptualizing the domestic impact of Europe, in K. Featherstone and C. M. Radaelli (eds), *The Politics of Europeanization*, pp.57–80. Oxford: Oxford University Press.

Bradbury, J. and Mitchell, J. (2005), Devolution: between governance and territorial politics, *Parliamentary Affairs*, Vol.58, No.2, pp.287–302.

Braun, D. (2009), Verfassungsänderung trotz vieler Veto-Spieler: Föderalismusreform in der Schweiz, in T. Bräuninger, S. Shikano and J. Behnke (eds), *Jahrbuch für Handlungs- und Entscheidungstheorie*, pp.87–118. Wiesbaden: VS Verlag.

Broschek, J. (2011), Conceptualizing and theorizing constitutional change in federal systems: insights from historical institutionalism, *Regional & Federal Studies*, Vol.21, No.4–5, pp.539–559.

Buchanan, J.M. and Tullock, G. (1962), *The Calculus of Consent. Logical Foundations of Constitutional Democracy*. Ann Arbor: University of Michigan Press.

Burkhart, S., et al. (2008), A more efficient and accountable federalism? An analysis of the consequences of Germany's 2006 constitutional reform, *German Politics*, Vol.17, No.4, pp.522–540.

Bußjäger, P. (2004), Der Österreich-Konvent als Chance oder Inszenierung? - der Bundesstaat Österreich vor einem neuen Anlauf der Verfassungsreform, in Europäisches Zentrum für Föderalismusforschung (ed), *Jahrbuch des Föderalismus 2004*, pp.248–263. Baden-Baden: Nomos.

Choudhry, S. (ed) (2008), *Constitutional Design for Divided Societies: Integration or Accommodation?* Oxford: Oxford University Press.

Deschouwer, K. (2009), *The Politics of Belgium. Governing a Divided Society*. Basingstoke: Palgrave Macmillan.

Detterbeck, K. (2012), *Multi-level Party Politics in Western Europe. Comparative Territorial Politics*. New York: Palgrave Macmillan.

De Winter, L. and Baudewyns, P. (2009), Belgium: towards the breakdown of a nation-state in the heart of Europe? *Nationalism and Ethnic Politics*, Vol.15, No.3–4, pp.280–304.

Erk, J. (2008), *Explaining Federalism. State, Society and Congruence in Austria, Belgium, Canada, Germany and Switzerland*. London and New York: Routledge.

Farrell, H. and Héritier, A. (2007), Codecision and institutional change, *West European Politics*, Vol.30, No.2, pp.285–300.

Feld, L.P. (2010), Sinnhaftigkeit und Effektivität der deutschen Schuldenbremse, *Perspektiven der Wirtschaftspolitik*, Vol.11, No.3, pp.226–245.

Freiburghaus, D. (2002), Neuer Finanzausgleich und Föderalismusreform in der Schweiz, in Europäisches Zentrum für Föderalismus-Forschung (ed), *Jahrbuch des Föderalismus 2002*, pp.374–387. Baden-Baden: Nomos Verlagsgesellschaft.

Gagnon, A.-G. and Tully, J. (eds) (2001), *Multinational Democracies*. Cambridge: Cambridge University Press.

Geißler, R., et al. (eds) (2015), *Das Teilen beherrschen. Analysen zur Reform des Finanzausgleichs 2019*. Baden-Baden: Nomos.

Georgii, H. and Borhanian, S. (2006), *Zustimmungsgesetze nach der Föderalismusreform*. Berlin: Wissenschaftliche Dienste des Deutschen Bundestages.

Gerber, E. and Kollman, K. (2004), Introduction – authority migration: defining an emerging research agenda, *PS: Political Science and Politics*, Vol.37, No.3, pp.397–401.

Gerring, J. (2008), Case selection for case study analysis: qualitative and quantitative techniques, in J. Box-Steffensmeier, H. Brady and D. Collier (eds), *Oxford Handbook of Political Methodology*, pp.645–684. New York: Oxford University Press.

Hall, P.A. and Taylor, R.C.R. (1996), Political science and the three new institutionalisms, *Political Studies*, Vol.44, pp.936–957.

Hombrado, A. (2011), Learning to catch the wave? Regional demands for constitutional change in contexts of asymmetrical arrangements, *Regional & Federal Studies*, Vol.21, No.4–5, pp.479–501.

Hooghe, L. (2003), Belgium: from regionalism to federalism, in J. Coakley (ed.), *The Territorial Management of Ethnic Conflict*, pp.73–98. London: Frank Cass.

Höreth, M. (2007), Zur Zustimmungsbedürftigkeit von Bundesgesetzen: Eine kritische Bilanz nach einem Jahr Föderalismusreform I, *Zeitschrift für Parlamentsfragen*, Vol.38, No.4, pp.712–733.

Hrbek, R. (ed) (2003), *Deutschland vor der Föderalismus-Reform*. Tübingen: EZFF Selbstverlag.

Hueglin, T. (2000), From constitutional to treaty federalism: a comparative perspective, *Publius: The Journal of Federalism*, Vol.30, No.4, pp.137–153.

Hueglin, T. (2013), Treaty federalism as a model of policy making: comparing Canada and the European Union, *Canadian Public Administration*, Vol.56, No.2, pp.185–202.

Jeffery, C. (2009), Devolution in the United Kingdom: problems of a piecemeal approach to constitutional change, *Publius*, Vol.39, No.2, pp.289–313.

Kastrop, C., et al. (eds) (2010), *Die neuen Schuldenregeln im Grundgesetz*. Berlin: Berliner Wissenschafts-Verlag.

Keating, M. and McEwen, N. (2005), Introduction: devolution and public policy in comparative perspective, *Regional and Federal Studies*, Vol.15, No.4, pp.413–421.

Kropp, S. (2015), Federalism, people's legislation, and associative democracy, in C. Fraenkel-Haeberle, S. Kropp, F. Palermo and K.-P. Sommermann (eds), *Citizen Participation in Multi-level Democracies*, pp.48–66. Amsterdam, Leiden: Brill Nijhoff.

Kropp, S. (2010), The ubiquity and strategic complexity of grand coalition in the German federal system, *German Politics (Special Issue: Kenneth Dyson and Thomas Saalfeld (eds.): Grand Coalition as Systemic Transformation? The German Experience)*, Vol.19, No.3/4, pp.286–311.

Lieberman, R.C. (2002), Ideas, institutions, and political order: explaining political change, *American Political Science Review*, Vol.96, No.4, pp.697–712.

Lorenz, A. (2011), Constitutional negotiations in federal reforms: interests, interaction orientation and the prospect of agreement, *Regional & Federal Studies. Special Issue: Federalism and Constitutional Change: Theoretical and Comparative Perspectives*, Vol.21, No.4–5, pp.407–425.

Mahoney, J., et al. (2009), The logic of historical explanation in the social sciences, *Comparative Political Studies*, Vol.42, No.1, pp.114–146.

Mahoney, J. and Thelen, K. (eds) (2010), *Explaining Institutional Change. Ambiguity, Agency, and Power*. New York: Cambridge University Press.

Mayntz, R. and Scharpf, F.W. (1995), Der Ansatz des akteurszentrierten Institutionalismus, in R. Mayntz and F.W. Scharpf (eds), *Gesellschaftliche Selbstregelung und politische Steuerung*, pp.39–72. Frankfurt/M.: Campus.

McGarry, J. and Moore, M. (2005), Karl Renner, power sharing and non-territorial autonomy, in E. Nimni (ed), *National Cultural Autonomy and Its Contemporary Critics*, pp.74–94. London and New York: Routledge.

Meguid, B. (2005), Competition between unequals: the role of mainstream party strategy in niche party success, *American Political Science Review*, Vol.99, No.3, pp.347–359.

Mitchell, J. (2009), *Devolution in the United Kingdom*. Manchester: Manchester University Press.

Münch, U. and Zinterer, T. (2000), Reform der Aufgabenteilung zwischen Bund und Ländern: Eine Synopse verschiedener Reformansätze zur Stärkung der Länder 1985 bis 2000, *Zeitschrift für Parlamentsfragen*, Vol.3, pp.657–680.

Nee, V. (2005), New institutionalism, economic and sociological, in N. J. Smelser and R. Swedberg (eds), *The Handbook of Economic Sociology*, pp.49–74. Princeton, NJ: University of Princeton Press.

Orren, K. and Skowronek, S. (1994), Beyond the iconography of order: notes for a "new institutionalism", in L.C. Dodd and C. Jillson (eds), *The Dynamics of American Politics*, pp.311–330. Boulder, CO: Westview Press.

Petersohn, B., et al. (2015), Negotiating territorial change in multinational states: party preferences, negotiating power and the role of the negotiation mode, *Publius: The Journal of Federalism*, pp.pjv016.

Pierson, P. (2000a), Increasing returns, path dependence, and the study of politics, *American Political Science Review*, Vol.94, No.2, pp.251–267.

Pierson, P. (2000b), The limits of design: explaining institutional origins and change, *Governance: An International Journal of Policy and Administration*, Vol.13, No.4, pp.475–499.

Pierson, P. (2004), *Politics in Time. History, Institutions, and Social Analysis*. Princeton, NJ: Princeton University Press.

Poirier, J. (2002), Formal mechanisms of intergovernmental relations in Belgium, *Regional and Federal Studies*, Vol.12, No.3, pp.24–54.

Radaelli, C.M. (2003), The Europeanization of public policy, in K. Featherstone and C.M. Radaelli (eds), *The Politics of Europeanization*, pp.27–56. Oxford: Oxford University Press.

Russell, P.H. (2004), *Constitutional Odyssey*. Toronto: University of Toronto Press.

Scharpf, F.W. (1985), Die Politikverflechtungs-Falle: Europäische Integration und deutscher Föderalismus im Vergleich, *Politische Vierteljahresschrift*, Vol.26, pp.323–356.

Scharpf, F.W. (1997), *Games Real Actors Play. Actor-centered Institutionalism in Policy Research*. Boulder, CO: Westview Press.

Scharpf, F.W. (2000), *Interaktionsformen: Akteurszentrierter Institutionalismus in der Politikforschung*. Wiesbaden: VS Verlag für Sozialwissenschaften.

Scharpf, F.W. (2009), *Föderalismusreform. Kein Ausweg aus der Politikverflechtungsfalle?* Frankfurt a.M.: Campus Verlag.

Schmidt, V. (2008), Discursive institutionalism: the explanatory power of ideas and discourse, *Annual Review of Political Science*, Vol.11, No.1, pp.303–326.

Schneider, H.-P. (2013), *Der neue deutsche Bundesstaat. Bericht über die Umsetzung der Föderalismusreform I*. Baden-Baden: Nomos.

Scott, R.W. (2014), *Institutions and Organizations. Ideas, Interests, and Identities* (Vol.4). New York: Sage.

Shepsle, K.A. (2006), Rational choice institutionalism, in R.A.W. Rhodes, et al. (eds), *The Oxford Handbook of Political Institutions*, pp.23–38. Oxford: Oxford University Press.

Sturm, R. (2010), More courageous than expected? The 2006 reform of German federalism, in J. Erk and W. Swenden (eds), *New Directions in Federalism Studies*, pp.34–49. Abingdon: Routledge.

Swenden, W., et al. (2006), The politics of Belgium: institutions and policy under bipolar and centrifugal federalism, *West European Politics*, Vol.29, No.5, pp.863–873.

Swenden, W. and Maddens, B. (2009), Introduction. Territorial party politics in Western Europe: a framework for analysis, in W. Swenden and B. Maddens (eds), *Territorial Party Politics in Western Europe*, pp.1–30. New York: Palgrave Macmillan.

Taylor, C. (1992), *Multiculturalism and the Politics of Recognition: An Essay*. Princeton, NJ: Princeton University Press.

Toubeau, S. and Massetti, E. (2013), The party politics of territorial reforms in Europe, *West European Politics*, Vol.36, No.2, pp.297–316.

Tully, J. (1995), *Strange Multiplicity. Constitutionalism in an Age of Diversity*. Cambridge: Cambridge University Press.

The effects of federalism reform on the legislative process in Germany

Christian Stecker

ABSTRACT

When the reform of German federalism was enacted in 2006, the right of the second chamber, *Bundesrat*, to veto large parts of national legislation had long been identified as a dysfunctional element of the federal system. The need to compromise with an often opposition-controlled *Bundesrat* was perceived as hurting democratic principles and worsening Germany's policy performance. Hence, a variety of constitutional amendments was adopted in 2006 to curb the veto threat. This paper sketches how the expansion of the *Bundesrat* veto emerged and how the reform tried to reduce it. Covering all federal legislation between 1978 and 2016 this paper then analyses the actual effects of the reform. It is shown that the veto threat has been reduced by around 17% but that it remains unchanged at around 65% in the area of tax law.

Introduction

Separating legislative tasks between the federal and *Land* level and reducing the impact of the *Bundesrat* (BR) veto on federal legislation was one of the main goals of federalism reform. Since the 1950s, for more than half of its bills the federal government had to seek the approval of the *Bundesrat*, a chamber rarely featuring government-friendly majorities. Federal decision-making was marked by an excessive need for compromise which – according to a widely shared perception – blurred the clarity of responsibility and pro-moted ineffective and inefficient public policies.

Therefore, the reform was aimed at re-allocating legislative powers and considerably changing veto rights: The Framework legislation (Art. 75) was abolished and respective responsibilities were allocated to either the *Länder* (see Dose in this issue) or federal level. Moreover, the *Länder* were allowed to deviate from federal legislation in specific areas (Art. 72 and 74). Most, importantly, the rule that any federal regulation on how the *Länder* were to implement federal laws triggers the consent requirement (Art. 84.1) was suspended. At the same time, however, important triggers were left intact and the *Bundesrat* was even granted a new veto right over laws that induced direct costs for the *Länder* (Art. 104a.4).

Against this background, this paper sketches the triggers of the reform and the specific changes that were implemented to curb the veto power of the Bundesrat. Furthermore, it offers a long-term analysis of the actual effect of the reform on the legislative process in Germany (see also Burkhart and Manow, 2006; Georgii and Borhanian, 2006; Risse, 2007; Zohlnhöfer, 2008b). In a longitudinal design comprising all 4450 published federal laws between 1 January 1978 and 9 August 2016 several questions are answered: To what extent did federalism reform reduce the share of consent laws? More specifically, did the reform effectively curb the veto threat in areas of important and contentious legislation? Are there significant differences of reform effects across policy areas? In answering these questions the paper also highlights aspects that are particularly interesting for comparative federalism research, showing that the applicability of the BR veto is not simply a clear legal decision but contentious between political actors during the legislative process. Overall, a mixed assessment of the reform effects is presented. While there has been a considerable drop of the veto threat from 55% to 39% of all laws, the consent rate remains high in the area of salient laws and even stagnates at around 66% for taxation laws.

As Behnke and Kropp argue in the introduction, the different variants of institutionalist theories (Aspinwall and Schneider, 2000) offer different fruitful avenues for an understanding of the reform of federal arrangements and the respective effects. In this spirit, I will make explicit and implicit use of arguments from particularly the rational choice, historical and sociological institutionalism when covering the triggers, contents and effects of federalism reform in Germany. In the next section, I discuss how the huge impact of the *Bundesrat* veto resulted from institutional designers' ignorance of the future which gave rise to unintended consequences and finally sparked a constitutional reform. I then revisit the reform process with a focus on the *Bundesrat* veto. The empirical section analyses the reform effects in a longitudinal perspective on all adopted federal laws between 1978 and 2016.

The *Bundesrat* veto: unintended consequence and reform trigger

As Behnke and Kropp discuss in more detail in the analytical framework to this issue, federal systems may come under pressure when its processes and institutions are perceived as dysfunctional and inferior to alternative arrangements. The reform of the national legislative process as a core part of Germany's wider federal structure exemplifies how such a perception manifested itself among the political elite and paved the way towards constitutional change.

The dominant perceptions of the merits and problems of Germany's federalism have changed several times over the course of history since 1949 (Benz, 1985; Scharpf, 1988; Lehmbruch, 2000; Wachendorfer-Schmidt, 2005; Schneider, 2013). Yet, when the 'Joint Commission on the Modernisation of the Federal State' was set up in October 2003, a negative assessment had long prevailed among journalists, political scientists and the political elite: The legislative process embedded in the federal structure was seen as dysfunctional and as a central reason for a variety of undesired policy effects. By the end of the 1990s, a main cause for Germany's increasing budget deficit, high unemployment rate and low economic growth was seen in a logjam of reforms (*Reformstau*) not least resulting from the allegedly cumbersome federalized decision-making (Zohlnhöfer, 2008a). Next to the entanglement of legislative tasks between federal and *Land* level (Kropp, 2010), a main institutional culprit for this situation was seen in the right of the *Bundesrat* to veto a large share of federal legislation. This veto power is based on a constitutional differentiation between two types of federal laws. For objection laws (*Einspruchsgesetze*) an absolute majority of votes in the *Bundesrat* may invoke a suspensive veto that can be overturned by an absolute majority in the *Bundestag*.[1] For consent laws (*Zustimmungsgesetze*), however, the active approval of an absolute majority of all votes in the *Bundesrat* is indispensable (making abstentions effectively count against a law's passage). Since reunification, the share of these consent laws has ranged between 50% and 60% (see Figure 1), and

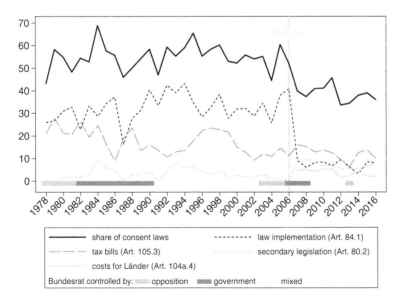

Figure 1. The share of consent laws and individual constitutional triggers (1978–2016).

included the majority of politically important laws (Reutter, 2007: 313).[2] According to the dominant narrative, the *Bundesrat*'s veto over such a high share of important legislation violated democratic principles and worsened the quality of decisions.

With regard to the veto's effect on democratic principles, the directly elected majority supporting the government in the *Bundestag* was severely constrained in its ability to shape public policy.[3] Before the reform, the government had to seek *Bundesrat* approval for more than half of its bills. At the same time, the government could command a clear-cut absolute majority in the *Bundesrat* for only less than 17% of the time since reunification. The government was, thus, constantly forced to hammer out compromises with those opposition parties in the *Bundestag* that controlled a significant share of votes in the *Bundesrat*. In fact, Manow and Burkhart (2007: 180) suggest that the government parties absorbed the *Bundesrat* veto by forming oversized legislative coalitions in the *Bundestag* before a bill was sent to the second chamber. This institutionally coerced 'legislative self-restraint' of the government's majority not only violated the majoritarian principle (Christiano, 1996), it also reduced the transparency of decision-making, blurred the clarity of responsibility and undermined the democratic goal of accountability (Powell, 2000). German voters had a hard time in attributing responsibility for the resulting policy packages as laws were rarely made by an identifiable minimal-winning coalition in the *Bundestag* but by an informal 'grand coalition' (Schmidt, 1996) of government and opposition parties or even by ad-hoc agreements with individual *Länder*. Moreover, although the formal use of the BR veto was an exception, it lead to some outright deadlocks in matters of high importance such as tax reforms (Zohlnhöfer, 1999; Lehnert et al., 2008).

In addition to these violations of democratic goals, the perceived quality of legislative decisions also suffered. As decision-making under the presence of the BR veto was effectively supermajoritarian, the scope for action was limited. In the jargon of veto player theory (Tsebelis, 2002), the winset between *Bundestag* and *Bundesrat* was often heavily circumscribed, preventing those major policy changes that were seen as adequate responses to the social and economic challenges Germany faced since reunification. Rather, policy changes tended to be, on the one hand, incremental as the preferences of many different veto actors had to be accommodated (but see Saalfeld, 2006). On the other hand, larger policy changes had to come in packages entailing potentially incoherent side payments and logrolls. Observing federal law-making in Germany, Swenden (2006: 216) notes that "in order to strike a deal, the 'pie' is enlarged rather than the shares among the actors redistributed". This was famously exemplified by the last major reforms of the tax (2000) and pension (2001) system (see Kropp, 2004, 2006) enacted by a coalition of Social Democrats and Greens. Facing a hostile majority in the *Bundesrat*, the then Chancellor Schroeder secured the reform's passage by offering side payments to individual *Länder* within the party-politically defined blocking coalition inside the *Bundesrat*. Thereby, the reform was linked to various incoherent federal subsidies, such as for the modernization of Berlin's largest sports stadium or the construction of a power plant in the northern *Land* Mecklenburg-Vorpommern. Finally, there has been a general impression that the legislative process was too slow for adequate policy reactions to emerging challenges. While this hardly finds empirical backing as a general assessment (König and Bräuninger, 2005: 66; Reutter, 2007; Burkhart et al., 2008), it is certainly true for specific areas of legislation such as for the transposition of European law that often requires legislative acts at both the federal and *Land* levels (Szukala, 2012). In sum, Germany's federalism in general and the *Bundesrat* veto in particular performed poorly with regard to democratic principles and policy performance. As both the federal arrangement's input and output legitimacy (Scharpf, 1999) stood in question, pressures for reform grew enormously.

Against this background, it is surprising to note that when the Parliamentary Council drafted the new constitution in 1948/49 it expected no more than 10% of all federal laws to be subject to the approval of the *Bundesrat* (Bryde, 1989: 862). How could the applicability of the *Bundesrat*'s veto expand so drastically and leave such a huge imprint on legislative decision-making? The answer to this question points to one of the core insights of historical institutionalism: institutional designers often have to frame rules under limited information about the future context in which these rules are to operate – an uncertainty promoting unintended institutional effects (Pierson, 2004: 15, 117; Behnke/Kropp in the introduction). In this article, only a few highly selective parts of the complex causal chain leading to the BR veto's unintended effects can be discussed (see Lehmbruch, 2000; Laufer and Münch, 2010).

To begin with, it is helpful to analytically differentiate between the institutional environment and the specific actor constellation operating under this environment. With regard to the institutional environment two things deserve highlighting: first, the Parliamentary Council's estimate of a consent rate of around 10% was based on the expectation that there would be little federal interference with matters assumed to be regulated by the *Länder* (concurrent legislation). Yet, in the absence of any salient territorially anchored cleavage, a strong unitary consensus of both citizens and elites (Oberhofer et al., 2011) carried a swift process of 'unitarisation'. One the one hand, this 'unitarisation' centralized legislative competencies over the most important policy areas, including taxation, at the national level. On the other hand, it strengthened the participation of the *Bundesrat* in a now centralized federal law-making process (Schneider, 2011: 27–28). By contrast, the subsequent creation of new consent triggers in the constitution (e.g. in the 1960s) contributed only marginally to the growth of the consent rate (Dästner, 2001).

Second, a founding feature of Germany's federalism lies in the fact that it divides legislative functions between the different levels of government instead of competencies over separate policy areas as is the case in an ideal-type dual federalism (Swenden, 2006: 49). Whereas the federal level makes (most) law, the *Länder* implement it 'in their own right' (Art. 83) by establishing the required authorities and regulating administrative procedures. This notion of the administrative authority of the *Länder* (*Verwaltungshoheit*) can be traced back to as early as the German Empire forming in 1871 (Schneider, 2011: 21). Under this tradition, the new German constitution protected the *Länder's* administrative authority by making rules on the implementation of laws subject to the approval of the *Bundesrat* (Art. 84.1). At the outset a veto over administrative rules seemed hardly at risk to hinder the legislative intent of the federal law-maker. Yet, in 1958 a ruling by the Federal Constitutional Court[4] expanded the applicability of Art. 84.1 from the administrative legal norms of a bill to its legal norms on substantive policy. The court's interpretation, the so-called *Einheitstheorie,* stipulated that any law passed by the *Bundestag* had to be treated as an inseparable unit, meaning that both legal norms on the substantive intent and implementation were subject to the consent of the *Bundesrat.*

Neither did the Parliamentary Council foresee changes that were to significantly alter the actor constellation operating in this institutional environment. The core idea behind the specific construction of the *Bundesrat* was that it should act as a counterbalance to party politics in the first chamber – yet, not counterbalance in the sense of a Madisonian anti-majoritarian veto but more as an 'objective', issue-oriented chamber transcending everyday partisan conflict in the first chamber (Lehmbruch, 2000: 77). In fact, the situation during the work on the new constitution gave many reasons to expect that the *Bundesrat* would fulfil this role. After the defeat of Nazi Germany quite disparate party systems formed in the *Länder,* where parties were not yet well-integrated into federal party organizations (Rohe, 2002) and where partly non-partisan cabinets were supported by broad all-party-coalitions of 'national unity'. Both the political incentives and party system-structure that could turn the *Bundesrat* into an arena of coordinated partisan action were lacking. Nonetheless, these conditions were soon created by a quick concentration of the regional party systems around the two catch-all parties, Christian Democrats and Social Democrats, and an increasing adjustment of party competition at the federal and regional level (Rudzio, 2015: 107–128). By the end of the 1950s, both federal and regional party systems were marked by a bipolar structure, and regional and federal party organizations were increasingly well-integrated (Renzsch, 1999; Detterbeck, 2012). Now, federal and *Land* parties began to adopt joint strategies in the *Bundesrat.* In the 1970s the *Bundesrat's* potential as party-political minority veto fully unfolded for the first time when the Christian Democrats turned their *Bundesrat's* majority against the federal government of SPD and FDP. It was this impression that inspired Lehmbruch's (2000) famous notion that two competing actor-orientations clashed in the *Bundesrat* and paralysed the polity: a cooperative and problem-solving attitude required for the smooth working of the federal system and an antagonistic and polarizing bargaining attitude induced by the logic of party competition.

Moreover, electoral dynamics often laid the *Bundesrat*'s veto in the hands of federal opposition parties. Due to the unitary focus on party competition at the federal level, regional elections were more or less referenda on the popularity of national parties (Decker and von Blumenthal, 2002; Hough and Koß, 2009). With the tides of government popularity at the federal level, parties of the federal opposition often gained votes in the staggered regional elections and, by entering a *Land* government, also added seats in the *Bundesrat* (Burkhart, 2005). Hence, a German-style mid-term effect stacked the deck against a government-friendly *Bundesrat* – since 1949 non-governmental majorities had been prevalent for 72% of the time. Since reunification, though regional disparities have grown and regional party systems have diversified (Niedermayer, 2010). This has generated more heterogeneous government constellations in the *Länder* (Jeffery, 1999; Jun, 2011: 123) among which governmental majorities in the *Bundesrat* are even harder to find.[5] In addition, the *Bundesrat* veto has also become an important instrument in intra-party competition. During the coalition of CDU/CSU and FDP between 2009 and 2013, for example, Christian-democratic led *Länder* governments increasingly used the veto threat against laws of the federal government (Glaab, 2010: 141; Höreth, 2010: 119).

In short, while partly unforeseen constitutional developments created the opportunity for the *Bundesrat* veto to become a powerful instrument in federal party competition, a changing constellation and orientation of actors created the incentives necessary to put this instrument to work. Certainly, a stylized account of the *Bundesrat* as a blunt party-political instrument paints a distorted picture. Rather, *Bundesrat*'s members are pursuing mixed motives, balancing the territorial interest of their *Land* and political interests of their party (Bräuninger et al., 2010; Kropp, 2010: 31; Leunig and Träger, 2012). The *Bundesrat* is, hence, an arena for both regional representation (Swenden, 2006: 196) and federal party competition (Stecker, 2015). Yet, the latter part has gotten out of hand to an extent which is considered to be largely dysfunctional.

Reforming the *Bundesrat* veto

In 2003, political actors embarked on the reform of federalism with quite ambitious rhetoric. 'The mother of all reforms'[6] was to enable Germany to operate 'faster, better and more efficiently'.[7] Under the *Leitbild* of disentanglement (*Entflechtung*), the reform commission envisaged a clearer separation of tasks between the *Land* and the federal level (Auel, 2008; Scharpf, 2008; Auel, 2010; Behnke, 2010) and a significant reduction of the *Bundesrat*'s veto power. The following discussion focusses on reform dynamics relating to the latter goal.[8]

Art. 84.1 was the central theme of reform discussions as it was the main consent trigger. Many members attached the overall success of the commission to an adequate change of this provision. Various possibilities for amendment were considered. Law experts proposed to cut the consent requirement of Art. 84.1 back to its original meaning – the legal norms covering the administrative parts of a bill (Scharpf, 2009: 79–80).[9] Yet, *Länder* prime ministers – particularly those with ambitions at the federal level – were reluctant to trade a veto over contentious policies with a veto over administrative technicalities as this would have reduced their clout and credibility in negotiations at the federal level (Scharpf, 2006: 7; Scharpf, 2007: 201).

A central question underlying the different reform options of Art. 84.1 was whether and to what extent binding provisions on administrative procedures and the establishment of authorities were necessary to secure the unbiased realization of a federal law's substantive intention. On the one hand, representatives of the *Länder* argued that their autonomous administrative authority would not hurt the legislative intent of federal laws and some even proposed to ban federal provisions on law implementation altogether. On the other hand, federal representatives, mostly specialists from the ministerial bureaucracy, emphasized the inextricable connection between a law's substantive intent and its implementation, at least with regard to specific policies.

The final constitutional amendment codified three options that differentiated between consent and consent-free bills: Firstly, a law is consent-free if it does not include rules on law implementation. Secondly, it is also consent-free if it includes rules on law implementation but allows for deviating implementation rules by the *Länder*.[10] Thirdly, the law requires the *Bundesrat*'s consent if the federal government 'in exceptional cases, owing to a special need for uniform federal legislation' sets implementation rules and prohibits deviating provisions by individual *Länder*. In fact, only the second option, that is, allowing deviating implementation rules by the *Länder*, created an entirely new option.

The effectiveness of this amendment was immediately questioned. In fact, keeping laws free from implementation rules and thereby consent-free had already been a viable strategy before the reform. It seems reasonable to expect that federal governments would always chose this option if they deemed binding implementation rules not essential for their substantive legislative intent (Burkhart et al., 2008: 531). However, it cannot be ruled out either, that under the new provision the *Länder*, especially those with limited administrative resources (e.g. Saarland or Bremen), would by default adopt the voluntary implementation rules provided by the national legislator. In sum, the quantitative reduction of this specific consent trigger would be decided by the extent to which the federal legislator would combine its bills with uniform and binding implementation rules.

It has to be noted that the change of Art. 84.1 came at a price for the federal level as the *Länder* could sell the sustained possibility for binding federal implementation rules as a concession. As the *Länder* were now bereft of a veto over laws incurring budget costs, they demanded a 'functional equivalent' and pushed for the inclusion of a new provision. This article (104a.4) introduced a new consent trigger for laws that 'oblige the *Länder* to provide money grants, benefits in kind, or comparable services to third persons'.

By most assessments, this provision clearly strengthened the *Bundesrat* veto. Whereas the pre-reform constitution stipulated that laws required *Bundesrat* consent if the *Länder* had to carry more than 25% of the resulting costs, the constitutional amendment lacked any specific limit. Moreover, it was feared that the article's vague wording carried the risk of an incalculable expansion of the veto. In fact, depending on the imponderability of constitutional court rulings, any bill incurring costs to the *Länder* (e.g. on child care or social expenditures) could now prompt the consent requirement. For some observers Art. 104a.4 has, thus, the potential of becoming an even more effective partisan tool in the hands of an opposition-controlled *Bundesrat* than the old Art. 84.1 did (Scharpf, 2006: 7; Höreth, 2008: 419).

Further criticism drew on the fact that other influential consent triggers were not touched by the commission, among them the issue of taxation laws (Art. 105.3 GG) and secondary legislation (Art. 80.2). Some feared that not having addressed these and other triggers could backfire, as Art. 84.1 was under the suspicion of being an 'umbrella' trigger. The suspicion was that Art. 84.1 was declared applicable for many bills whose consent requirement was in fact overdetermined by additional triggers 'hiding' in the background (Höreth, 2007: 731).

After an initial stalemate in December 2004, the reform was finally pushed through with a huge majority and the political will of the grand coalition of CDU/CSU and SPD that formed in September 2005. Quickly adopted in the *Bundestag* and *Bundesrat*, the constitutional amendments took effect on 1 September 2006.

While the reform – by quantitative standards – resulted in the largest postwar constitutional amendment, most observers concluded that it had failed in achieving a major overhaul of the federal system. Two nascent defects were identified by two prominent experts of federalism, Arthur Benz and Fritz W. Scharpf, who also served as advisors to the commission. First, with the goal of disentanglement an inadequate *Leitbild* or solution concept was chosen (Benz, 2008: 443; Scharpf, 2008: 515–516). Disentanglement seemed neither adequate for many policy areas that were best addressed in the joint coordination of different levels nor possible given the financial entangle-ment of the federal and *Land* level. Second, the constitutional reform game was essentially played by the same actors that also played the daily political game under the existing and future rules. Hence, not even a thin veil of ignor-ance could protect the negotiations from the intrusion of outright self-inter-est. With too much bargaining and too little problem-solving-orientation among the commission, federalism reform itself might have stepped into a joint-decision trap (Auel, 2008).

Fewer consent laws and also more scope for government action?

Federalism reform quickly generated a remarkable interest in the effects it would have on the federal legislative process. It was especially the quantifi-able share of consent laws that offered an easy yardstick for the evaluation of a very complex reform. A first counterfactual analysis by the *Bundestag* research unit (Georgii and Borhanian, 2006) estimated the hypothetical impact of the constitutional amendments in the pre-reform years between 1998 and 2005, predicting a 50% drop of the consent rate to about 27% of all federal legislation. In a subsequent study by Burkhart and Manow (2006), this assessment was criticized as overly optimistic. They argued, that more rea-listic assumptions about actor's behaviour and the consideration of a bill's contentiousness would suggest a more modest drop to around 50%. Empirical studies of the first year following the reform estimated the consent rate at 42.7% (Risse, 2007: 709), 47.4% (Höreth, 2007: 727) and 44.2% (federal govern-ment's reply to a parliamentary question[11]).

Ten years after the reform took effect, the present study offers a long-term assessment of the upshot of it. The analysis draws on an original dataset on federal legislation in Germany including all bills that entered the legislative process between 1 January 1978 and 9 August 2016. For the analysis of the consent rate, the sample of bills is restricted to all 4450 laws that were pub-lished during that period in order to maximize accuracy and temporal com-parability of the data.[12] Using computer scripts implemented in R (Nolan and Temple Lang, 2014; Munzert et al., 2015), the bulk of the data was har-vested from the official homepage of the Bundestag that publishes infor-mation on each bill in semi-structured text.[13] Additional information (e.g. on the voting behaviour of parties) had to be manually coded from the plenary protocols. The data were cross-checked with different existing sources and aggregate statistics published by the Bundestag (Feldkamp and Ströbel, 2005) in order to maximize accuracy. The dataset comprises a wealth of information about bill characteristics (e.g. initiator, policy area), pro-cessing information (e.g. date of readings) and behavioural indicators from different stages of a bill's legislative career (e.g. length of first reading, voting behaviour of parties during 2nd and 3rd reading). Most importantly for the present purpose, it identifies the exact constitutional provision prompting the requirement for *Bundesrat* consent. The question of consent requirement and the respective constitutional provisions are considered by the *Bundesrat*'s committees, sometimes in consultation with officials from the federal government, when a bill, after being adopted by the *Bundestag*, arrives at the *Bundesrat* for the so-called second passage (*2. Durchgang*) (Risse, 2007: 709). The respective information is condensed in the Order papers of *Bundesrat* sessions and in the official database on federal legislation administered by the *Bundestag*.

To put the following results in context, two points are worth considering. First, it is well established that – with certain constraints accepted – political actors try to bend rules to their own favour (e.g. Vanberg, 2005), since most rules leave some room for interpretation. This is no less true for the consent triggers enumerated in the German constitution. Hence the consent rate cannot be interpreted as a direct mapping of constitutional rules. Rather, at least a small part of it results from a competition between political parties about the 'right' classification of a bill as a consent or a consent-free bill (Höreth, 2007: 716). What is perceived as the 'right' classification depends on the question of who would gain or lose from the activation of the *Bundesrat* veto. A government facing hostile majorities in the *Bundesrat* will favour an interpretation as a consent-free bill in order to avoid the veto threat while the opposition will push for the consent requirement. By contrast, in the situation of unified government or largely consensual legislation, the question of the 'right' classification loses salience. In this case, one could expect an uncontested 'objective' interpretation of the constitution (Höreth, 2007). Yet, there is some evidence that, though not clearly applicable, Art. 84.1 was cited for bills that were not conflictual between the government and the opposition in the pre-reform time as then determining an exact constitutional trigger seemed irrelevant anyway (Georgii and Borhanian, 2006: 34). The share of consent laws triggered by Art. 84.1 before the reform, therefore, might be overestimated. While these claims are hard to substantiate empirically, there is some evidence for a modest but significant effect of a contest over the 'right' classification of a bill. Overall, conflict about a bill's classification occurred for 3.5% of all announced laws in the sample, differing between 3.3% during a government-controlled *Bundesrat* and 5.9% during an opposition-controlled *Bundesrat*.

Second, in their strive for votes parties try to build up a reputation for 'getting things done' (Ganghof and Bräuninger, 2006). In the case of federalism reform, this reputation depended crucially on the public image of a successful reform, at least for the CDU/CSU and SPD. Therefore, it cannot be ruled out that the grand coalition especially tended to bend the rules in favour of a lower consent rate in order to facilitate the public's perception of success.

Figure 1 visualizes the reform effects presenting the yearly share of consent laws and of individual consent triggers. These descriptive statistics may be seen as the most appropriate representation of the underlying data, not least because more complex quantitative models would pretend a degree of precision that is impossible to reach with the data at hand (Schrodt, 2014: 288). Nevertheless a logistic regression, which models the probability of a bill to be adopted as a consent bill depending on different covariates, can be found in the appendix. It corroborates the descriptive results presented here (Figures A2 and A3).

The upper thick black line in Figure 1 represents the yearly percentage of all federal laws that required the consent of the *Bundesrat*. The thinner lines below give the share of four relevant consent triggers on all published laws: consent due to federal rules on law implementation (Art. 84.1), tax bills (Art. 105.3), secondary legislation (Art. 80.2) and the newly established trigger for laws that incur costs for the *Länder* (Art. 104a.4). In order to control for the potential over-determination of consent requirements, all cited triggers of a consent law are included.[14] Finally, the vertical grey line for the year 2007 divides pre- and post-reform era[15] and the differently grey-shaded boxes above the horizontal time line indicate whether the *Bundesrat* was (predominantly) controlled by a governmental, oppositional or mixed majority in that year.

Evidently before the reform, the consent requirement was the norm rather than the exception. On average, 55% of all published laws had been subject to the *Bundesrat*'s veto, reaching peaks in the mid-1980s and 1990s. It is noteworthy that the consent rate had already climbed to around 50% during the second term of the *Bundesrat* between 1953 and 1957 (Dästner, 2001).[16] Since the reform has taken effect, the quota dropped within a year considerably from 51.1% (January to September 2006) to 39.9% (September 2006 to December 2007). On average, after the reform the Bunderat's approval is now required for 39% of all laws processed under the reformed legislative procedure.

Regarding individual consent triggers, the dominance of Art. 84.1 before the reform stands out. According to the data, federal rules on how the *Länder* were to implement laws were solely responsible for 40.2% of all consent laws with another 7% added when in conjunction with other triggers. In fact, the reduction of the consent rate after 2007 mainly resulted from 'disarming' Art. 84.1. Since then it has prompted the consent requirement for only 8.9% of all passed laws. Obviously, the federal level has been very sparing with stipulating binding and uniform implementation rules since the reform. These referred mainly to matters where uniform implementation rules were unavoidable, for example, in the area of environmental protection and European law (Robbe et al., 2009: 9). At the same time, there is little evidence that the *Länder* deviate from the voluntary federal implementation rules that now come as part of consent-free objection laws. A study by the *Bundestag* research unit reported only three such cases before July 2009 (Robbe et al., 2009). Overall, the change of Art. 84.1 seems to have increased the discretion of the federal legislator in making policy without incurring losses in the stage of policy implementation by the Länder.

This considerable effect of the slight change of Art. 84.1 seems puzzling given that laws could already be kept consent-free by omitting implementation rules before the reform. Yet, it has been suggested that the German ministerial bureaucracy (predominantly staffed with jurists) has a strong tendency to draft both substantial and administrative parts of a bill (Georgii and Borhanian, 2006: 20). Before the reform this tendency always triggered the consent requirement. After the reform, not formally committing the Länder to the implementation rules avoids the consent requirement.

For the time being, the data alleviate concerns that the newly established consent trigger for laws inducing direct costs to the Länder (Art. 104a.4) could take the place of Art. 84.1 as a gateway for the consent requirement.[17] At least as of August 2016, it has only activated the consent requirement of 4% (51) of all laws. Yet, the historical experience of the expansion of the applicability of Art. 84.1 by a constitutional court ruling is a reminder of the future possibility of such a development. When the incentives to present the reform as a success to the public begin to fade, the vague wording of Art. 104a.4 might open new ways for the Bundesrat veto (Burkhart et al., 2008: 532–533). Finally, the figure mirrors the persistence of other prominent consent triggers. The rate of consent laws prompted by the untouched Art. 105.3 (tax laws) remained stable, while Art. 80.2 (secondary legislation) caused more rather than fewer consent laws.

Overall, this first look at the data invites a positive evaluation of the legislative effect of federalism reform: it has not lived up to the aspiration of reducing the share of consent laws by 25% (Georgii and Borhanian, 2006) but has led to a considerable drop of around 17%. Nonetheless, a valid assessment of whether the reform succeeded in strengthening the discretion of legislative majorities in the Bundestag requires a more nuanced look. As it has been emphasized in many studies (Burkhart et al., 2008: 527; Höreth, 2008; Zohlnhöfer, 2008b), a more adequate yardstick for success is whether and to what extent the Bundestag majority has been freed from the veto threat in the area of salient and/or contentious legislation. The more the drop of the consent rate is constrained to consensual or unimportant legislation, the more the reform would appear to have made a merely cosmetic formal change. To shed light on this question, Figure 2 combines different measures of a law's salience and contentiousness into the analysis of how the consent rate developed. It is important to note that these categories are not mutually exclusive and that each of these indicators has its strength and weaknesses.

The lines with arrowheads represent the development of the consent rate within a specific category of bills while the numbers give the absolute

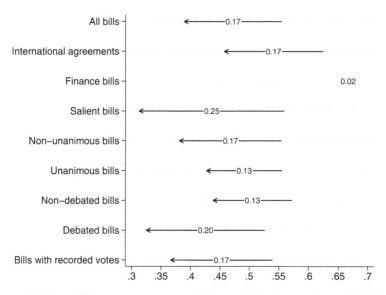

Figure 2. Reform effects on consent rates within specific bill categories (1978–2016).

difference between the pre-reform and post-reform average consent rate in that category. As a baseline the development of the overall consent rate is given at the top. At the bottom of the figure, the change is given for bills that experienced a recorded vote during their 2nd or 3rd reading. In the *Bundestag* ordinary bills are only voted upon via recorded votes (*Namentliche Abstimmung*) on request of a party group. Most often, this request indicates that a matter is important and contentious (Stecker, 2010; Bergmann et al., 2016). The category of debated bills comprises those bills that were debated during the first reading in the *Bundestag*. While technical and uncontroversial matters are often immediately transferred to a committee ('non-debated bills') without debate (*Überweisungen im vereinfachten Verfahren ohne Debatte*), increasing debate length indicates that parties attach importance to a bill and invest parliamentary time to present their views on it to the public (Linn and Sobolewski, 2010: 47). The advantage of this measure over voting data is that it is unaffected by the strategic anticipation of the *Bundesrat* veto. Unanimous bills are those that were adopted by an all-party consensus in the second or third reading in the *Bundesrat*. This measure is, of course, affected by the varying party composition of the *Bundestag*. I coded bills as salient when they received a debate during the first reading and fall under policy areas that lie at the heart of party competition in Germany. Specifically, these areas are finance, labour, economic, health and social policies. As a sub-group of salient bills, values are also presented for finance bills. Finally, information is given on bills ratifying international agreements.

As can be seen, except for finance bills federalism reform has affected all categories to a similar extent. With regard to salient bills, before the reform,

56% were processed under the veto threat. With 25%, the drop down to 31% within this category was above average. Yet, this result should not be overstated as the measurement of salient bills is inherently difficult. The result for non-unanimous bills also indicates that the reform not only had a mere formal impact. The drop of the consent rate of non-unanimous bills is near the average for all bills.

Strikingly, there has been no effect of federalism reform within the category of finance bills. The consent requirement for finance bills stagnates at a very high share of 65%. While this is problematic with regard to the overall reform of Germany's federalism, it is also not surprising. The deep fiscal entanglement of the *Land* and federal level was deliberately excluded as creating too much of a conflict from the reform negotiations.

As can be seen in the appendix (Figure A3), there are no cabinet-specific effects on the consent rate. Most importantly, the grand coalition with its huge majority after the reform is no different from the bourgeois coalition of CDU/CSU and FDP lead by Angela Merkel with a comparable slim majority. Moreover, there is no robust indication that different government constellations before the reform substantially influenced the consent rate.

Conclusion

Reducing the veto threat of the *Bundesrat* was at the heart of federalism reform that took effect in September 2006. In the decades before the reform, the veto was increasingly perceived as a dysfunctional part of Germany's federal system. It was accused of hurting democratic principles by favouring the status quo and blurring political accountability as well as of contributing to inferior policy results. While the reform commission succeeded in changing the main consent trigger related to the administrative authority of the *Länder*, it left intact quite a few triggers and even created a new consent trigger for laws incurring costs to the *Länder* budgets.

This study has presented a first long-term analysis of the reform's effect on the consent rate, analysing all federal bills published between 1978 and 2016. The reform reduced the average consent rate significantly from 55% to around 39%, including bills that can be regarded as salient based on different indicators. Yet, the reform's inability to address the financial entanglement between *Land* and *Bund* is strikingly mirrored by an unchanged consent rate of about 65% for finance laws.

Finally, a look at factors beyond the legislative statistics invites a hesitant interpretation of the overall reduction of the consent rate by 17%. By the end of data collection in August 2016, the reform might not yet have been put to a crucial test. Since September 2006 a grand coalition of CDU/CSU and SPD has governed 55% of the time. Grand coalitions most likely clear a lot of those conflicts in intra-coalitional bargaining that are usually staged in the *Bundesrat*. During the (minimal-winning) CDU/CSU/FDP-coalition, incentives to create the public impression of success for a still young reform might have kept partisan strategies in the Bundesrat on a shorter leash than usual. Hence, we might have to wait for a smaller minimal-winning coalition in the *Bundestag* facing hostile *Bundesrat* majorities to see whether old and/or especially new consent triggers are proof against situations of divided government and the unpredictability of constitutional court rulings.

Notes

1. More specifically, objections by the *Bundesrat* can only be overturned by the absolute majority of all members of the *Bundestag*, the so-called Chancellor's majority. Furthermore, if the *Bundesrat* invokes an objection with two thirds of its members the *Bundestag* would need a majority of the same size to overturn.
2. Compiling different data collections on legislative key decisions between 1972 and 2005 (Beyme, 1997; König and Bräuninger, 2005), Reutter (2007) estimated the share of consent laws at around 63%.
3. Auel (2010) rightly adds, that some instances of perceived stalemate were caused more by intra-coalitional conflicts than by the *Bundesrat*'s veto (see also Lorenz and Riese, 2014).
4. BVerfGE 8, 274, Tz. 89
5. As a strong, often in coalition agreements codified convention, *Länder* coalition governments abstain in the *Bundesrat* when in disagreement (Debus, 2007; Kropp, 2001). Due to the absolute majority requirement, these abstentions work effectively against the passage of a consent law.
6. Edmund Stoiber, the then prime minister of Bavaria and co-leader of the reform commission.
7. Matthias Platzeck, the then prime minister of Brandenburg and former leader of the SPD.
8. All information about the content and progress of the Reform Commission's deliberations are based on (Bundestag, 2005)
9. Interestingly, such an option was also re-opened two years earlier by a constitutional court ruling explicitly allowing a separation of a bill into a consent-free substantive part and an administrative part requiring the Bundesrat's consent. Puzzlingly, this option had been largely ignored by the federal government (Scharpf 2009: 81). It is also worth mentioning that lowering the bar for *Bundesrat* approval to simple majorities, making abstentions count in favour of a consent bill's passage (Wagschal and Grassl, 2004), was also not seriously considered.
10. In such a case the respective federal law would not enter into force for six months allowing other *Länder* to consider passing deviating administrative procedures.
11. http://dip21.Bundestag.de/dip21/btd/16/086/1608688.pdf
12. Information on legislation are most precise for published laws. Furthermore, the consent requirement and triggers are most accurate for published bills. On the one hand, consent requirements and triggers are only formally documented after the adoption by the Bundestag during the so-called second passage (*2. Durchgang*) in the Bundesrat. On the other hand, disputes over the consent requirement are only resolved by the Federal Constitutional Court for adopted bills.

13. http://dipbt.bundestag.de/dip21.web/bt
14. On average, 1.07 constitutional triggers are cited for a consent law.
15. For the sake of illustrating the reform effects all 73 laws that entered the last stage in the *Bundesrat* between 1 September 2006 (when the reform came into force) and 31 December 2006 are assigned to the year 2007 in the figure.
16. In the first term of the Bundestag (1949–53) the consent rate already reached 41.8%.
17. It is also not obvious that Art. 84.1 acted as an 'umbrella' trigger and other triggers were to appear after its refinement.

Acknowledgements

I thank Sebastian Riedl for valuable research assistance and Nathalie Behnke, Georg Heilmann and Sabine Kropp for helpful comments and discussions.

Disclosure statement

No potential conflict of interest was reported by the author.

Funding

This work was supported by Deutsche Forschungsgemeinschaft [grant number STE 2353/1-1].

References

Aspinwall, M. D. and Schneider, G. (2000), Same menu, separate tables: the institutionalist turn in political science and the study of European integration, *European Journal of Political Research*, Vol.38, pp.1–36.

Auel, K. (2008), Still no exit from the joint decision trap: the German federal reform(s), *German Politics*, Vol.17, No.4, pp.424–439.

Auel, K. (2010), Between Reformstau and Länder strangulation? German co-operative federalism re-considered, *Regional & Federal Studies*, Vol.20, No.2, pp.229–249.

Behnke, N. (2010), Föderalismusreform in Deutschland, der Schweiz und Österreich, in J. Blumenthal and S. Bröchler (eds), *Föderalismusreform in Deutschland. Bilanz und Perspektiven im internationalen Vergleich*. 1. Aufl. ed., pp.37–58. Wiesbaden: VS Verlag für Sozialwissenschaften.

Benz, A. (1985), *Föderalismus als dynamisches System*. Opladen: Leske+Budrich.

Benz, A. (2008), From joint decision traps to over-regulated federalism: adverse effects of a successful constitutional reform, *German Politics*, Vol.17, No.4, pp.440–456.

Bergmann, H., et al. (2016), Namentliche Abstimmungen im Deutschen Bundestag, 1949–2013, *Zeitschrift für Parlamentsfragen*, Vol.47, No.1, pp.26–50.

Beyme, K. von. (1997), *Der Gesetzgeber. Der Bundestag als Entscheidungszentrum*. Opladen: Westdeutscher Verlag.

Bräuninger, T., et al. (2010), Sachpolitik oder Parteipolitik? Eine Bestimmung des Parteidrucks im Bundesrat mittels bayesianischer Methoden, *Politische Vierteljahresschrift*, Vol.51, pp.223–249.

Bryde, O. (1989), Das Gesetzgebungsverfahren. Stationen, Entscheidungen und Beteiligte im Gesetzgebungsverfahren, in H.-P. Schneider and W. Zeh (eds), *Parlamentsrecht und Parlamentspraxis*, pp.859–881. Berlin and New York: De Gruyter.

Bundestag, D. (2005), *Dokumentation der Kommission von Bundestag und Bundesrat zur Modernisierung der bundesstaatlichen Ordnung*. Paderborn: Media-Print.

Burkhart, S. (2005), Parteipolitikverflechtung. Über den Einfluss der Bundespolitik auf Landtagswahlentscheidungen von 1976–2000, *Politische Vierteljahresschrift*, Vol.46, No.1, pp.14–38.

Burkhart, S. and Manow, P. (2006), Was bringt die Föderalismusreform? Wahrscheinliche Effekte der geänderten Zustimmungspflicht, *MPIfG Working Paper*, 6:6.

Burkhart, S., et al. (2008), A more efficient and accountable federalism? An analysis of the consequences of Germany's 2006 constitutional reform, *German Politics*, Vol.17, No.4, pp.522–540.

Christiano, T. (1996), *The Rule of the Many. Fundamental Issues in Democratic Theory*. Boulder, CO: Westview Press.

Dästner, C. (2001), Zur Entwicklung der Zustimmungsbedürftigkeit von Bundesgesetzen seit 1949, *Zeitschrift für Parlamentsfragen*, Vol.32, No.2, pp.290–309.

Debus, M. (2007), *Pre-electoral Alliances, Coalition Rejections, and Multiparty Governments*. Baden-Baden: Nomos.

Decker, F. and von Blumenthal, J. (2002), Die bundespolitische Durchdringung der Landtagswahlen. Eine empirische Analyse von 1970 bis 2001, *Zeitschrift für Parlamentsfragen*, Vol.33, No.1, pp.144–165.

Detterbeck, K. (2012), *Multi-level Party Politics in Western Europe*. Basingstoke: Palgrave Macmillan.

Feldkamp, M. F. and Ströbel, B. (2005), *Datenhandbuch zur Geschichte des Deutschen Bundestages 1994 bis 2003*. Baden-Baden: Neue Verlagsgesellschaft.

Ganghof, S. and Bräuninger, T. (2006), Government status and legislative behaviour. Partisan Veto Players in Australia, Denmark, Finland and Germany, *Party Politics*, Vol.12, No.4, pp.521–539.

Georgii, H. and Borhanian, S. (2006), Zustimmungsgesetze nach der Föderalismusreform: Wie hätte sich der Anteil der Zustimmungsgesetze verändert, wenn die vorgeschlagene Reform bereits 1998 in Kraft gewesen wäre? *Wissenschaftliche Dienste des Deutschen Bundestages*, 06:37.

Glaab, M. (2010), Political Leadership in der Großen Koalition. Führungsressourcen und -stile von Bundeskanzlerin Merkel, in C. Egle and R. Zohlnhöfer (eds), *Die zweite Große Koalition*, pp.123–155. Wiesbaden: VS Verlag für Sozialwissenschaften.

Höreth, M. (2007), Zur Zustimmungsbedürftigkeit von Bundesgesetzen: Eine kritische Bilanz nach einem Jahr Föderalismusreform I, *Zeitschrift für Parlamentsfragen*, Vol.38, No.4, pp.712–733.

Höreth, M. (2008), A successful failure? The contested implications of Germany's federal reforms, *German Politics*, Vol.17, No.4, pp.408–423.

Höreth, M. (2010), Die Föderalismusreform in der Bewährungsprobe unter Schwarz-Gelb: Warum der Blick zurück die Prognose des Scheiterns erlaubt, in J. Blumenthal and S. Bröchler (eds), *Föderalismusreform in Deutschland. Bilanz und Perspektiven im internationalen Vergleich*. 1. Aufl. ed., pp.117–138. Wiesbaden: VS Verlag für Sozialwissenschaften.

Hough, D. and Koß, M. (2009), Territory and electoral politics in Germany, in W. Swenden and B. Maddens (eds), *Territorial party politics in Western Europe*, pp.47–62. New York: Palgrave Macmillan.

Jeffery, C. (1999), Party politics and territorial representation in the federal republic of Germany, *West European Politics*, Vol.22, No.2, pp.130–166.

Jun, U. (2011), Der Bundesrat und die politischen Parteien: Mitwirkungs- oder Blockadeinstrument? in U. Jun and S. Leunig (eds), *60 Jahre Bundesrat : Tagungsband zum Symposium an der Friedrich-Schiller-Universität Jena vom 12. bis 14. Oktober 2009*. 1. Aufl. ed., pp.106–133. Baden-Baden: Nomos-Verl.

König, T. and Bräuninger, T. (2005), *Gesetzgebung im Föderalismus*. Speyer: Forschungsinstitut für Öffentliche Verwaltung.

Kropp, S. (2001), *Regieren in Koalitionen. Handlungsmuster und Entscheidungsbildung in deutschen Länderregierungen*. Wiesbaden: Westdeutscher Verlag.

Kropp, S. (2004), Gerhard Schröder as 'coordination chancellor': the impact of institutions and arenas on the chancellor's style of governance, in W. Reutter (ed), *Germany on the Road to Normalcy. Policies and Politics of the Red–Green Federal Government (1998–2002)*, pp.67–88. New York: Palgrave MacMillan.

Kropp, S. (2006), Rot-Grün im Reformkorsett? Parteien, Wahlen und Föderalismus, in E. Jesse and R. Sturm (eds), *Bilanz der Bundestagswahl 2005. Voraussetzungen, Ergebnisse, Folgen*, pp.235–258. Wiesbaden: VS Verlag für Sozialwissenschaften.

Kropp, S. (2010), *Kooperativer Föderalismus und Politikverflechtung*. Wiesbaden: VS.

Laufer, H. and Münch, U. (2010), *Das föderale System der Bundesrepublik Deutschland*. München: Bayrische Landeszentrale für Politische Bildung.

Lehmbruch, G. (2000), *Parteienwettbewerb im Bundesstaat*. Wiesbaden: Westdeutscher Verlag.

Lehnert, M., et al. (2008), Never say never again: legislative failure in German bicameralism, *German Politics*, Vol.17, No.3, pp.367–380.

Leunig, S. and Träger, H. (eds) (2012), *Parteipolitik und Landesinteressen. Der deutsche Bundesrat 1949–2009*. Münster: Lit-Verlag.

Linn, S. and Sobolewski, F. (2010), *The German Bundestag. Functions and Procedures*. Rheinbreitbach: NDV.

Lorenz, A. and Riese, D. (2014), The ambiguity of veto power in coalitions: German liberals' role as a watchdog in justice and home affairs and their failure to sell stalemate as success in the federal elections of 2013, *German Politics*, Vol.23, No.4, pp.1–15.

Manow, P. and Burkhart, S. (2007), Legislative self-restraint under divided government in Germany, 1976–2002, *Legislative Studies Quarterly*, Vol.32, No.2, pp.167–191.

Munzert, S., et al. (2015), *Automated Data Collection with R. A Practical Guide to Web Scraping and Text Mining*. Chichester: John Wiley & Sons.

Niedermayer, O. (2010), Von der Zweiparteiendominanz zum Pluralismus: Die Entwicklung des deutschen Parteiensystems im westeuropäischen Vergleich, *Politische Vierteljahresschrift*, Vol.51, No.1, pp.1–13.

Nolan, D. and Temple Lang, D. (2014), *XML and Web Technologies for Data Sciences with R*. New York and Heidelberg: Springer.

Oberhofer, J., et al. (2011), Citizenship im unitarischen Bundesstaat, *Politische Vierteljahresschrift*, Vol.52, No.2, pp.163–194.

Pierson, P. (2004), *Politics in Time. History, Institutions, and Social Analysis*. Princeton, NJ: Princeton University Press.

Powell, G. B. (2000), *Elections as Instruments of Democracy: Majoritarian and Proportional Visions*. New Haven, CT: Yale University Press.

Renzsch, W. (1999), Party competition in the German federal state: new variations on an old theme, *Regional & Federal Studies*, Vol.9, No.3, pp.180–192.

Reutter, W. (2007), Struktur und Dauer der Gesetzgebungsverfahren des Bundes, *Zeitschrift für Parlamentsfragen*, Vol.38, No.2, pp.299–315.

Risse, H. (2007), Zur Entwicklung der Zustimmungsbedürftigkeit von Bundesgesetzen nach der Föderalismusreform 2006, *Zeitschrift für Parlamentsfragen*, Vol.38, No.4, pp.707–712.

Robbe, P., et al. (2009), Auswirkungen der Föderlismusreform I, *Infobrief. Wissenschaftliche Dienste Deutscher Bundestag*, pp.321/09.

Rohe, K. (2002), Entwicklung der politischen Parteien und Parteiensysteme in Deutschland bis zum Jahre 1933, in O. W. Gabriel, et al. (eds), *Parteiendemokratie in Deutschland*, pp.39–58. Bonn: Bundeszentrale für Politische Bildung.

Rudzio, W. (2015), *Das politische System der Bundesrepublik Deutschland*. Wiesbaden: Springer VS.

Saalfeld, T. (2006), Conflict and consensus in Germany's bi-cameral system: a case study of the passage of the agenda 2010, *Debatte*, Vol.14, No.3, pp.247–269.

Scharpf, F. W. (1988), The joint-decision trap: lessons from German federalism and European integration, *Public Administration*, Vol.66, No.3, pp.239–278.

Scharpf, F. W. (1999), *Governing in Europe. Effective and Democratic?* Oxford and New York: Oxford University Press.

Scharpf, F. W. (2006), Föderalismusreform: Warum wurde so wenig erreicht? *Aus Politik und Zeitgeschichte*, Vol.50, pp.6–11.

Scharpf, F. W. (2007), Nicht genutzte Chancen der Föderalismusreform, in C. Egle and R. Zohlnhöfer (eds), *Ende des rot-grünen Projektes. Eine Bilanz der Regierung Schröder 2002–2005*. 1. Aufl. ed., 197–214. Wiesbaden: VS.

Scharpf, F. W. (2008), Community, diversity and autonomy: the challenges of reforming German federalism, *German Politics*, Vol.17, No.4, pp.509–521.

Scharpf, F. W. (2009), *Föderalismusreform. Kein Ausweg aus der Politikverflechtungsfalle?* Frankfurt and New York: Campus.

Schmidt, M. G. (1996), The grand coalition state, in J. M. Colomer (ed), *Political Institutions in Europe*, pp.62–98. London and New York: Routledge.

Schneider, H.-P. (2011), Die 'Länderkammer' im Wandel der Zeiten, in U. Jun and S. Leunig (eds), *60 Jahre Bundesrat : Tagungsband zum Symposium an der Friedrich-Schiller-Universität Jena vom 12. bis 14. Oktober 2009*. 1. Aufl. ed., 17–29. Baden-Baden: Nomos-Verl.

Schneider, H.-P. (2013), *Der neue deutsche Bundesstaat. Bericht über die Umsetzung der Föderalismusreform I*. Baden-Baden: Nomos.

Schrodt, P. A. (2014), Seven deadly sins of contemporary quantitative political analysis, *Journal of Peace Research*, Vol.51, No.2, pp.287–300.

Stecker, C. (2010), Causes of roll call vote supply. Evidence from the German Länder, *Journal of Legislative Studies*, Vol.16, No.4, pp.438–459.

Stecker, C. (2015), Parties on the chain of federalism. Position-taking and multi-level party competition in Germany, *West European Politics*, Vol.38, No.6, pp.1305–1326.

Swenden, W. (2006), *Federalism and Regionalism in Western Europe: A Comparative and Thematic Analysis*. Basingstoke and New York: Palgrave Macmillan.

Szukala, A. (2012), *Das Implementationssystem europäischer Politik*. Wiesbaden: VS Verlag für Sozialwissenschaften.

Tsebelis, G. (2002), *Veto Players. How Political Institutions Work*. Princeton, NJ: Princeton University Press.

Vanberg, G. (2005), *The Politics of Constitutional Review in Germany*. Cambridge, UK and New York: Cambridge University Press.

Wachendorfer-Schmidt. (2005), *Politikverflechtung im vereinigten Deutschland*. Wiesbaden: VS Verlag für Sozialwissenschaften.

Wagschal, U. and Grasl, M. (2004), Die modifizierte Senatslösung. Ein Vorschlag zur Verringerung von Reformblockaden im deutschen Föderalismus, *Zeitschrift für Parlamentsfragen*, Vol.35, No.4, pp 732–752.

Zohlnhöfer, R. (1999), Die große Steuerreform 1998/99: Ein Lehrstück für Politikentwicklung bei Parteienwettbewerb im Bundesstaat, *Zeitschrift für Parlamentsfragen*, Vol.30, No.2, pp.326–345.

Zohlnhöfer, R. (2008a), An end to the reform logjam? The reform of German federalism and economic policy-making, *German Politics*, Vol.17, No.4, pp.457–469.

Zohlnhöfer, R. (2008b), Föderalismusreform und die Entwicklung der Zustimmungsbedürftigkeit von Bundesgesetzen. Versuch einer Klärung, *Zeitschrift für Parlamentsfragen*, Vol.39, No.2, pp.415–419.

Appendix

In order to further corroborate the descriptive results in Figure 1 a multivariate analysis controls for other factors that might also affect the consent rate. The unit of analysis is whether a bill was adopted as an objection or consent bill. Accordingly, this binary dependent variable is modelled in a logistic regression. Dummy variables identify the period after the reform, oppositional and mixed control of the Bundesrat with government control as baseline, as well as specific categories of bills that are explained in more detail in the main text. The coefficient plot in the left pane of Figure A2 reports confidence intervals and odds ratios. Coefficients below 1 indicate that an increase in the independent variable reduces the likelihood that an opposition party votes against the government. Coefficients above 1 increase the likelihood of a bill being adopted as a consent bill. As can be seen the reductive effect of the reform remains substantial and significant. This is further visualized in the right pane of Figure A2 that plots the

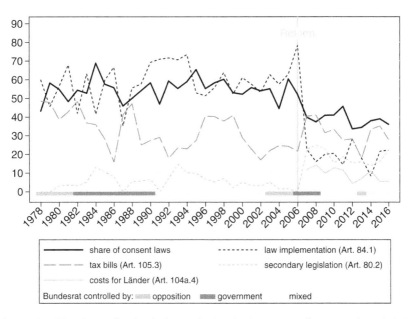

Figure A1. The share of individual constitutional triggers on all consent laws (1978–2016).

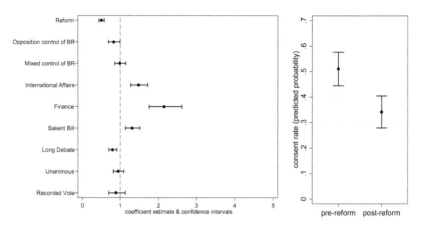

Figure A2. The share of individual constitutional triggers on all consent laws (1978–2016).

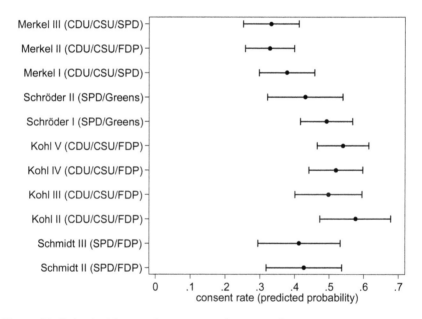

Figure A3. Federal cabinets and consent rate (1978–2016).

predicted probability of a bill to be adopted as a consent bill (under the assumption of mixed control of the BR and non-financial legislation while all other dummy variables are set to 1). The predicted probability is 51% before and 34% after the reform.

Figure A3 presents the predicted probability of a bill to be adopted as a consent bill depending on the cabinet that was in place. Additional covariates are included as in the logistic regression underlying Figure A2. Cabinets are chronologically ordered along the y-axis. The reform was enacted during the cabinet Merkel I. As can be seen, pre- and post-reform cabinets do see a significantly different consent rate. However, there are no significant different consent rates across cabinets within the pre- and post-reform area.

The effect of reformed legislative competences on *Länder* policy-making: determinants of fragmentation and uniformity

Nicolai Dose and Iris Reus

ABSTRACT
The Federalism Reform I (2006) transferred some additional legal competences to the German *Länder* to provide them with more autonomy. Our analysis is guided by the question as to how fragmentation and uniformity concerning the content of the new *Länder* laws can be explained. To this end, we develop a theoretical framework based on a short review of the literature on the field. Subsequently, the framework is tested empirically on the basis of four selected legislative competences. Our results show that differences in party positions and problem pressures result in the fragmentation of laws. This applies also to competition under budgetary constraints, whereas competition superimposes the first two factors. Uniformity was influenced by similar party positions, and particularly by networks of experts.

Introduction

Owing to the Federalism Reform I in 2006, the German *Länder* gained the responsibility for a number of additional legislative competences. These matters range from public sector pay or amusement arcades to the penitentiary system. The literature review reveals that almost ten years after the coming into effect of the reform, legislative activity has increased manifold. However, we observe contradictory developments with respect to the content of the laws. In some policy fields, the *Länder* made use of their new leeway and followed their own ideas of policy-making, resulting in increasing fragmentation of laws. In contrast, other policy fields are still marked by uniformity of laws like before the implementation of the reform in 2006. However, the literature mainly analyses the new *Länder* laws from the perspective of other disciplines, while only a few detailed case studies explain

---

Supplemental data for this article can be found in the Appendix (referred to as the Online Appendix in the text).

Länder legislation from a political science perspective (e.g. Reus, 2016; Rowe and Turner, 2016). In particular, studies comparing all the *Länder* and several policies systematically are still scarce. Based on the identified research gap, this article seeks to pinpoint the most important factors explaining the fragmentation and uniformity of laws and to reveal their relative explanatory power. Therefore, in short the research question is as follows: which factors can explain the different degrees of the fragmentation of laws in different policies?

To answer this question, we will proceed in the following manner: first, we will reflect on the theoretical background of *Länder* policy-making and on this basis develop our analytical framework, that is, potential determinants of fragmentation and uniformity. Second, we will discuss the chosen research design and the employed methods. Third, four new *Länder* competences –'penitentiary system', 'shop closing time', 'civil service career law', and 'civil servants' pay' – are analysed empirically with regard to the analytical framework. The final part summarizes the empirical results in the light of the theoretical considerations.

Theoretical background

The transfer of competences strengthened the self-rule of the *Länder* in order to facilitate sub-national diversity and strengthening of competition among the *Länder* (Dose, 2016: 27–28). Sturm (2008: 37) argues convincingly that German federalism is no longer determined by a path dependency that is based on symmetric developments and unitarianism, as Hesse (1962: 18) had observed as early as the 1960s (differently Decker, 2011: 233). Instead, diversity as well as asymmetric developments and outcomes have become accepted concepts of German federalism. Jeffery et al. (2016: 166–168) even go so far as to argue that to a lower extent diversity has always been present, which Jeffery and Rowe (2014: 53) capture by the expression "the two faces of German federalism". The growing significance of diversity might lead to more flexibility, democracy, transparency of decision-making and accountability (Sturm, 2008: 37). Moreover, after the Federalism Reform had gone into effect, the *Länder* governments received a certain leeway in terms of region-specific policy decisions.

This posed a challenge to the 'uniformity narrative', which is backed by Art. 72, para. 2 of the German Basic Law, which stresses nationwide equivalent living conditions. Thus, the 'uniformity narrative' – which was and still might be prevalent in German federalism working in the direction of uniform *Länder* laws – was questioned by the notion of competition (Sturm, 2008: 34–40; Jeffery et al. 2016: 169; cf. Keating and Cairney, 2012: 240). The new diversity narrative, set up against the older uniformity narrative (Schmidt, 2016: 311), is one that is recognized across Europe (Loughlin, 2013: 12).

Although there is substantial doubt concerning the extent of autonomy that is connected with the new legislative competences (Scharpf, 2008: 514–515; Reus and Zohlnhöfer, 2015: 268; Hildebrandt and Wolf, 2016: 5–7), the *Länder* have made increasing use of their new leeway over the last ten years and substituted the former federal law with their own laws. Concerning the content of these laws, four years after the Federalism Reform had come into effect, Blumenthal (2010: 177) observed a relatively high degree of uniformity, while two years after that a research project of the German Institute for Federalism Research (Schneider, 2012: 230) registered increasing variance between the *Länder* policies. The latest overview (Reus and Zohlnhöfer, 2015: 262–264) shows that there is no consistent picture but huge differences across competences.

Examining the factors that explain the results of *Länder* policy-making, Jeffery et al. (2014) revealed substantial variation of outcomes by analysing four policies and attributed the differences between laws to structural causes (differences in economic performance and to a certain extent differences in the institutional configuration of the *Länder*, that is, the number of actors in the policy-making process), as well as to differing positions of the governing parties (Jeffery et al. 2014: 1360, Appendix C). Similarly, Wolf and Hildebrandt (2016: 391) conclude from a cross-section analysis of policy field-oriented studies that socio-economic factors and to a lesser extent party politics make the most important difference.

Overall, the diversity of important determinants having the potential to influence public policy-making in the *Länder* is significant (Schmidt, 2016: 302–303). Different demographic constellations (age, ethnic structure, and crime rates), different socio-economic situations including the percentage of those living on transfer income and the per capita government debt naturally have some impact on policy diversity. Moreover, variations of public opinion seem to have an influence on the degree of diversity (Jeffery et al. 2016: 168).

The plurality of determinants may be structured by grouping factors like demographic constellation, socio-economic circumstances, public or published opinion, and the government's fiscal capacity with reference to functionalist demands (problem pressure) and problem-solving capacities (cf. Wilensky, 1975; Obinger, 2015). On the one hand, problem pressure arises due to the effects of societal modernization. On the other hand, these problems can only be solved considering the governmental problem-solving capacities, which are to a great extent influenced by institutions and financial resources (cf. Obinger, 2015: 35, 39). The striking point, however, is the assumption that modern societies converge with an increasing level of economic growth (Wilensky, 1975: 18). This should be even more the case if there is some competition between the different states (Holzinger and Knill, 2005: 789). Likewise, similar problem pressure might lead to convergence

(Obinger and Starke, 2007: 472). Conversely, if the problem pressure is different in the different *Länder*, we have to expect different laws.

Analytical framework: determinants of fragmentation and uniformity

The underlying rationale of the analytical framework employed in this study is that different conditions in the *Länder* and different electoral demands, which translate into different party compositions of the *Länder* governments, influence the degree of fragmentation of policy-making. If policies are denoted by different characteristics in the different *Länder*, we should expect, *ceteris paribus*, a higher degree of fragmentation of the laws.

However, as indicated, many additional factors might also influence the degree of fragmentation (Keating and Cairney, 2012: 240). Based on the short literature review above, we chose those factors that have been identified as having the greatest explanatory power, factors that are the partisan composition of government on the one hand and socio-economic factors on the other.

Moreover, we have to consider that sometimes the *Länder* have to compete for scarce resources in their striving to solve the problems that put pressure on them. In general, competition between the *Länder* should foster uniformity, but if it goes along with budgetary constraints, it may lead to fragmentation.

Dependent variable: degree of fragmentation

The objective of this article is to explain the level of fragmentation or uniformity of the law in those policy fields for which the *Länder* gained legislative competences after the Federalism Reform I of 2006. In order to measure the dependent variable, we use the following combinations of two characteristics: the degree of similarity between the laws and the amount of *Länder* involved. Both will be revealed through a systematic comparative analysis of the respective laws in all 16 *Länder*.

Highly uniform:	Essential features of the law are similar; the differences are minor for all the *Länder*.
Uniform:	There is a bigger group of *Länder* denoted by a law with similar essential features; the differences for the rest of the *Länder* are moderate.
Slightly uniform:	There is a bigger group of *Länder* denoted by a law with similar essential features; the differences for the rest of the *Länder* are substantial.
Slightly fragmented:	There is no bigger group of *Länder* denoted by a law with similar essential features; the differences for all the *Länder* laws are moderate.
Fragmented:	There is no bigger group of *Länder* denoted by a law with similar essential features; the differences for all the *Länder* laws are substantial.
Highly fragmented:	The differences in the essential features for all the *Länder* laws are very substantial; there are only minor similarities.

Independent variable: parties

The 'parties-do-matter hypothesis' argues that the partisan composition of governments has implications for the choice of policies (Hibbs, 1977; Page, 1991; Schmidt, 1996). The different party positions can be traced back to different clientele groups with which parties are connected as well as to different ideas and values (Zohlnhöfer, 2005: 51–54). Differing party compositions of the *Länder* governments should eventually result in the fragmentation of laws grouped by *Land* governments with the same partisan composition (Schmidt, 2016: 308–310). However, in order to make a difference, parties must have differential policy preferences (Schmidt, 1996: 163, 168–169).

Other researchers observe a regionalization of party competition, meaning different positions of *Land* parties though belonging to the same political camp. According to Bräuninger and Debus (2012: 203–204), their positions are influenced by the socio-structural composition and the ideological orientation of the electorate in the respective *Land*. The latter is based on common cultural beliefs, in particular the religiousness of citizens. The impact on policy decisions has rarely been analysed so far, but authors such as Turner (2011: 224) show that for several policies there is an impact of intraparty differences relating to CDU *Länder* parties. In general, such 'federal partisan effects' should lead to fragmentation, even between *Länder* governed by parties belonging to the same political camp. In line with respective studies, we will operationalize party politics by the party composition of the *Länder* governments.

> H1: The more different the party positions of *Länder* governments are in a cross-*Länder* comparison, the higher we expect the fragmentation of the *Länder* laws to be.

Independent variable: problem pressure

With respect to the socio-economic factors, some clarifications have to be made. We recognize such functional demands as demographic constellations, degree of population living on transfer payments, etc. In order to encompass all these demands, we will refer in accordance with parts of the literature to the term 'problem pressure'. Besides, other analytical frameworks have already incorporated problem pressure into their outline for research (Grande, 1998: 819–821; Rothgang and Wessel, 2008: 163; Blumenthal, 2010: 180; Wenzelburger and Zohlnhöfer, 2015: 29). Generally, problem pressure stemming from globalization, Europeanization, or the demographic development may be in absolute terms the same across all the *Länder*. Since, however, the specific constellations in the *Länder* are often different, the *Länder* might perceive different pressures, and hence different needs, to adapt (Grande, 1998: 821). With regard to the *Land*-specific situation, Blumenthal (2010: 180, our translation) suggests, in line with the above literature review, including "all variables which are relevant for the respective policy", ranging from the structure of the economy to demographic aspects or the proportion of migrants. Thus, we can expect to observe policies tailored to the specific situations in each *Land* (Jeffrey, 1999: 340). The heterogeneity of circumstances should subsequently be reflected in the differing policies, that is, in fragmentation of the laws.

While, for instance, social transfer rates above average indicate some problem pressure, many incidents call for a qualitative method of measuring this factor. In the end, it is important to know whether decision-makers perceive a situation as problematic rather than whether it is problematic from the viewpoint of a researcher.

> *H2*: The more different the problem pressure in a cross-*Länder* comparison is, the higher we expect the fragmentation of the law to be.

Independent variable: competition between Länder *combined with* budgetary constraints

Generally, competition is regarded as the cause of change, efficiency, and innovation (Hayek, 2002; Stucke, 2011). Correspondingly, the proponents of the economic theory of federalism argue that a division of competences into federal and state levels encourages competition between the *Länder* for taxpayers. This, in turn, induces efficient government (Oates, 1972: 12–13), because the states strive for attracting taxpayers through efficient public services (education, security, absence of corruption, immediate and reliable response to demands, etc.) and attractive regulations (unspoiled and healthy environment, attractive business regulation, etc.). However, achieving the respective benefits requires that certain assumptions be given (Tiebout, 1956: 419; Olson, 1969: 483; Oates, 1972: 13). In our context, the most important one is that the *Länder* have equal capacity to provide public services (Benz, 2002: 36–37). If this assumption were not a given, substantial inequality would develop between the *Länder* (Hausner, 2005: 59). Certainly, the German *Länder* face very different budgetary constraints. The pressure exerted by state debt on policy-making is substantially different across the *Länder* (Dose and Wolfes, 2016: 279–281). Moreover, as the short literature review already revealed, the budgetary room for policy-making seems to make a difference (Hildebrandt and Wolf, 2016: 3; Jeffery et al. 2016: 169). While budgetary constraints might also be perceived as a kind of problem pressure, there is a significant difference: problem pressures (such as high lung cancer rates or pressure on the labour market) call for public action. How this action might look like is sometimes, but not always, a question of budgetary constraints. Moreover, if there is any competition between the *Länder* for scarce resources such as the supply of qualified personnel, this will have an impact on public action.

If a state suffers from considerable state debt, it would seem logical that this state makes use of new legal competences if the legal matters of these competences allow reducing the debt or at least do not increase it. Thus, it should be appropriate to operationalize this factor by the ratio of the state debt and the respective GDP. High state debt limits governmental activities (Jeffery et al. 2016: 169). Conversely, a low ratio of state debt to GPD allows government spending, for example, raising pay levels to be an attractive employer. The differences of ratios will result in fragmentation. Since, however, absolute figures of the state debt would level the differing potential to pay back a certain amount of debt between small and large *Länder*, it makes sense to employ the proportion of *Länder* debt to its GDP (Dose and Wolfes, 2016: 279–281). The overall argument gains special momentum if one takes into account that, according to Art. 109, para. 3 of the German Basic Law, the *Länder* are constitutionally obliged to have a net borrowing rate of zero beginning with the year 2020. Based on this reasoning, we derive the following hypothesis (cf. Keating and Cairney, 2012: 241):

> *H3*: Competition under the condition of equal budgetary constraints of the *Länder* or without budgetary constraints being important leads to uniformity, while competition without equal or similar budgetary constraints leads to fragmentation.

Research design and methods

We will employ a Most Similar Systems Design including all 16 *Länder* and covering a time span of roughly ten years after the Federalism Reform in 2006. Overall, the relatively great commonality among the German *Länder* allows to focus the analysis on those variables that seem to make a difference (Peters, 1998: 23), without being disturbed by the effects of variables not systematically observed and included in the analysis (Keman, 2014: 54–55). Thus, generally the institutional setting can be assumed as constant in our cross-country comparison. This does not mean that institutional variables do not make a difference, as may be revealed by deep case studies. However, in a cross-country analysis, we are not able to attribute any differences to them because the institutional context is hardly changing.

Concerning the selection of legislative competences, we have chosen policy fields with considerable legislative activity that allow a comparative analysis of all or most of the 16 *Länder*. Moreover, the competences should promise to produce variance with regard to the dependent and independent variables of the theoretical framework. Our final selection comprises 'penitentiary system', 'shop closing time', 'public service law', and 'public sector pay'.

While Table 1 presents only an initial rough estimate of the degree of fragmentation of each policy field, we will start the empirical analysis with a

Table 1. Variance of the variables in different policy fields.

	Penitentiary system	Shop closing time	Civil service career law	Civil servants pay
Is there competition between the *Länder* and are budgetary constraints important?	No	No	Yes	Yes
Do governing parties in the *Länder* have different positions?	Yes	Yes	No	Yes
Are there different problem pressures in the *Länder*?	No	Yes	Yes	Yes
Degree of fragmentation (preliminary and rough)	Slightly uniform	Fragmented	Slightly fragmented	Highly fragmented

thorough description of the value of our dependent variable by comparing the content of the laws of the 16 *Länder*. In order to estimate the degree, we will refer to a number of essential aspects of the policy. The influence of the explanatory factors is investigated by qualitative as well as quantitative analysis.

In order to collect the data, we have followed a triangulation approach. Besides the *Länder* laws, we have drawn upon parliamentary documents (draft bills, minutes of plenary debates, etc.), a systematic analysis of newspaper articles via the Nexis and WISO newspaper collections, as well as press releases. In addition, we conducted interviews with ministerial officials and representatives of interest groups.

Empirical analysis of *Länder* legislation after the federalism reform

Penitentiary system[1]

With regard to the degree of fragmentation, we observe two groups (see Graph 1 and Online Appendix). The laws of Bavaria, Baden-Württemberg, Hamburg, Hesse, and Lower Saxony contain, without coordination, similar regulations in many respects. These laws are marked by a high overall degree of restrictiveness, close to the former federal law. Ten *Länder* (Brandenburg, Berlin, Bremen, Mecklenburg-Western Pomerania, Rhineland-Palatinate, Schleswig-Holstein, Saarland, Saxony, Saxony-Anhalt, and Thuringia) set up a workgroup to coordinate their laws. The result was a sample draft bill with a low overall degree of restrictiveness. Finally, these *Länder* stayed close together; only Brandenburg went significantly beyond it in several respects. Ten out of 24 aspects are completely the same in these laws; deviations

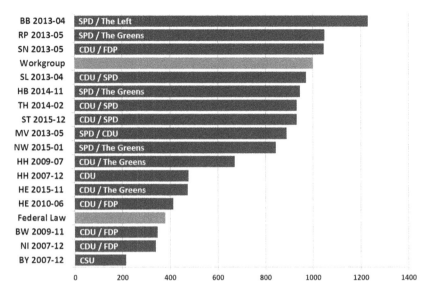

Graph 1. Ranking of laws according to overall degree of restrictiveness (low score = restrictive, high score = supportive). Source: authors' compilation, www.bundeswahllei-ter.de. Comment: Law (Land/date) in the first column, partisan composition of government within bars (white); bars show total score of each law derived from an additive index capturing essential aspects of the policy. These include, for instance, the number of visiting hours, the amount of payment for work, leisure activities made available or the number of prisoners per room (for detailed information see Online Appendix). Abbreviations of the 16 *Länder*: BB = Brandenburg, BE = Berlin, BW = Baden-Württemberg, BY = Bavaria, HB = Bremen, HE = Hesse, HH = Hamburg, MV = Mecklenburg Western-Pomerania, NI = Lower Saxony, NW = North Rhine-Westphalia, RP = Rhineland-Palatinate, SH = Schleswig-Holstein, SL = Saarland, SN = Saxony, ST = Saxony-Anhalt, TH = Thuringia.

vary between three and eight aspects per law. Later, North Rhine-Westphalia passed a law close to the workgroup, and Hamburg and Hesse also came closer with amendments. Therefore, thanks to the high degree of uniformity within but huge differences between the groups, we assign the value 'slightly uniform'.

On looking at the analytical framework, based on systematic process tracing of the legislation in all *Länder*, it turned out that 'Parties' were the central factor. In accordance with our hypothesis, parties caused fragmentation of laws on the one hand due to different positions (between the groups) and, on the other hand, caused uniformity due to similar positions (within the groups). Although there were still some differences between the different regional party associations, we observed the effects of parties of the same camp. Except Saxony, all CDU/CSU and CDU-FDP governments passed comparatively restrictive laws, while all governments in which the SPD was involved passed less restrictive laws (see Graph 1). Arguments related to party ideology dominated the political discussions. All CDU parties emphasized security issues more strongly than all other parties, which included both the protection of the public and safety as well as order inside the prisons. On the basis of that reasoning, some CDU parties demanded deviations from the sample draft bill of the workgroup, particularly concerning the possibility of long-term leave for prisoners sentenced to life-long imprisonment (cf. Saxony, plenary protocol 5/77: 7935; Saxony-Anhalt, plenary protocol 6/84: 6978; Thuringia, plenary protocol 5/144: 13 628). In contrast, SPD parties and the Greens focused mainly on social rehabilitation, claimed more support, and tried to strengthen the position of the prisoners. The impact was most visible in North Rhine-Westphalia, where the CDU-FDP government had kept the restrictive federal law, whereas the SPD-Green government later passed a law close to the workgroup. In Hamburg, the Greens also reached several modifications after they had entered government, while in Hesse the Greens could only achieve minor modifications against their coalition partner CDU.

A further important factor explaining the high uniformity of the laws of the workgroup *Länder* was the possibility to build on former experiences of existing networks. Table 2 shows that most of these *Länder* had already worked together twice, and pointed to the 'successful cooperation'.[2] Given the increasing number of violent criminals and drug abusers (cf. Dünkel, 2010: 14), the experts involved in the workgroup unanimously demanded more therapy and support for prisoners. The coordination procedure established a common view and set standards so that there were only a few deviations from the sample draft bill in the *Länder* laws and a high degree of uniformity within the group.

Competition did not at all matter in this case, as the *Länder* do not compete for prisoners. Budgetary constraints were sometimes mentioned in the discussions, but not seen as an essential criterion for legislation. The factor 'problem pressure' was present insofar as almost all politicians generally emphasized the need for measures of social rehabilitation to avoid recurrences of prisoners (e.g. Brandenburg, plenary protocol 5/75: 6069; Hamburg, plenary protocol 18/95: 5033; Saxony-Anhalt, plenary protocol 6/84: 6980). However, the pressure (as well as the measures connected with it) was perceived differently, which facilitated fragmentation of laws, but it mattered to a significantly lesser extent than the factor 'parties'.

Table 2. Participation of *Länder* in workgroups concerning the three parts of the penitentiary system.

	BB	BE	HB	HE	HH	MV	RP	SH	SL	SN	ST	TH
Adolescents 2007	BB	BE	HB			MV	RP	SH	SL		ST	TH
Remand 2008	BB	BE	HB	HE	HH	MV	RP	SH	SL	SN	ST	TH
Adults 2011	BB	BE	HB			MV	RP	SH	SL	SN	ST	TH

Source: Authors' compilation.

Shop closing time

As Graph 2 shows, fragmentation is first of all reflected by the rather even distribution of *Länder* laws over the entire spectrum concerning the overall degree of state-regulation. Fragmentation is limited on both sides as follows: on the one hand, we find a general tendency towards liberalization as all the *Länder* allowed longer opening times than the former federal law would. On the other hand, the Federal Constitutional Court (01.12.2009, 1 BvR 2857/07, 1 BvR 2858/07) restricted the possible extent of liberalization by protecting Sundays and particularly declared shop opening on all four Sundays in advent in Berlin unconstitutional. However, within this spectrum, we find a huge variety of regulations regarding the different aspects of the laws (see Online Appendix). Even laws with a similar overall degree of state-regulation contain different arrangements in detail that again increase the degree of fragmentation. Thus, we consider this policy to be 'fragmented'.

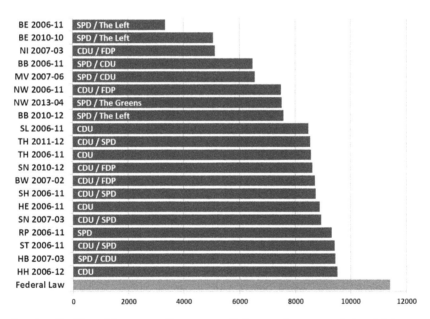

Graph 2. Ranking of laws according to overall degree of state-regulation (high score = state-regulated, low score = economically liberal). Source: Authors' compilation, www.bundeswahlleiter.de. Comment: Law (Land/date) in the first column, partisan composition of government within bars (white); bars show total score of each law derived from an additive index capturing essential aspects of the policy. These include, for instance, opening hours on weekdays, regulations regarding Sundays and Public Holidays, exceptions for certain places like stations as well as exceptions for certain products like tourist supply (for detailed information, see Online Appendix).

Systematic Process Tracing of the legislation in the *Länder* revealed that the discussions were strongly based on arguments connected with party ideology. The partisan composition of government did matter significantly and in all the *Länder* the following party differences could be observed: FDP parties demanded extensive liberalization, SPD parties voted for restrictive laws for worker protection, and the CDU parties supported restrictive regulations concerning Sundays for religious reasons. However, Graph 2 shows that there are finally no clear partisan effects visible in this way. This was due to the huge differences that emerged between the positions of parties with the same label in the different *Länder*. In Baden-Württemberg, for instance, the CDU parliamentary group turned out to be "almost more Catholic than the Catholic church itself" (Süddeutsche Zeitung, 01.12.2006, authors' own translation), and due to its resistance – against Prime Minister Oettinger and the coalition partner FDP – shop opening on Sundays was limited to three, and all Sundays in advent were excluded from shop opening. In contrast, in Saxony the CDU supported shop opening on all four Sundays in advent based on the view that contrary to the traditional position more and more families enjoyed Christmas shopping on Sundays (plenary protocol 4/65: 5133). These differences occurred particularly within the CDU, but also in other parties. For instance, in early discussions in Baden-Württemberg, the FDP had demanded shop opening on four Sundays per year (Stuttgarter Zeitung, 01.12.2006), while in Lower Saxony the FDP had claimed unrestricted shop opening on Sundays in general (Bremer Nachrichten, 10.10.2006). The different positions of different governing parties as well as different regional party associations of the same political camp led to the fragmentation of laws.

Across *Länder*, politicians mentioned pressure to liberalize shop opening times due to varied working hours and changed shopping habits, which facilitated some uniformity. Yet, different perceptions of this problem pressure, coupled with partisan differences, led again to the fragmentation of laws. The land-specific problem situation was dominant in Berlin, which passed an extremely liberal law. The draft bill of the SPD/Left-government was even more liberal than the FDP proposal and justified due to the status as capital city and metropolis (plenary protocol 16/2: 99). Similarly, Mecklenburg-Western Pomerania opted for extensive exceptions for the economically significant tourist cities. In contrast, Saarland kept the restrictive federal regulation on weekdays because the government feared that liberalization could disadvantage smaller shops that competed with large supermarkets (plenary protocol 13/29: 1641).

While budgetary constraints were not important, competition did exert some influence on neighbouring *Länder*, because more liberal regulations in the neighbouring *Land* could mean losing purchasing power. However, this factor was prevalent only in Brandenburg due to the high attractiveness of the neighbour city Berlin. For instance, the government had originally planned to restrict shop opening in advent to two Sundays but later increased, against its partisan preferences, the number to four like Berlin to avoid economic disadvantages (plenary protocol 4/40: 2825). Overall, such competition led to more uniformity between some *Länder*, but finally involved only few aspects of the laws.

Civil service career law

As Burmester (2015: 34–47) has shown, after having started generally with the same federal regulations, which have been effective across the *Länder* before Federalism Reform I in 2006, the regulations of the civil service career laws remain fairly different. Analysing the degree of fragmentation by referring to the most important aspects, we find three different groups. As shown in Table 3, the German coastal *Länder* are denoted by fairly similar laws. Three additional *Länder* have opted for at least parts of the civil service career systems of the coastal *Länder*. Therefore, in many aspects, their laws resemble those of the coastal *Länder*. The third group comprises eight *Länder* with widely different regulations. Only the standard retirement age is the same for all of them. According to the above definition of the degree of fragmentation, the civil service career laws are slightly fragmented.

Table 3. Characteristics of the civil service career law in a cross-*Länder* comparison.

Bundesland	No. of career tracks	No. of subject areas	Weekly working hours	Maximum age for appointment as civil servant	Modular qualification 0 = no; 1 = yes	Standard retirement age
Northern coastal *Länder*						
Bremen	2	10	40	45	0	67
Hamburg	2	10	40	45	0	67
Mecklenburg-Western Pomerania	2	10	40	40	0	67
Lower Saxony	2	10	40	45	0	67
Schleswig-Holstein	2	10	41	45	0	67
Länder that opted for at least parts of the coastal *Länder* model						
Berlin	2	9	40	50	0	65
Saxony	2	9	40	47	0	67
Saxony-Anhalt	2	54	40	45	0	65
Länder with highly fragmented laws						
Baden-Wuerttemberg	3	48	41	42	0	67
Bavaria	1	6	40	45	1	67
Brandenburg	4	48	40	47	0	67
Hesse	3	11	42	50	0	67
North Rhine-Westphalia	2	4	41	40	1	67
Rhineland-Palatinate	1	6	40	45	1	67
Saarland	4	11	40	40	0	67
Thuringia	3	11	40	47	0	67

Source: Burmester (2015) with some updates by the authors.

The most convincing independent variable explaining the degree of fragmentation is the competition between the *Länder* and with the private sector for qualified personnel. In this case, it is a competition for qualified staff which will increase significantly in the future (cf. Frank and Heinicke, 2009: 39; Helmrich et al. 2012: 10). As is also known to the government, the demographic development will increasingly bring about a shortage of qualified personnel (Lower Saxony, printed matter 16/655: 74). Owing to this development, *Länder* governments are not only in competition with each other for qualified personnel but also with the private sector (Schünemann, 2007: 23, North Rhine-Westphalia, printed matter 16/9500: 15). Thus, the *Länder* have to modernize their public sector law if they want to attract a sufficient number of applicants.[3]

However, the problem pressure varies. In *Länder* like the booming ones in the south that are characterized by a low unemployment rate, the problem pressure is higher than in those *Länder* that are marked by a relatively high unemployment rate. The unequal problem pressure allows taking measures, which differ in their potential to make the civil service career system more attractive. Moreover, the *Länder* compete with each other for qualified personnel. However, creating a substantial upward mobility in the system does not come without financial costs. Bavaria, the frontrunner in this process, invested a substantial amount of money in creating 34,400 possibilities for promotion (Bayerisches Staatsministerium der Finanzen, 2013: 86, 105). In contrast, North Rhine-Westphalia, which had also set up an attractive qualification system, could not afford, due to budgetary constraints, to create additional promotion possibilities (DBB NRW, 2015: 1–2; DGB NRW, 2015: 4). Therefore, finally a highly attractive civil service is dependent, among other things, on a financially sound state budget as in Bavaria. As can be seen, the unequal budgetary constraints explain the fragmentation of the laws.

As already mentioned, the German coastal *Länder* are characterized by fairly uniform regulations. This is due to some coordinating activities starting at the beginning of the reform process in order to guarantee mobility of the civil servants between these *Länder* (Seeck and Rieger, 2011: 1–2). The question is why the coastal *Länder* have been successful in coordinating their reform processes despite being under similar competitive pressure as the rest of the *Länder*. The difference can be explained by a long tradition of corporation in various fields that even has been spelt out in a state contract between them (cf. Hamburg, plenary protocol 16/31: 1443; printed matter 16/2263). Except for Lower Saxony, the coastal *Länder* lacked administrative capacities to develop sound concepts for reform processes. In order to hold their ground in comparison to the bigger *Länder* like Bavaria and North Rhine-Westphalia, they pooled their capacities.[4]

Partisan effects seem not to have influenced the fragmentation of public sector law. Due to the complexity of the civil service career law, this subject was not suitable either for party competition or for a remarkable coverage in the media, as a media analysis revealed.

Civil servants' pay

Starting with the dependent variable, the field of public sector pay has to be considered as highly fragmented, although in 2006 it was mostly the same across the different *Länder*. Bavaria is the highest-paying *Land* in Germany, while Berlin is characterized by the lowest pay level. In the career track A 13 (e.g. first-grade high school teacher), the difference in yearly pay between Bavaria (€62,501) and Berlin (€56,165) amounts to €6,336 or 11.3% in 2016 (cf. DGB Bundesvorstand, 2016: 13).[5] A similar picture holds true for career track A 9 (e.g. detective superintendent). Here the difference between the highest-paying country (Bavaria paying €41,281) and the lowest-paying *Land* (Berlin €36,909) stands at €4,372 or 11.8% (cf. DGB Bundesvorstand, 2016: 13). No two *Länder* show the same pay level, whereas the differences in the pay scales are substantial. Even the Constitutional Court of North Rhine-Westphalia has declared the system of civil servants' pay in this *Land* as unconstitutional for being too fragmented in its internal structure to ensure constitutionally guaranteed traditional principles of the civil service (VerfGH NRW 21/13 from 1 July 2014). Overall, it seems justified to assess the degree of fragmentation as high.

In this case, the competition for qualified personnel gave rise to a process that led to highly diverse public sector pay levels in the different *Länder*. For instance, the impact of competition became evident from the growing difficulties Berlin faces to attract qualified civil servants. The neighbouring government of Brandenburg and especially the federal government based in the same city pay better than Berlin the *Land*. In response to its weak position in the competition for the most qualified civil servants, in August 2016 Berlin will start increasing the civil servants' pay at least by 0.5 percentage points above the average pay increase in the other *Länder* (DGB, 2015: 28).

Compared to the case of the civil service career law, budgetary constraints were even more important. Since the public sector employs a workforce of 4.6 million, of which 1.8 million are civil servants, a major public cost factor, the attempt to limit any increase in the pay level seems understandable. Thus, especially *Länder* with high budget deficits have to limit them very significantly. However, the already existing and the impeding shortage of qualified personnel in the labour market makes it necessary to build a more attractive civil service system, a part of which is the pay level. As in the case with the civil service career law, the problem pressure is differently distributed across the *Länder*. More affluent *Länder* such as Bavaria, which are marked by a tense labour market for qualified personnel, feel the pressure stronger than less booming *Länder*. At the same time, they suffer less from budgetary constraints.

Following this line of thought, Dose and Wolfes (2016: 279–281) worked with a model that incorporates not only the *Länder* public debt as percentage of its GDP, but also the partisan dominance in the governments of the different *Länder*. By calculating a regression analysis using data of the mid-range career track A 13, they explained about 60% of the variance and attributed a substantially higher explanatory power (Beta = −.655) to the ratio of *Länder* debt to GDP than to being governed by a left-wing government (Beta = −.329). Thus, the *Länder* governments that are dominated by the CDU and the sister party CSU pay their civil servants slightly better than left-wing/Green governments.

Conclusion

This paper aimed to explain the degree of fragmentation or uniformity of *Länder* laws based on four of the new legislative competences that the *Länder* gained with the Federalism Reform I in 2006. Referring to our hypotheses, we can summarize our empirical results as follows.

As assumed in Hypothesis 1, the *Länder* laws show a higher degree of fragmentation if there are different positions of the governing parties. This holds true for the differences between parties as well as for the differences between regional party associations of the same political camp (see the case studies on shop closing time and on the penitentiary system). Naturally, if a party has not developed its own position, this variable does not make any difference (see civil service career law). Likewise, as Hypothesis 2 posits, different problem pressures across the *Länder* increase the degree of fragmentation of the laws. However, on the basis of the selected cases, we cannot attribute the extent of explanatory power because there was no sufficient variance. Finally, Hypothesis 3 could be provisionally confirmed. In two of the case studies, we observed highly fragmented or at least slightly fragmented laws due to competition between the *Länder* under unequal budgetary constraints. Especially, if the budgetary constraints are important, competition results in a high degree of fragmentation. Comparing the three factors, namely parties, problem pressure, and competition, the latter superimposes the others. If the *Länder* fear economic disadvantages, even partisan beliefs step back to some extent.

However, there is an additional factor not yet included in our analytical framework, which seems to have an influence on the degree of fragmentation of laws. In the case of the penitentiary system as well as in the case of civil service career law, the existence of expert networks has developed a substantial explanatory power in the direction of uniformity. In this case, the influence of "brotherhoods of experts", as already stated by Frido Wagener in 1979, was again confirmed. It appears that such networks are even able to superimpose the impact of the factor of 'competition under the condition of budgetary constraints'. Thus, further research should take up this 'new' factor.

Finally, with regard to the impact of the Federalism Reform on *Länder* politics, we notice an indication for a certain change towards 'more federalism' compared to the traditional 'uniformity narrative'. Although there is still some uniformity, the majority of cases in our analysis were characterized by a remarkable degree of fragmentation.

Notes

1. The penitentiary system consists of three parts: adults, adolescents, and imprisonment on remand. This analysis concentrates on 'adults' as it is the main part of the policy.
2. Press release, http://www.bsbd-thueringen.de/aa_pdf/PDF218_MI___LStVollzG. pdf (accessed 18 August 2016).
3. See the statement of the high-ranking civil servant of the Bavarian Ministry of Finance Ministerialdirigent Wilhelm Hüllmantel during an event of the Beamtenbund Tarifunion (BBW) on 1 April 2009; http://www.bbw.dbb.de/begegnungen/090401_dienstrechtsreform.php (accessed 22 November 2015).
4. Expert interviews with a ministerial official 01-2015 and a representative of an interest group 02-2015.
5. In both *Länder* the weekly working hours are the same.

Disclosure statement

No potential conflict of interest was reported by the authors.

Funding

This work was supported by the Hans-Böckler-Foundation [2014-738-4].

References

Bayerisches Staatsministerium der Finanzen (2013), *Bericht des Bayerischen Staatsministeriums der Finanzen zur Evaluation des Neuen Dienstrechts. o.O.* München: Bayerisches Staatsministerium der Finanzen.

Benz, A. (2002), Themen, Probleme und Perspektiven der vergleichenden Föderalismusforschung, in A. Benz and G. Lehmbruch (eds), *Föderalismus. Analyse in entwicklungsgeschichtlicher und vergleichender Perspektive*, pp.9–50. Wiesbaden: Westdeutscher Verlag.

Blumenthal, J. v. (2010), Im Zweifel für die Einheit(lichkeit)? Determinaten landespolitischer Entscheidungen, in J. V. Blumenthal and S. Bröchler (eds),

Föderalismusreform in Deutschland, pp.177–196. Wiesbaden: VS Verlag für Sozialwissenchaften/Springer Fachmedien.

Bräuninger, T. and Debus, M. (2012), *Parteienwettbewerb in den deutschen Bundesländern*. Wiesbaden: VS Verlag für Sozialwissenschaften.

Burmester, C. (2015), *Mobilität von Beamten der allgemeinen Verwaltung von Lehrern und Polizisten. Vorschriftenanalyse zu den Auswirkungen der Föderalismusreform I. Duisburger politik- und verwaltungswissenschaftliche Arbeitspapiere*. Duisburg: Lehrstuhl für Politikwissenschaft und Verwaltungswissenschaft.

DBB NRW (2015), *Entwurf eins Dienstrechtsmodernisierungsgesetzes für das Land Nordrhein-Westfalen. Stellungnahme des DBB NRW - Beamtenbund und Tarifunion*. Düsseldorf: DBB NRW.

Decker, F. (2011), *Regieren im "Parteienbundesstaat". Zur Architektur der deutschen Politik*. Wiesbaden: VS-Verlag für Sozialwissenschaften.

DGB Bundesvorstand (2016), *Besoldungsreport 2016. Die Entwicklung der Einkommen der Beamtinnen und Beamten von Bund, Ländern und Kommunen, DGB diskurs*. Berlin: DGB Bundesvorstand.

DGB NRW (2015), *Stellungnahme des DGB Bezirks NRW zum Entwurf der Kerngesetze eines Dienstrechtsmodernisierungsgesetzes*. Düsseldorf: DGB NRW.

Dose, N. (2016), Ökonomische Theorie des Föderalismus und die Föderalismusreformen. Die Bundesländer im Wettbewerb und die Beamten, in K.-P. Sommermann (ed.), *Öffentliche Angelegenheiten - interdisziplinär betrachtet. Forschungssymposium zu Ehren von Klaus König*, pp.27–48. Berlin: Duncker & Humblot.

Dose, N. and Wolfes, F. (2016), Die Höhe der Beamtenbesoldung in den Ländern. Der Versuch einer Erklärung: Parteiendifferenzhypothese oder Verschuldungsdruck?, *Zeitschrift für Vergleichende Politikwissenschaft*, Vol.9, No.4, pp.267–293.

Dünkel, F. (2010), Strafvollzug in Deutschland – Rechtstatsächliche Befunde, *APuZ* 7/2010, pp.7–14.

Frank, G. and Heinicke, T. (2009), Die Auswirkungen der Föderalismusreform auf das öffentliche Dienstrecht – das neue Spannungsfeld von Solidarität, Kooperation und Wettbewerb zwischen den *Ländern, Zeitschrift für Beamtenrecht*, Heft 1/2, pp.34–39.

Grande, E. (1998), Globalisierung und die Zukunft des Nationalstaats: Eine vergleichende Untersuchung zur reflexiven Modernisierung moderner Staatlichkeit, in SFB 536 (ed.), *Reflexive Modernisierung. Antrag auf Finanzierung für die Jahre 1999-2002*, pp.809–852. München: SFB 536

Hausner, H. (2005), Die Ökonomische Theorie des Föderalismus, *Wirtschaftsdienst*, 85.Jhrg., Heft 1, pp.55–60.

Hayek, F. A. (2002), Competition as a dicovery procedure, *Quarterly Journal of Austrian Economics*, Vol.5, No.3, pp.9–23.

Helmrich, R., Zika, G., Kalinowski, M. and Wolter, M. I. (2012), Engpässe auf dem Arbeitsmarkt: Geändertes Bildungs- und Erwerbsverhalten mildert Fachkräftemangel, *BIBB-Report*, Heft 18, pp.1–14.

Hesse, K. (1962), *Der unitarische Bundesstaat*. Karlsruhe: Verlag C. F. Müller.

Hibbs, D. A. J. (1977), Political parties and macroeconomic policy, *The American Political Science Review*, Vol.71, No.4, pp.1467–1487.

Hildebrandt, A. and Wolf, F. (2016), Politik in den BundesLändern unter reformierten institutionellen Rahmenbedingungen, in A. Hildebrandt and F. Wolf (eds), *Die Politik der Bundesländer: Zwischen Föderalismusreform und Schuldenbremse*. 2. Aufl. 2016. pp.1–9.

Holzinger, K. and Knill, C. (2005), Causes and conditions of cross-national policy convergence, *Journal of European Public Policy*, Vol.12, No.5, pp.775–796.

Jeffrey, C. (1999), From cooperative federalism to a "sinatra doctrine" of the Länder?, in C. Jeffrey (ed.), *Recasting German Federalism. The Legacies of Unification*, pp.329–342. London and New York: Pinter.

Jeffery, C., Pamphilis, N. M., Rowe, C. and Turner, E. (2014), Regional policy variation in Germany: the diversity of living conditions in a "unitary federal state", *Journal of European Public Policy*, Vol.21, No.9, pp.1350–1366.

Jeffery, C., Pamphilis, N. M., Rowe, C. and Turner, E. (2016), Introduction to the special issue: reframing German federalism, *German Politics*, Vol.25, No.2, pp.165–175.

Jeffery, C. and Rowe, C. (2014), The reform of German federalism, in S. Padgett, W. Paterson and R. Zohlnhöfer (eds), *Development of German Politics 4*. Basingstoke: Palgrave Macmillan, pp.35–56.

Keating, M. and Cairney, P. (2012), Introduction: policy-making, learning and devolution, *Regional & Federal Studies*, Vol.22, No.3, pp.239–250.

Keman, H. (2014), Comparative research methods, in D. Caramani (ed.), *Comparative Politics*. 3rd ed., pp.47–59. Oxford and New York: Oxford University Press.

Loughlin, J. (2013), Reconfiguring the nation-state. hybridity vs. uniformity, in J. Loughlin, J. Kincaid and W. Swenden (eds), *Routledge Handbook of Regionalism and Federalism*, pp.1–18. Abingdon and New York: Routledge.

Oates, W. E. (1972), *Fiscal Federalism*. New York, Chicago, San Francisco and Atlanta: Harcourt Brace Jovanovich.

Obinger, H. (2015), Funktionalismus, in G. Wenzelburger and R. Zohlnhöfer (eds), *Handbuch Policy-Forschung*, pp.35–54. Wiesbaden: Springer.

Obinger, H. and Starke, P. (2007), Sozialpolitische Entwicklungstrends in OECD-Ländern 1980–2001: Konvergenz, Divergenz oder Persistenz?, in K. Holzinger, H. Jörgens and C. Knill (eds), *Transfer, Diffusion und Konvergenz von Politiken*, pp.470–495. PVS-*Sonderheft 38*/2007. Wiesbaden: VS Verlag für Sozialwissenschaften.

Olson, M. C. (1969), The principle of "fiscal equivalence": the division of responsibilities among different levels of government, *American Economic Review*, Vol.59, pp.479–487.

Page, E. C. (1991), Die "Do parties make a difference"- Diskussion in Großbritannien, in B. Blanke and H. Wollmann (eds), *Die alte Bundesrepublik. Kontinuität und Wandel*, *Leviathan-Sonderheft 12*/1991, pp.239–252. Opladen: Westdeutscher Verlag.

Peters, B. G. (1998), *Comparative Politics. Theory and Methods*. Houndmills, Basingstoke, Hampshire, London: Macmillan Press.

Reus, I. (2016), On a successful road to "more federalism" in *Länder* Politics? The case of smoking bans after Germany's federalism reform, *German Politics*, Vol.25, No.2, pp.210–226.

Reus, I. and Zohlnhöfer, R. (2015), Die christilich-liberale Koalition als Nutznießer der Föderalismusreform? Die Rolle des Bundesrates und die Entwicklung des Föderalismus unter der zweiten Regierung Merkel, in R. Zohlnhöfer and T. Saalfeld (eds), *Politik im Schatten der Krise*, pp.245–272. Wiesbaden: Springer VS.

Rothgang, H. and Wessel, A. C. (2008), Sozialpolitik in den Bundesländern, in A. Hildebrandt and F. Wolf (eds), *Die Politik der Bundesländer. Staatstätigkeit im Vergleich*, pp.137–172. Wiesbaden: VS Verlag für Sozialwissenschaften.

Rowe, C. and Turner, E. (2016), Let's stick together? Explaining boundaries to territorial policy variation: the case of Germany's prisons legislation, *German Politics*, Vol.25, No.2, pp.193–209.

Scharpf, F. W. (2008), Community, diversity and autonomy: the challenges of reforming German federalism, *German Politics*, Vol.17, No.4, pp.509–521.

Schmidt, M. G. (1996), When parties matter: a review of the possibilities and limits of partisan influence on public policy, *European Journal of Political Research*, Vol.30, No.2, pp.155–183.

Schmidt, M. G. (2016), Conclusion: policy diversity in Germany's federalism, *German Politics*, Vol.25, No.2, pp.301–314.

Schneider, H.-P. (2012), Die Föderalismusreform I auf dem Prüfstand: Ein Zwischenbericht über Teilbereiche ihrer Umsetzung, in Europäisches Zentrum für Föderalismus-Forschung (ed.), *Jahrbuch des Föderalismus 2012. Föderalismus, Subsidiarität und Regionen in Europa*, pp.222–233. Baden-Baden: Nomos Verlagsgesellschaft.

Schünemann, U. (2007), *Talk of the Minister for the Interior and Sport of the Land Lower Saxony delivered at the symposium "Dienstrechtsreform in Niedersachen". Dokumentation der Veranstaltung am 30. August 2007*, pp.20–26.

Seeck, E. and Rieger, R. (2011), Neues Laufbahnrecht der Norddeutschen Küstenländer, *Recht im Amt*, Vol.1, No.2011, pp.1–9.

Stucke, M. E. (2011), Reconsidering competition, *Mississippi Law Journal*, Vol.81, No.2, pp.107–188.

Sturm, R. (2008), Von der Symmetrie zur Asymmetrie - Deutschlands neuer Föderalismus, in Europäisches Zentrum für Föderalismus-Forschung Tübingen (eds), *Jahrbuch des Föderalismus 2007. Föderalismus, Subsidiarität und Regionen in Europa*, pp.27–41. Baden-Baden: Nomos Verlagsgesellschaft.

Tiebout, C. M. (1956), A pure theory of local expenditures, *Journal of Political Economy*, Vol.64, No.5, pp.416–424.

Turner, E. (2011), *Political parties and public policy in the German Länder: when parties matter*. Basingstoke: Palgrave Macmillan.

Wagener, F. (1979), Der öffentliche Dienst im Staat der Gegenwart, *Veröffentlichung der Vereinigung der Deutschen Staatsrechtslehrer*, Vol.37, pp.215–266.

Wenzelburger, G. and Zohlnhöfer, R. (2015), Konzepte und Begriffe der Vergleichenden Policy-Forschung, in G. Wenzelburger and R. Zohlnhöfer (eds), *Handbuch Policy-Forschung*, pp.15–32. Wiesbaden: Springer.

Wilensky, H. L. (1975), *The Welfare State and Equality. Structural and Ideological Roots of Public Expenditures*. Berekely: University of Carlifornia Press.

Wolf, F. and Hildebrandt, A. (2016), Länderpolitik revisited. Zwei Föderalismusreformen und ihre Folgen, in A. Hildebrandt and F. Wolf (eds), *Die Politik der Bundesländer : Zwischen Föderalismusreform und Schuldenbremse*. 2. Aufl. 2016. pp.391–399.

Zohlnhöfer, R. (2005), Globalisierung der Wirtschaft und nationalstaatliche Anpassungsreaktionen. Theoretische Überlegungen, *Zeitschrift für Internationale Beziehungen*, Vol.12, pp.41–75.

Online-Appendix

The effect of reformed legislative competences on Länder policy-making: determinants of fragmentation and uniformity

Nicolai Dose, Iris Reus

The basis of our analysis is the presentation of the content of the laws in a way which is suitable for systematic comparison. Therefore, an additive index was developed for the competences 'penitentiary system' and 'shop closing time'. The total score of the index allows ranking the Länder laws according to their overall design.

- In the case of 'penitentiary system' the overall design refers to the degree of restrictiveness, whereas the scale of the index ranges from 'supportive' (high score) to 'restrictive' (low score).
- In the case of 'shop closing time' the overall design refers to the degree of state-regulation, whereas the scale of the index ranges from 'state-regulated' (high score) to 'economically liberal' (low score).

Thus, the total score shows whether a law is, on the whole, designed to be more or less restrictive (penitentiary system) or liberal (shop closing time). As different arrangements in detail can lead to the same total score, it is just as important to look at the detailed scores.

The index is constructed as follows:

First, essential aspects of the policy are identified which are represented by the different components of the index. Subsequently, in each component scores are assigned to the different regulations in the laws. The index is built on empirical differences, which means that both the components and the values are directly obtained from the laws. The components grasp all essential differences in the laws. Similar formulations concerning the different values are treated as equal. The index is additive, which means that the scores for each component are summed up to a total score for each law. All scores are standardised before summing up so that each component has the same weight.

The first columns of the following tables contain the Länder laws. For instance, BB 2013-04 stands for a law which was passed by Brandenburg in April 2013.

Abbreviations of Names of the 16 Länder:

BB = Brandenburg

BE = Berlin

BW = Baden-Württemberg

BY = Bavaria

HB = Bremen

HE = Hesse

HH = Hamburg

MV = Mecklenburg Western-Pomerania

NI = Lower Saxony

NW = North Rhine-Westphalia

RP = Rhineland-Palatinate

SH = Schleswig-Holstein

SL = Saarland

SN = Saxony

ST = Saxony-Anhalt

TH = Thuringia

Dependent Variable: Penitentiary System

The index can range from 0 to 1440 (total score if max. scores in each component). Low score marks a restrictive law, i.e. with more restrictions for prisoners. High score marks a supportive law offering more rights and development opportunities to prisoners.

Table 4. Penitentiary System: detailed scores and total scores of laws according to the index

	A	B	C	D	E	F	G	H	I	J	K	L	M	N	O	P	Q	R	S	T	U	V	W	X	Total
BB 2013-04	1	5	2	1	1	1	3	1	1	4	3	5	3	4	1	1	1	4	1	1	1	2	5	2	1230
RP 2013-05	1	4	2	1	1	1	1	1	1	2	3	2	3	3	1	1	1	4	1	0	2	2	3	2	1049
SN 2013-05	1	4	2	1	1	1	1	1	1	2	3	2	3	4	1	1	1	4	1	0	1	2	4	2	1046
Work-group	1	3	2	1	1	1	1	1	1	2	3	4	3	2	1	1	1	4	1	0	1	2	2	2	1000
SL 2013-04	1	3	2	1	1	1	3	1	1	1	3	2	3	0	1	1	1	3	1	0	1	2	3	2	972
HB 2014-11	1	3	2	0	1	1	1	1	1	2	3	2	3	1	1	3	1	4	1	0	1	2	2	2	945
ST 2015-12	1	3	2	0	1	1	3	1	0	2	0	2	3	2	1	2	1	4	1	0	2	2	3	2	932
TH 2014-02	1	3	2	0	1	1	1	1	1	2	3	2	3	2	1	1	1	4	1	0	1	2	3	2	932
MV 2013-05	1	3	2	0	1	1	1	1	1	2	3	2	3	2	1	1	1	2	1	0	1	2	2	2	890
NW 2015-01	2	4	1	0	1	0	2	1	2	2	2	2	1	3	1	1	1	2	0	1	0	3	3	2	844
HH 2009-07	1	1	0	0	2	1	2	1	1	2	2	6	0	0	1	1	0	3	0	0	1	4	2	1	671
HH 2007-12	0	0	0	0	2	1	2	1	1	0	1	0	0	0	1	1	0	3	0	0	0	4	1	1	477
HE 2015-11	1	2	1	0	1	1	0	0	0	0	0	0	2	0	0	1	0	4	1	0	1	1	2	1	473
HE 2010-06	1	2	1	0	1	1	0	0	0	0	0	0	2	0	0	1	0	4	0	0	0	1	2	1	413
Federal law	1	0	2	0	0	0	2	2	2	3	0	2	0	0	0	1	0	4	0	0	0	3	0	0	380
BW 2009-11	2	1	2	0	0	0	2	0	1	2	0	2	0	0	0	0	0	0	0	0	1	3	0	0	347
NI 2007-12	1	0	1	0	0	0	2	0	0	1	0	2	0	0	0	2	1	1	0	0	0	0	0	1	340
BY 2007-12	0	0	1	0	0	0	2	0	1	1	0	1	0	0	0	0	0	0	0	0	0	4	0	1	215

Source: authors' compilation

Explanation and possible values of components:

A) Goals of execution

- 0 = protection of the public equivalent to social rehabilitation
- 1 = social rehabilitation prior to protection of the public
- 2 = social rehabilitation only

B) Principles of execution (i.e. rights of the prisoners)

Examples of such principles: respect the individual personality of each prisoner, encourage self-reliance of prisoners, take different needs of prisoners (age, religion, sexual identity, sex, origin) into account, support connection to social life

- 0 = 3 principles/rights
- 1 = 6 principles/rights
- 2 = 8 principles/rights
- 3 = 10 principles/rights
- 4 = 12 principles/rights
- 5 = 14 principles/rights

C) Duty of prisoner to cooperate and participate

- 0 = duty
- 1 = recommendation
- 2 = no duty

D) Obligation to work

- 0 = yes
- 1 = no

E) Number of holidays per year

- 0 = 18 days
- 1 = 20 days
- 2 = 22 days
- 3 = 24 days

F) Time when holidays are granted for the first time

- 0 = after a waiting period of one year
- 1 = after a waiting period half a year

G) Minimum amount of pay for work

- 0 = no minimum amount
- 1 = at least 60% of a certain reference value ('Eckvergütung')
- 2 = less than 75% of a certain reference value ('Eckvergütung') only if work performance does not meet the standards
- 3 = at least 75% of a certain reference value ('Eckvergütung')

H) Pocket money paid to prisoner

- 0 = ‚appropriate', no minimum amount
- 1 = fixed, 14% of a certain reference value ('Eckvergütung')

I) Payment for operating costs

(in particular the electricity consumed by electronic devices like stereo systems or game consoles)

- 0 = prisoner has to pay for entire operating costs
- 1 = appropriate share
- 2 = no pay for operating costs

J) 'Closed prison' vs. 'open prison'

'Open prison' means that the prisoners can move more freely inside the building, while in 'closed prisons' the private rooms of the prisoners are normally locked and only open during certain times. Furthermore, 'open prisons' allow working outside the prison as well as certain other relaxations of execution with regard to the social rehabilitation of the prisoners.

- 0 = 'closed prison' is regular form of execution, prisoner 'may' be accommodated in 'open prison', if meeting the standards
- 1 = 'closed prison' as regular form of execution, prisoner 'should' be accommodated in 'open prison', if meeting the standards
- 2 = both 'closed prison' and 'open prison' are regular forms of execution, prisoner 'should' be accommodated in 'open prison', if meeting the standards
- 3 = priority of 'open prison', if meeting the standards
- 4 = claim for 'open prison', if meeting the standards

K) Long-term leave: number of days

A certain kind of relaxation of execution with regard to social rehabilitation:

The prisoner is allowed to spend several days (and nights) completely outside the prison.

- 0 = max. 21 days
- 1 = max. 22 days
- 2 = max. 24 days
- 3 = no limit

L) Long-term leave for prisoners sentenced to lifelong imprisonment

- 0 = after 10 years
- 1 = after 12 years or when accommodated in ‚open prison‘ or when suitable for 'open prison'
- 2 = after 10 years or when accommodated in ‚open prison‘
- 3 = after 10 years or when accommodated in ‚open prison‘ or when suitable for 'open prison'
- 4 = after 5 years or when accommodated in ‚open prison‘
- 5 = no minimum time, agreement of regulatory authority required
- 6 = no minimum time

M) Long-term leave in preparation for release: number of days

- 0 = max. 7 days
- 1 = max. 10 days
- 2 = max. 3 months
- 3 = max. 6 months

N) Visits: number of hours

- 0 = at least 1 hour per month
- 1 = at least 2 hours per month + 1 additional hour for children < 14 years
- 2 = at least 2 hours per month + 2 additional hours for children < 14 years
- 3 = at least 2 hours per month + 2 additional hours for children < 18 years
- 4 = at least 4 hours

O) Long-term visits (= visits of several hours of spouses which are not monitored)

- 0 = not possible
- 1 = possible

P) Telephone calls

- 0 = can be allowed in urgent cases
- 1 = can generally be allowed
- 2 = should be allowed in urgent cases
- 3 = can be allowed, conversations with family members have to be allowed

Q) Other forms of communication (Email, Internet)

- 0 = not allowed
- 1 = prison director can allow use after regulatory authority has approved

R) Claim for single room

- 0 = no claim both in 'closed prison' and 'open prison' (only recommendation)
- 1 = claim both in 'closed prison' and 'open prison', no claim if the room situation demands it
- 2 = claim in 'closed prison' and not in 'open prison'
- 3 = claim in 'closed prison' and 'open prison'; not in 'open prison' if room situation demands it
- 4 = claim both in 'closed prison' and 'open prison'

S) Living groups

- 0 = possible
- 1 = not possible

T) Claim for vegetarian food

- 0 = no
- 1 = yes

U) Shopping

- 0 = only products offered by prison, limited to food and cosmetics
- 1 = only products offered by prison, no limitation of products
- 2 = additionally mail order allowed

V) Number of leisure activities prisons have to offer

Examples: different kind of sports, library, cultural events, continuing education, etc.

- 0 = 1 activity
- 1 = 2 activities
- 2 = 4 activities
- 3 = 5 activities

W) Number of disciplinary measures available to impose on prisoners

Examples: deprivation of radio, deprivation of television, limitation of shopping, reduction of pay for work, limitation of visiting hours, arrest

- 0 = 11 disciplinary measures
- 1 = 10 disciplinary measures
- 2 = 9 disciplinary measures
- 3 = 8 disciplinary measures
- 4 = 7 disciplinary measures
- 5 = 6 disciplinary measures

X) Procedure concerning offences and disciplinary measures

- 0 = minimal requirements: clarification of situation, hearing of prisoner, oral explanation of the decision to the prisoner, written notice including short justification
- 1 = additional requirements: duty to inform the prisoner on the offence as well as his/her right (not) to comment, consultation of other staff involved in the prisoner's therapy in case of serious offence, determination of incriminating and exonerating material, comprehensive documentation
- 2 = additional: dispute resolution by mutual agreement (with disciplinary measures) possible

Dependent variable: Shop closing time

The index can range from 0 to 14280 (total score if max. score in each component). Low score marks a (economically) liberal law with few restrictions for shop owners, high score marks a high degree of state-regulation and thus more restrictions for shop owners.

Table 5. Shop closing time: detailed scores and total scores of laws according to index

	A	B	C	D	E	F	G	H	I	J	K	L	M	N	O	P	Q	Total
BE 2006-11	0	0	3	0	3	2	2	0	5	0	0	0	0	0	5	1	1	3345
BE 2010-10	0	0	3	0	1	2	3	2	5	1	1	5	0	0	5	1	1	5053
NI 2007-03	0	0	0	0	5	0	1	6	6	3	0	1	2	1	1	4	0	5118
BB 2006-11	0	0	2	1	3	4	4	0	3	1	1	0	3	1	4	3	5	6463
MV 2007-06	1	1	3	3	5	4	4	5	6	0	0	1	1	0	0	3	1	6546
NW 2006-11	0	0	3	1	5	0	3	3	4	3	0	1	3	1	6	3	7	7496
NW 2013-04	0	1	3	1	0	1	5	3	4	3	0	1	3	1	6	3	7	7510
BB 2010-12	0	0	2	1	3	4	4	2	3	1	1	5	3	1	4	3	5	7583
SL 2006-11	4	4	3	3	5	0	0	5	5	3	2	1	0	0	3	3	4	8477
TH 2011-12	2	2	3	3	5	0	4	4	1	2	1	2	0	2	4	3	7	8537
TH 2006-11	2	2	3	3	5	0	4	5	0	2	1	2	0	2	4	3	7	8572
SN 2010-12	3	3	3	1	4	3	4	0	8	2	2	4	0	1	2	2	5	8624
BW 2007-02	0	0	3	1	6	0	5	6	2	3	2	1	3	1	3	4	6	8710
SH 2006-11	0	0	3	3	5	4	4	6	4	3	2	1	2	0	0	3	7	8736
HE 2006-11	0	0	3	3	5	5	5	6	6	2	1	1	3	1	3	2	2	8874
SN 2007-03	3	3	3	1	5	5	3	0	8	2	2	4	0	1	2	2	5	8932
RP 2006-11	3	3	1	1	5	5	3	6	8	3	0	2	3	1	6	0	5	9300
ST 2006-11	2	2	3	3	5	4	4	0	4	3	1	3	0	2	4	3	7	9412
HB 2007-03	0	0	3	1	5	0	5	6	4	3	2	2	3	1	6	4	7	9428
HH 2006-12	0	0	1	2	5	4	4	6	7	3	2	1	3	1	7	3	5	9511
Federal Law	4	4	3	2	5	4	5	6	0	3	2	1	3	1	6	5	5	11400

Source: Authors' compilation

Explanation and possible values of components:

A) Opening hours from Monday to Friday / all shops

- 0 = 0:00 – 24:00
- 1 = 0:00 – 22:00
- 2 = 0:00 – 20:00
- 3 = 6:00 – 22:00
- 4 = 6:00 – 20:00

B) Opening hours on Saturdays / all shops

- 0 = 0:00 – 24:00
- 1 = 0:00 – 22:00
- 2 = 0:00 – 20:00
- 3 = 6:00 – 22:00
- 4 = 6:00 – 20:00

C) Goods which shops at stations are allowed to sell out of opening hours

- 0 = travel necessities + gift items + small quantities of daily goods + clothes + jewellery
- 1 = travel necessities + gift items + small quantities of daily goods
- 2 = travel necessities + gift items
- 3 = travel necessities only

D) Goods which shops at airports are allowed to sell out of opening hours

- 0 = travel necessities + gift items + small quantities of daily goods + additional goods
- 1 = travel necessities + gift items + small quantities of daily goods
- 2 = travel necessities + administration may allow gift items and small quantities of daily goods
- 3 = travel necessities only

E) Exceptionally opening on Sundays / all shops: number of days per year

- 0 = 11 days
- 1 = 10 days
- 2 = 8 days

- 3 = 6 days
- 4 = 5 days
- 5 = 4 days
- 6 = 3 days

F) Exceptionally opening on Sundays / all shops: number of Sundays per city

(increase of exceptionally opening on Sundays when different days in different parts of the city are possible because of higher total number per city)

- 0 = different days in different parts of the city possible
- 1 = different days in different parts of the city possible, max. 11 in total per city
- 2 = max. 2 days may be different
- 3 = max. 1 day may be different, max. 8 in total per city
- 4 = no explicit limitation by law, discretionary powers of municipalities
- 5 = explicitly same days

G) Exceptionally opening on Sundays / all shops: choice of days

- 0 = shop owners themselves decide
- 1 = at request of the majority of shop owners in the district
- 2 = without special occasion by the municipality + two days by shop owners themselves by reason of special occasions
- 3 = without special occasion by the municipality
- 4 = by reason of special occasions by the municipality
- 5 = by reason of certain special occasions (e.g. markets, regional festivals, important anniversaries) by the municipality

H) Shop opening on Sundays in advent

- 0 = all (four) allowed
- 1 = three allowed
- 2 = two allowed
- 3 = one allowed + free choice of the day
- 4 = one allowed + choice between first and second advent
- 5 = one allowed + only first advent
- 6 = none allowed

I) Exceptional opening on Sundays / all shops: Public Holidays excluded from exceptional opening

- 0 = 2 public holidays
- 1 = 3 public holidays
- 2 = 4 public holidays
- 3 = 7 public holidays
- 4 = 8 public holidays
- 5 = 9 public holidays
- 6 = 10 public holidays
- 7 = 12 public holidays
- 8 = 15 public holidays

J) Exceptional opening on Sundays / all shops: number of hours

- 0 = unlimited
- 1 = max. 7h
- 2 = max. 6h
- 3 = max. 5h

K) Exceptional opening on Sundays / all shops: in the evenings

- 0 = unlimited
- 1 = max. 20:00
- 2 = max. 18:00

L) Exceptional opening on Sundays / all shops: in the mornings

- 0 = unlimited
- 1 = not at the time of the main church service
- 2 = from 11:00 on
- 3 = from 11:00 on + not at the time of the main church service
- 4 = from 12:00 on
- 5 = from 13:00 on

M) Exceptional opening on Sundays / tourist cities: number of days

- 0 = all Sundays of the year
- 1 = not Sundays in December after the first advent

- 2 = not between 31.10 and 15.12.
- 3 = max. 40 days

N) Exceptional opening on Sundays / tourist cities: number of hours

- 0 = unlimited
- 1 = max. 8h
- 2 = max. 6h

O) Exceptional opening on Sundays / tourist cities: number of product groups allowed to sell

- 0 = unlimited
- 1 = 16 product groups
- 2 = 15 product groups
- 3 = 14 product groups
- 4 = 12 product groups
- 5 = 11 product groups
- 6 = 10 product groups
- 7 = 8 product groups

P) General opening on Sundays / special goods like newspapers, flowers or rolls: number of hours

- 0 = unlimited
- 1 = max. 9h
- 2 = max. 6h
- 3 = max. 5h
- 4 = max. 3h
- 5 = max. 2h

Q) General opening on Sundays / special goods like newspapers, flowers or rolls: number of product groups

- 0 = 10 product groups
- 1 = 9 product groups
- 2 = 8 product groups

- 3 = 7 product groups
- 4 = 6 product groups
- 5 = 5 product groups
- 6 = 4 product groups
- 7 = 3 product groups

Dependent variable: Civil servants' pay (May 2016)

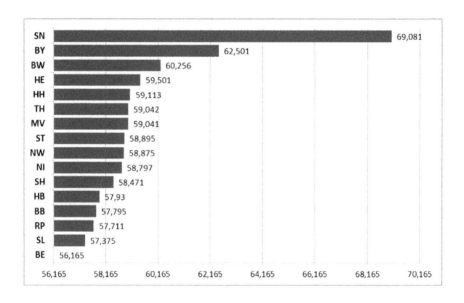

Graph 3. Level of yearly payment for career track A13 in Euros (gross).

Source: DGB Bundesvorstand 2016: 11

Comment: Yearly base salary, last promotional step, all general bonuses included. For reasons of presentation the bars start with the lowest pay level (Berlin)

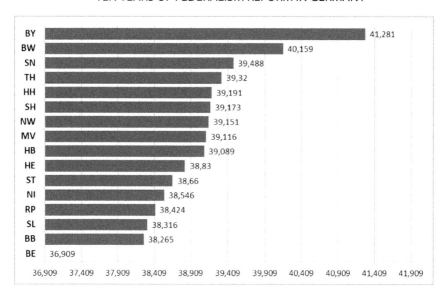

Graph 4. Level of yearly payment for career track A9 in Euros (gross).

Source: DGB Bundesvorstand 2016: 10

Comment: Yearly base salary, last promotional step, all general bonuses included. For reasons of presentation the bars start with the lowest pay level (Berlin)

The Role of Party and Coalition Politics in Federal Reform

Klaus Detterbeck

ABSTRACT

The article analyses the role of the German political parties as actors of federal change. Parties perceive federal processes through their own organizational lenses, giving priority to electoral logics, programmatic ideas or territorial interests. Each of the three reform steps in the German case was shaped by a specific blend of the three logics. Looking at the sequences of reform, the analysis shows that parties have remained central for organizing federal processes but have become less capable of arriving at cohesive and unified party positions. There have been struggles over which of the strategies was to prevail both within individual parties and across the party divide. The territorial power balances within parties, the timing of the reform, that is, the constellation of political majorities at federal and regional levels in the moment of reform, and the policy issues in question are important framing conditions for the choice of particular party strategies.

Introduction

The aim of the article is to analyse the role of political parties as actors of federal change in Germany. In doing so, it adds a party political perspective to the literature on constitutional reform processes. As in other parliamentary democracies, parties are crucial for organizing political processes in the Federal Republic. They represent societal interests, provide electoral choices for voters, shape political agendas, recruit political elites for public offices and organize parliamentary work by structuring government and opposition. While there has been much debate on how well parties perform with regard to their representative and governmental functions, the centrality of parties in running state institutions has remained basically undisputed (Ware, 1996; Mair, 2008). Processes of federal constitutional change will thus inevitably be shaped by parties and their leading protagonists. Parties may start and drive reform processes, or they may oppose and delete such moves. The pro-grammatic positions, competitive strategies and organizational structures of parties have a massive impact on the accommodation or exacerbation of ter-ritorial cleavages in a political system (Filippov et al., 2004; Swenden and Maddens, 2009).

How do parties act in federal reform? Party agency reflects the primary goal of parties, leading to vote-seeking, office-seeking, or policy-seeking strategies (Strom, 1990). Applying this framework to the territorial dimension of party politics, three distinct logics of party behaviour can be identified (Toubeau and Massetti, 2013). Parties may either give priority to a pure electoral logic in pursuing advantages in electoral and parliamentary competition, they may follow general programmatic ideas on the right balance between regional autonomy and federal unity, or they may put the territorial interests of specific regions first. The ways in which parties decide on these issues, however, is shaped by the institutional context in which they act, by govern-ment formation and coalition politics, and by their own internal power bal-ances (Hepburn and Detterbeck, 2013). The first part of the paper will outline this theoretical framework in some more detail.

The second part of the paper will look at the sequential process of federal reform in Germany from the early years of the new millennium. The theoreti-cal framework will be applied to a case in which many important parameters of party politics have been modified over the course of the last few decades. This is as true to the structures of party competition and coalition politics as it is true to the relationship between federal and *Land* party levels. As a conse-quence, severe strains on the vertical integration of German parties have developed. The analysis will show that the parties have remained central for organizing federal processes but have become less capable of arriving at cohesive and unified party positions.

Party Agency in Federal Reforms

Political Parties and Federalism

There is a long-standing normative and conceptual debate on the mutual interaction between federalism and political parties (see Detterbeck, 2012: 14–29). In democratic theory, liberal thinkers have seen in the federal division of powers a device to temper party rule, whereas majoritarian positions have feared the constraining effects of federalism on the expression of the popular will. On a conceptual level, parties have been seen as either reflecting or shaping institutional and societal environments. Looking at the proactive role of parties, Riker (1964) laid the ground for a party-based theory of feder-alism. He suggested that federal dynamics result from the strategic choices of party politicians and based on two factors—the degree of partisan harmony of federal and constituent governments and the level of intra-party discipline. In a similar vein, Stepan (2001) saw state-wide parties as necessary motors of democratic innovations, capable of producing effective and 'demos-enabling' policy solutions in multi-level settings. Both authors stressed the importance of intra-party coordination for federal developments.

In recent accounts on territorial reform, parties figured prominently as actors of change by linking the different state institutions and political levels, managing negotiation processes, articulating and/or aggregating terri-torial demands, and determining the political agenda with respect to the timing and contents of reform (Behnke and Benz, 2009; Lorenz, 2011; Benz and Broschek, 2013; Petersohn et al., 2015). The preferences and strategies of parties in the politics of territorial reform are essential for understanding processes and outcomes. But what drives the positions that parties take with regard to constitutional and territorial issues? How do we account for the relative salience that parties attach to these issues *vis-á-vis* other political topics?

The Three Logics of Party Agency

Toubeau and Massetti (2013) have developed a threefold typology on the logics of party agency in territorial politics. According to their argument, parties decide on positions and salience in the light of their general values and objectives. They take a stance on whether to pursue territorial reform or not, and define the direction (centralization versus decentralization) that they want potential change to take. With regard to party competition, parties may opt to put territorial issues high on their political agenda or pay little attention to them. They may choose to compete on these policy areas against their political rivals or look for other battlefields. Whatever these decisions may be they are reflective of a party's primary goal (for similar accounts, see Jeffery, 1999a; Scharpf, 2005; Turner and Rowe, 2013). The three logics of action can be outlined as follows:

(a) *Electoral logic*: parties give clear priority to vote-seeking and office-seeking strategies (Strom, 1990). As rational utility –maximizing actors, their territorial party policies are determined exclusively by the pursuit of advantages in electoral and parliamentary competition. There is a stra-tegic interest in defeating the political purposes of the electoral opponents, for example, in voting down government bills in bicameral legislation (Bräuninger and Debus, 2012). Territorial demands may also be derived from the wish to enlarge the party's share of the electoral market. A new commitment to transfer fiscal revenues to the poorer regions may be a case in point here, but so too the political intention to reduce the level of fiscal equalization. Equally important, government formation and coalition politics may drive the positioning on territorial issues. The degree to which the same party governs at different levels affects territorial dynamics (Riker, 1964). With respect to competitive strategies, parties may be willing to pursue specific territorial policies in order to accommodate coalition partners or to attract new partners by signalling policy proximity (Kropp, 2010). In short, with electoral logic territorial demands are simply a means to other ends.[1]

(b) *Programmatic logic*: parties follow basic ideological principles and seek policy solutions that are in accordance with their programmatic platforms and concepts (Strom, 1990). As socially bound actors, parties pursue territorial politics that are guided by shared collective norms while also acting as 'norm entrepreneurs' in promoting new ideas (see Peters, 2012: 112–142). There are substantive policy preferences that parties seek to fulfil when dealing with territorial issues (Bräuninger et al., 2010). These preferences are shaped by party identities and core values, such as social equality, traditional order, religious faith, liberal freedom or sustainable development. In that sense, there is a statewide perspective to the programmatic logic of party agency. Parties advance particular territorial arrangements for the positive benefits they can yield to the polity as a whole. Territorial demands for a legitimate and efficient balance between regional autonomy and federal unity serve the pursuit of overarching political and ideological objectives.

(c) *Territorial logic*: parties seek policy solutions that are beneficial for particular regions or constituent entities in multi-level systems. As advocates of distinct territorial communities, parties emphasize the salience of geographically-based political cleavages. Party identities very much revolve around issues of territorial empowerment (De Winter et al., 2006; Hepburn, 2009). Partisan aspirations may range from unilateral secession to enlarged political autonomy and cultural recognition. Next to constitutional demands, the pursuit of material advantages for the region may constitute the terms of territorial representation. This involves the redistribution of resources within the system and/or demands for a stronger support from the political centre. What is striking about the territorial logic is the claim of parties to stand up for the 'genuine' interests of the territorial community in question. In putting territorial interests first, parties readjust the patterns of political competition.

As the description of the three logics of party agency shows, these are constructed as ideal types. We would expect to find real-life parties operating on a mix of these different strategies. Moreover, actual party behaviour may vary with regard to the policy area in question and to the timing of the electoral calendar. For instance, it may prove easier to maintain party solidarity in education policy than in fiscal equalization. Similarly, electoral considerations are more likely to dominate territorial party politics in the run-up to federal elections than at other times (Scharpf, 2005: 6–7). We should also be aware that there may be difficulties to disentangle the 'true' motivations behind specific partisan actions calling for specific research strategies.[2] Taking these considerations into account, there are strong arguments for studying the three logics of party agency as a dynamic process which evolves over time. Going one step further and looking at the causes why parties prioritize a specific logic, we will have to take intra-party conditions, the role of non-state-wide parties, coalition effects and institutional contexts into account. The next section will outline these four factors that set the framing conditions for the choice of specific party strategies in territorial politics.

Framing Party Strategies: Intra-Party Conditions, Non-State-Wide Parties, Government Formation, Coalition Patterns and Institutional Context

Parties are no unitary actors. This is particularly true in multi-level settings, in which there are distinct national and regional arenas of electoral and parliamentary party competition (Deschouwer, 2006; Jeffery, 2010). State-wide parties have responded quite differently to the challenge of maintaining internal unity while still allowing for regional variation in federal and decentralized political systems. Some parties have installed hierarchical control of a strong central party over its regional branches; others have sought to establish federal-type linkages between the different territorial levels of party in which regional branches have their own autonomous areas of decision-making but are also involved in the steering bodies of the state-wide party; while others still have developed a strong separation of national and regional party levels in which each is governing its own affairs without much interaction between them (Swenden and Maddens, 2009; Hepburn and Detterbeck, 2013).

Territorial power balances within parties have a massive impact on how parties behave. Electoral and ideological logics of party agency presuppose a high degree of vertical coordination. State-wide and sub-state party elites will have to agree on common party lines and coherent action. To be able to do so, there is need for structural mechanisms of cooperation, common interests across levels and shared values that provide the 'glue' to hold the different party units together. Or, to put it differently, parties in which regional branches enjoy a large degree of autonomy may neither have the integrative capacity nor the political incentives to stick to a unified party strategy across the territory. The same is true for parties which operate at one political level only (truncated parties). In all of these cases, we may expect the prevalence of a territorial logic of party agency.

This is also true for the strategies of non-state-wide parties. Interestingly, most relevant non-state-wide parties in Europe, including the Bavarian CSU, are multi-level organizations simultaneously competing at central and sub-state political levels (Hepburn, 2009; Jeffery, 2010). Although these parties are focused on one or a few specific constituent units within the wider polity, they face tensions—similar to state-wide parties—between the various demands stemming from the different political levels. For example, the participation in governments at state-wide levels may lead to conflicts with the interests of the 'home region'. What is different from the state-wide parties, however, is the exclusive appeal to a distinct territorial community. Thus, there is no need to balance the interests of several constituent units within the party organization. Accordingly, speaking in comparative terms, non-state-wide parties have often been drivers of territorial reform (Toubeau and Massetti, 2013: 303–304).

The logics of party agency are also dependent on government formation and coalition politics in multi-level settings (Stefuriuc, 2009). This has two different dimensions. On the one hand, there is an intra-party dynamic which is of importance. Parties that govern at different levels simultaneously have stronger potential but also a stronger need for policy coordination. 'Partisan harmony' can fuel electoral and ideological logics. At the same time, it can also heighten tensions between public office-holders at different levels triggering territorial logics. If, however, parties have diverse governmental status across the territory, being in and out of office at different levels, the incentives for finding commonality and presenting a unified image may be less intense. Moreover, the choice of coalition patterns may be a contested issue between state-wide party leaderships striving for congruence and sub-state party leaderships pursuing freedom of action. Depending on the territorial balances of power within the multi-level organization, the control over coalition formation will be distributed differently across parties (Hepburn and Detterbeck, 2013).

On the other hand, the composition of coalition governments affects inter-party competition and intra-party logics. Parties that govern together have stronger motivations to agree on controversial issues and present a common political agenda. Concerning territorial demands, coalition parties may be inclined to respect the preferences of their partner(s) *vis-á-vis* political opponents. The same holds true for potential new partners signalling each other that there is room for accommodating their respective territorial interests and party logics. As has been outlined above, coalition games form part of the electoral logic of party agency. They may, however, also facilitate the strengthening of territorial logics in a multi-level system. This is especially the case when specific coalition partners, such as non-state-wide parties or strongly autonomous branches of state-wide parties, compete on a formidable territorial agenda (Toubeau and Massetti, 2013).

Finally, institutional context matters. The territorial structures of the state and the structures of the electoral process define the political context in which parties operate (Detterbeck, 2012: 70–77). The specific nature of the territorial arrangement, in particular the degree of interdependence between central and sub-state levels, has strong relevance for the logics of party agency. In federal and decentralized states, territorial levels can be heavily intertwined or more clearly separated. The distribution of legislative and administrative competences, fiscal relations and the nature of the second chamber are among the most relevant variables in this respect. In a system with a high degree of interdependence between territorial levels, parties may provide for the coordination that is needed to make these systems work (Swenden and Maddens, 2009).[3] If this is the case, we may expect parties to prioritize electoral and programmatic logics over the representation of territorial interests.

For studying the reform of German federalism, these theoretical considerations provide conceptual lenses on how to understand better the logics of party agency. Most importantly, we are talking about a sequential process of reform. At each point in time when decisions were to be taken, there have been distinct constellations of the framing conditions of internal power balances, territorial party representation, coalition politics and institutional incentives. Thus, we may expect that the struggles over the relative weight of electoral, programmatic and territorial strategies, both within individual party organizations and across the party divide, have changed over time.

Party Politics in Reunified Germany

Party Change and Federal Reform

Federal reform in Germany took place in a context of party change. For quite some time, and predating the debates on the need for federal change in the 1990s, both the party system and the individual party organizations have been undergoing significant transformation. It is important to take party change into account when studying party agency in federal reform. The emergence of more distinct modes of territorial party competition, more regionalized patterns of government formation and reduced levels of party cohesion have made vertical party integration more difficult to obtain. As a result, territorial logics have become a more salient feature of German party politics (Sturm, 1999; Detterbeck and Jeffery, 2009).

Party System Change and Party Organizational Change in Germany

For most of the post-war period, competition centred on the two major parties, the Christian Democrats (CDU/CSU, Christlich Demokratische Union/ Christlich-Soziale Union) and the Social Democrats (SPD, Sozialdemokratische

Partei Deutschlands), with a pivotal role for the smaller Liberal Party (FDP, Freie Demokratische Partei). With the entry of the Greens in the 1980s, a fourth relevant party joined the game. Thus, in a highly concentrated party system, two big and two smaller parties dominated both national and *Land* elections. Since the 1990s, the degree of party system fragmentation has grown, thereby weakening the predominance of the CDU and SPD. This has been accompanied by a higher level of regional variation in voting behaviour in *Land* elections and growing asymmetries between national and regional levels of party competition (see Detterbeck, 2012: 105–107).[4] For reunified Germany, both federal and party system change reflect the growing social, political and economic disparities among the *Länder* (Sturm, 1999; Scharpf, 2005).

As a result of the greater heterogeneity of regional party systems, the diversity of government formats and coalition alignments in the *Länder* has increased (see Jun et al., 2008). There now is a rather flexible patchwork of grand coalitions (CDU/SPD), bourgeois (CDU/FDP), social-liberal (SPD/FDP), black-green (CDU/Greens), red-green (SPD/Greens), red-red coalitions (SPD/ The Left) as well as some rare three-party experiments in regional government (see Kropp, 2010: 289–292). Accordingly, the chances of modelling regional coalitions along federal political lines have decreased. The post-unification period has seen the return of incongruent coalitions, bringing together partners which are political opponents at another territorial level. While congruence with federal government-opposition patterns still matters, the coalition strategies of the *Land* parties have become more autonomous since 1990 (Detterbeck and Renzsch, 2003).

This has had important repercussions for federal processes in the *Bundesrat*. Federal congruence has facilitated policy coherence in the interlocked federal system (Jeffery, 1999a). Having the same party political majorities in both chambers promised to push through legislation under the condition that federal and *Land* parties of the same political colour find common ground. However, it is true that for an extended period of time the federal opposition held the majority in the *Bundesrat*. But even in the context of divided government, the bipolar structure of party competition—SPD versus CDU—allowed for inter-party negotiations and mutual bargaining on an easily defined scheme (Renzsch, 1999; see also Lehmbruch, 2000). These certainties are gone. The heterogeneity of *Land* governments impedes the formation clear majorities of either the federal government or the opposition camp. Federal bargaining in the *Bundesrat* has become more flexible but also less predictable. Increasingly, the two major parties have to take into account the preferences of their various coalition partners (Kropp, 2010: 303–306).

The growth of territorial diversity in the party system has also affected the internal life of German parties (see Sturm, 1999). All major parties are active at both federal and *Land* levels and run, with the exception of the

Bavarian CSU, state-wide organizations across the territory. German parties are characterized by strong vertical linkages between party levels. The *Land* parties, as branches of state-wide parties, possess formal autonomy in governing their own affairs with respect to personnel, policies and strategies. At the same time, they are fervently involved in federal-level party structures. The strong inclusion of regional party leaders in federal party executives is particularly noteworthy here (Detterbeck, 2012). Vertical linkages within parties have been one of the most important mechanisms to ensure federal coordination. As cooperative federal systems *'en miniature'*, parties were to aggregate territorial interest and develop common positions across levels of government. Coordination works via internal party channels, for example, in the multi-level federal party executives, but also via the informal structuring of the federal second chamber. On a routine basis, *Bundesrat* sessions are preceded by party round-tables of the federal party and its representatives in *Länder* governments (Renzsch, 1999; Leonardy, 2004).

The growth in territorial diversity has made uniform party strategies less feasible and less rewarding. Inside the parties, cohesion across levels has become more difficult to maintain. The bonds which have provided the 'glue' to unite the various territorial party units, such as programmatic commitments, deference to party leaders and shared party values, have become weaker. As a result, parties have lost the capacity to integrate different territorial interests in the way they classically had done. Looking at the responses of the various German parties to political change, we see subtle adaptations to a more competitive environment rather than fundamental party reforms. The autonomy of *Land* party branches has grown, while the levels of vertical integration within the federal parties have remained high. With respect to the autonomy of *Länder* parties, formal organizational competences which had existed before are now being used more and more systematically with a stronger focus on specific regional contexts. Even when *Länder* parties most often remain within the spectrum of their federal party, discussions are framed more explicitly with the regional context in mind and there is a stronger regional flavour to the decisions taken by *Länder* parties.

On the other hand, vertical party linkages, namely the integration of sub-state party elites into the federal party leadership, have not declined since 1990. Despite the stronger differentiation of their institutional, competitive and social context, which has led to inherent strains between party levels and between *Land* organizations, German parties have held on to intra-party structures designed to facilitate close cooperation. In a nutshell, German parties have sought to maintain a fragile balance between uniformity and differentiation (Detterbeck and Jeffery, 2009).

Federal Reform in Germany: The Role of Party and Coalition Politics

The Failed Reform: The 'Federalism Convention' of 2003–04

Federal reform became a major political issue in Germany during the 1990s. This reflected the higher level of territorial diversity among the *Länder* in the reunified polity, intensified by the challenges of European integration and economic change. The trademark of German federalism, the strong degree of joint decision-making and interdependence between political levels, increasingly came to be perceived as no longer allowing for effective governance within the multi-level system (see Jeffery, 1999b). Under the political leadership of the modernizers in the 'rich South', the CDU and CSU-led *Land* governments of Baden-Württemberg, Hesse and Bavaria, albeit with widespread cross-party support, a federal convention was set up in October 2003. The task of the federal convention was to draft proposals for constitutional reform aimed primarily at disentanglement between political levels. By giving more legislative autonomy to the *Länder* while reducing their veto potential in the *Bundesrat,* more political leeway for both federal and regional policy-making was to be achieved (Scharpf, 2005; Behnke and Kropp, 2016).

With 32 voting members, half of them being federal MPs in proportional representation of the parliamentary party groupings in the *Bundestag* and the other half being the 16 *Land* prime ministers as members of the *Bundesrat*, the federal convention brought together the vital institutional and partisan veto players needed for constitutional reform.[5] This approach was also symbolized by the double chairmanship of the leader of the SPD Bundestag group, Franz Müntefering, and the CSU Bavarian prime minister, Edmund Stoiber. The composition of the convention resembled the federal conciliation committee with its good track record of resolving conflict between both chambers of legislation. The federal government had no voting member in the convention but federal ministers took part in the general debates and the working groups, as it was the same for representatives of the *Land* parliaments and the local government associations (Turner and Rowe, 2013: 386–387).

To some extent, party coordination structured the work of the federal convention. The *Bundesrat* routine business of having partisan preparatory meetings in advance of plenary sessions was also practised in the constitutional forum. Federal and regional members of the federal convention came together regularly to arrive at shared positions along party lines (SPD/Greens versus CDU/CSU/FDP). Working papers were presented and discussed. The traditional mode of accommodating territorial conflict within vertically integrated parties and of simplifying the terms of inter-party bargaining by having unified party positions shaped actorś expectations on how to deal with potential conflict (Benz, 2005; Scharpf, 2005).

At the end of the day, however, party coordination did not work out as planned. In December 2004, the two chairmen had to declare that the federal convention had failed to reach agreement on sensitive issues, most notably education policy. Constitutional reform, then, was buried. One of the academic experts who participated in the public hearings of the federal convention pointed out that the informal party round-tables were not able to generate binding consensus across party levels. Due to the lack of a coherent and detailed partisan vision on how to exactly reconstruct the relationship between political levels, these attempts remained by and large unsuccessful (Scharpf, 2009: 76).

Instead, the *Land* prime ministers turned to a horizontal form of coordination amongst themselves. At several crucial points during the negotiations, the *Länder* presented joint position papers, prepared by the collective efforts of their state chancelleries. In attempts to minimize territorial conflict between regional governments, the papers were drafted in tandems of large and economically strong CDU/CSU-*Länder* (Baden-Württemberg, Bavaria) with small and rather weak SPD-*Länder* (Berlin, Bremen). Accordingly, many of the discussions took the format of 'we', the *Länder*, against 'them', the federal government, rather than the format of a bi-polar partisan cleavage between Social Democrats and Christian Democrats (Scharpf, 2009: 75–78).

Despite this framing of conflict, horizontal coordination suffered from the economic and socio-cultural differences between the *Länder*. The stronger regions, the 'rich South', openly pushed for a more competitive federal system in which they would be allowed to retain the benefits of their own economic successes, and demanded greater autonomy in a set of important policy areas. At the same time, the weaker regions feared the loss of federal solidarity. The decision, taken early on by the *Land* governments to exclude some issues, notably the redrawing of *Land* boundaries and the restructuring of fiscal arrangements, from the agenda of the federal convention was an attempt to avoid fundamental conflict between the *Länder* (Burkhart, 2008: 163–164). Yet, right from the start, the divergence of territorial interests made it difficult to formulate negotiation positions which satisfied the hunger of the more ambitious *Länder* without overburdening the others.

During the final phase of the federal convention, these differences in *Land* interests constituted the main barrier to reform. In evaluating what had been offered by the federal government, the stronger *Länder* saw only marginal advantages ('peanuts') rather than substantial policy gains, while the weaker *Länder* (in line with federal policy experts) became concerned that the effects of the reform, for example, with respect to the recruitment of civil servants, would make them worse off. Consequently, the *Länder* turned away from the compromise in the hope of a better deal in the future (Benz, 2005; Scharpf, 2005; Auel, 2008).[6] Quite clearly, the *Land* prime ministers put their own distinct sub-state interests first.

This is particularly remarkable in the case of the seven SPD-led governments to which partisan incentives to break political deadlock in the negotiations could be attributed. Although there was no federal election ahead for some time to come (at least as was thought), constitutional reform would have strengthened the political legitimacy of the red-green federal government of Chancellor Gerhard Schröder. As we have seen, however, the SPD prime ministers preferred to seek partnership with other *Land* governments, irrespective of party colours. There was also little ideological cohesion on the side of the centre-left. On the critical policy issues of the framework legislation for university education and federal interventions in school education, the SPD *Land* governments sided with their CDU *Land* colleagues rather than with the SPD experts on education and the SPD federal minister for education, Edelgard Bulmahn (Scharpf, 2009: 101–103).[7]

Hence, the failure of the federal convention in 2004 can be interpreted as the triumph of distinct *Land* interests over electoral and programmatic party logics (Turner and Rowe, 2013). Each *Land,* or each group of *Länder*, pursued its own agenda in the hope of maximal territorial benefits. While the hardening of positions also reflected differences in electoral rationalities of appealing to sub-state electorates and, to some extent, differences in ideological preferences (e.g. in education policy), the main problem lay in the difficulties of overcoming antagonistic territorial interests (see Sturm, 2005).

Yet, there is also another conclusion to be drawn from the 2004 failure. The weakness of internal party coordination demonstrates the difficulties German parties face in arriving at cohesive and united party positions across political levels. As a result of the dynamics outlined above—the stronger diversity in territorial party competition, the loss of internal coherence and the more autonomous role played by the *Land* party branches—the accommodation of territorial interests via vertical party integration has become a much more difficult endeavour.

Federalism Reform I (2006)

The early federal elections of September 2005 which resulted in the formation of the grand coalition led by Chancellor Angela Merkel brought the issue of federal reform back on the table. Less than a year after the federal convention had collapsed, the coalition agreement between Christian Democrats and Social Democrats committed both partners to a set of reform proposals which strongly relied on the failed agreement of December 2004. Over the first months of the new government, the proposals were polished into constitutional amendments. Rather than installing a new commission, the fine-tuning took place in meetings of the federal cabinet, the *Land* prime ministers, and the parliamentary parties of CDU/CSU and SPD (Laufer and Münch, 2010: 111).

Once the legislative procedure started, the grand coalitions had no problems in pushing through constitutional reform given their comfortable majorities in both houses. In the *Bundestag*, close to 75% of the MPs supported the reform. Only a small minority of 15 SPD deputies joined the opposition in voting against federal reform. In the *Bundesrat*, all *Land* governments (62 out of 69 votes) supported the package with the exception of Mecklenburg-West Pomerania (governed by a SPD/PDS coalition) and, interestingly, Schleswig-Holstein (governed by a grand coalition).[8] In the summer of 2006, federal reform was achieved (Turner and Rowe, 2013: 389–391).

To a large extent, coalition politics explains the differences in outcome. From the start, the grand coalition put much political effort into making constitutional reform work. The Merkel government certainly wanted an early success to demonstrate its capacity to govern effectively. This provided clear incentives for following an electoral logic of party agency. Neither of the two major parties could be interested in failing a second time. This is also true for the *Land* governments, all of which were either led by a grand coalition also or involved one of the major parties as senior partner. While in 2004, the *Länder* could dare play the territorial card, in 2006, they would have risked fatal damage to the new federal coalition. Vertical party linkages within both the CDU/CSU and SPD have been used to convince all party representatives involved in the reform process about the need to arrive at a common solution. Although doubts about the reform may still have not been resolved, especially among the weaker *Länder*, this time strategic political interests trumped specific policy reservations (Heinz and Hornig, 2012: 15–16; Turner and Rowe, 2013: 394–395).

In addition, compared to 2004, the *Länder* achieved some concessions. Most importantly, the new federal government renounced the ambition of its predecessors to remain constitutionally entitled to intervene in education policy. In the light of some recent decisions by the constitutional court on these issues and the change of relevant actors in the policy area after the 2005 election, the federal level 'surrendered' to the claims of the *Länder*. The SPD federal parliamentary party managed to negotiate some exceptions during the legislative process (with regard to research funding and the supervision of school testing), but by and large the *Länder* could solidify their exclusive control over school education and extend their responsibilities in third-level education (Scharpf, 2009: 104–110).

With this extra prize, the surplus in autonomy in the field of education, approval of the federal reform became more attractive for the *Länder*. In return the *Länder* accepted, as they had already done in the federal convention, the (potential) reduction of joint decision-making powers in the *Bundesrat* (see Jun, 2010). Several of the weaker *Länder* also started to see some of the changes—for example, the new responsibility to determine the payment of civil servants—as an opportunity rather than a threat (Turner and Rowe, 2013: 394). Thus, the 2006 federal reform involved some elements of a territorial logic of party agency—the pursuit of specific *Land* interest. However, these motives played a much lesser role than they did during the 2003–04 federal convention.

Federalism Reform II (2009)

In December 2006, the second phase of the federalism reform, the modernization of fiscal arrangements between the federal level and the *Länder*, began. A new commission was appointed to deal with financial issues, structured along the lines of the first federal commission. Headed by the CDU prime minister of Baden-Württemberg, Günther Oettinger, and the SPD parliamentary leader in the *Bundestag,* Peter Struck, 16 representatives of each house plus some non-voting members convened to prepare proposals for constitutional reform (Laufer and Münch, 2010: 273–280).

As the commission was to discuss money, strong differences in territorial interests were to be expected from the outset: the central government wanted to see a reduction of the high levels of public debt and state borrowing. While the richer *Länder* pushed for lower payments in fiscal equalization schemes and higher financial self-responsibility at the regional level, the poorer *ones* sought to maintain the burden of sharing and fiscal solidarity. The broad agenda of fiscal relationships in the federal system was quickly reduced to the issues of budgetary discipline and debt control (Renzsch, 2010; Behnke and Kropp, 2016). Given the context of the global financial crisis from 2007 on, it seemed necessary to deal with these problems first in order to establish a more robust system of fiscal federalism for preventing economic disturbances in Germany (Turner and Rowe, 2013: 396).

The second reform commission thus worked under strong external pressure. Economic stability was perceived to depend on suitable mechanisms of balancing federal and *Land* budgets. Public concerns about the levels of public debt put additional pressure on the federal commission (see Petersen et al., 2008). Any attempts by the parties to block the reform would have been electorally dangerous. Following an electoral logic of party agency, the governing parties of CDU and SPD had strong incentives to internally close ranks and deliver results. This proved to be more difficult for the Social Democrats. Both among the SPD *Länder* and in the federal party, there were demands for some deficit spending and full parliamentary control over public budgets. The SPD established several intra-party working groups, bringing together federal and *Land* policy experts on finances, in an attempt to coordinate the partýs position (Renzsch, 2010: 390; Turner and Rowe, 2013: 397).

Alongside electoral logics, we also see programmatic and territorial logics playing a role. Both major parties, but in particular the Christian Democrats, welcomed the reform for reasons of inter-generational solidarity and as a response to the moral hazard problem of weaker *Länder* relaxing their efforts at the expense of the federation and the economically stronger regions. While the 'rich South' had employed such arguments for quite some time, the debates now also saw other CDU politicians such as Wolfgang Böhmer, the prime minister of Saxony-Anhalt, one of the poorest *Länder* in Germany, formulating similar positions. With respect to territorial logics, the weaker *Länder* could be won over by offering them additional funding for an interim period (2011–19). For the stronger *Länder*, the reform promised lower risks of paying for the debts of the poorer regions, a general reduction of public debt levels (both of which were also in the interest of the federal government) and a first step towards future taxation autonomy (Laufer and Münch, 2010: 276–277; Turner and Rowe, 2013: 397).

In 2009, the second federalism reform was put into place. Based on the recommendations of the Oettinger-Struck commission, constitutional amendments concerning public finances—most notably the 'debt brake' which obliges the federal level and the *Länder* to produce balanced budgets without revenues from credits—and constitutional amendments concerning public administration, were legislated by *Bundestag* and *Bundesrat* (Renzsch, 2010). As in 2006, the grand coalition had few problems in organizing the necessary two-third majorities in both houses. In the federal parliament, 19 SPD deputies joined the opposition in voting against the reform on programmatic reasons. In the second chamber, three weaker *Länder* either abstained (Schleswig-Holstein, Berlin), or rejected the reform (Mecklenburg-West Pomerania). Their arguments were partly inspired by territorial interests and the lack of adequate financial compensation, but also touched upon programmatic issues such as the sacrifice of the constitutionally enshrined budgetary responsibility of the German *Land* parliaments (Heinz, 2010: 10–11; Turner and Rowe, 2013: 400).

Federalism Reform III: On the Road to New Fiscal Arrangements

The second reform of the federal system in 2009 postponed the contentious issue of vertical and horizontal fiscal equalization, both of which needed to be addressed with the current scheme running out in 2019. Accordingly, the grand coalition, elected back in office in 2013, signalled in its coalition agreement that a third phase of reform was to tackle open questions of fiscal federalism, including the equalization mechanism between the *Länder*. In terms of political procedure, the decision was made to work through the established intergovernmental channels of the conference of *Land* prime ministers, involving regular talks between the federal and the regional governments. The *Land* ministers of finance were entrusted with the operative leadership of the reform. Thus, rather than having a third federal commission of both legislative chambers, political negotiations were placed in the hands of policy experts (Behnke, 2015; Renzsch, 2015).

Long before the formal process started, most of the *Land* governments had invested quite some resources in preparing their own positions and in feeding them into the more general discussion. As was to be expected, controversy over distinct territorial interests dominated the debate. The old rift between the strong and the weak *Länder* reappeared. Bavaria and Hesse, governed by the Christian Democrats (in the latter case, in coalition with the Greens since 2014), acted as the frontrunners in demanding a less redistributive system of horizontal equalization. Both *Länder* had already put their case before the constitutional court in 2013, while the third partner of the 'rich South', Baden-Württemberg, now governed by a green-red coalition, took a more cautious approach. At the other end of the spectrum, the East German *Länder* called on federal solidarity as a necessary element in their attempts to strengthen their economic potential and fulfil their policy obligations. Other *Länder*, such as North Rhine-Westphalia and the three city states, campaigned on their own specific demands (see Lenk, 2015).

Given the predominance of particular territorial interests, the negotiations proved to be very complicated. Several attempts to break the deadlock by the federal government and individual *Land* governments (e.g. Baden-Württemberg) failed. The initiatives were blocked by other *Land* governments with a view to expected negative financial consequences for their own budgets (Renzsch, 2015; Scheller, 2015). Given these difficulties, it rather came as a surprise that the *Länder* agreed upon a common solution in December 2015. The compromise motion was hampered out in secret deliberations among the *Land* governments, led by Hamburg (SPD) and Bavaria (CSU). The proposal, still to be accepted by the federal government, seeks to replace the old system of horizontal fiscal equalization for a new formula of tax revenues distribution. By externalizing some of the extra costs to the federal level, the *Länder* managed to overcome their internal differences.[9]

As with the former rounds of federal reform, internal party coordination had its role in finding common ground among the *Länder*. This is particularly evident in the case of the five CDU/CSU-led *Land* governments which in September 2015 proposed a new scheme of fiscal equalization, feigning to bridge the demands of the strong regions (Bavaria, Hesse), East Germany (Saxony, Saxony-Anhalt) and the smaller western states (Saarland). With some amendments that helped to win the support of the other *Land* governments, the CDU/CSU proposal paved the way for the final solution in December 2015 (see Renzsch, 2015: 668).

Conclusion

The aim of this article was to study the role of political parties in federal reform. From a theoretical perspective, we have outlined three logics of party agency: electoral, programmatic and territorial. In the German case, each of the three reform steps—federalism reform I, II and, still unfinished, III—was shaped by a specific blend of the three logics. There have been struggles over which of the strategies was to prevail both within individual parties and across the party divide. Looking at the federal reforms of 2006 and 2009, the left-wing 'rebels' in the SPD parliamentary party and the dissenting *Länder* votes in the second chamber give examples of political conflict over such issues. Hence, it is important to have a clear understanding of the territorial power balances within political parties when explaining party behaviour (see Hepburn and Detterbeck, 2013).

However, it is not only intra-party politics that matters. In 2004, when the federal convention discussed the distribution of legislative competences, territorial logics dominated the process. In 2006, support for the newly elected grand coalition made electoral logics paramount. In 2009, budget control seemed to be the right answer to the financial crisis, uniting political actors behind the electoral logic of satisfying public demands by 'getting things done'. In 2015, divergence in territorial fiscal interests delayed compromise on a third federal reform until the *Länder* found a formula which promised to put them all in a better position (at the expense of the federal centre).

Two general lessons on territorial party strategies can be drawn from the German case. First, the timing of the reform process is absolutely crucial. In 2004 and, to some extent, in 2015, parties prioritized a territorial logic as there was only limited pressure to close ranks. Neither an upcoming federal election nor coalition politics made it necessary to overcome differences in territorial interests. This was different in 2006 and 2009 when an electoral logic of party agency prevailed. On both occasions, federal reform was seen as necessary to prove the credibility and effectiveness of the grand coalition. Second, policies matter. In some fields, such as fiscal policy in the federalism reform III, *Land* governments have proved to put territorial interests first. In other areas, like education policy in 2004, programmatic logics have been more pronounced with parties seeking to live up to normative objectives. More generally, electoral rationalities shape party agency very strongly. Taking a stance on territorial issues has much to do with parties' perception of gaining or losing popular support.

Finally, the federal reforms in Germany throw an interesting light on of party coordination in federal systems. As the analysis of the German case shows, the accommodation of territorial interests via vertical party integration has become a much more difficult endeavour. In explaining this development, we have pointed to the stronger diversity in territorial party competition, the loss of internal coherence and the more autonomous role played by the *Land* party branches. This reflects a more general trend in multi-level systems towards a stronger separation between national and regional party systems. Yet, the organizational responses of parties in dealing with the increasingly asymmetrical nature of party competition differ widely. Accordingly, comparative research has shown strong differences to the capacity of parties for vertical integration (see Swenden and Maddens, 2009; Detterbeck, 2012).

Since the 1990s, the German parties have maintained strong linkages between party levels while allowing for more autonomy of the *Land* parties. With respect to federal coordination, the parties have increasingly been faced with problems in arriving at cohesive and united party positions across territorial levels. Despite the growth of intra-party frictions the structuring of federal bargaining processes, both in the *Bundesrat* and in the federal reform commissions, still works very much along party lines (see Lehmbruch, 2000; Turner and Rowe, 2013). Whether party coordination succeeds in solving federal conflict and in steering federal reform, however, is far from certain. Much depends on the logics that drive party agency. The choice of strategy has a strong impact on how successfully parties can play an integrative role in federal systems.

Notes

1. In multi-level contexts, electoral logics may differ between the state-wide and sub-state levels of party competition causing frictions between different territorial layers of the party organization. Thus, we need to analyse the internal power balances of multi-level parties to understand better their strategic electoral choices (see Hepburn and Detterbeck, 2013).

2. For analytical tools in quantitative research that may help distinguishing between the different logics of partisan action in federal processes, see Bräuninger et al. (2010). In qualitative research, case studies and interviews with politicians and civil servants are most frequently used to learn about actorś perception of their interests and priorities (see Turner and Rowe, 2013).

3. Electoral systems at state-wide and sub-state levels and the electoral cycles resulting from the timing of elections at different levels constitute another institutional layer for party agency. As with territorial arrangements, the crucial question is whether there is a high or a low degree of interconnectedness between territorial levels. Differences in electoral formulas and consecutive elections at various levels, distributed over time, can add to the distinctiveness of state-wide and sub-state party systems, whereas simultaneous elections fought under similar rules may produce more symmetrical results (Deschouwer, 2006). In any case, the various structures of the electoral process provide distinct framework conditions for the choice of partisan strategies.

4. The most visible single element of territorial heterogeneity in German party competition is the success of the PDS / Left Party, which is a major party in the East but has remained a rather small force in western Germany. But there are other factors as well: the relative weakness of the FDP and the Greens in

the East, the temporary inroads of the populist right made into some Land parliaments, the growing instability of voting behaviour resulting from a general
decline of partisan alignments, and, related to this, an increased tendency of
switching party preferences between elections at different territorial levels
(Sturm, 1999; Hough and Koß, 2009).

5. Changes to the German constitution, the Basic Law, require two-third majorities
in both houses, the *Bundestag* and the *Bundesrat*.

6. The decision of the *Land* governments to leave the federal convention without
result was influenced by rulings of the federal constitutional court in 2014 on
education policy (junior professorships, student tuition fees) which strengthened the position of the sub-state level. In curtailing federal legislation in
areas of concurrent matters, the court decision revitalized *Land* responsibilities
without federal constitutional reform (see Benz, 2008: 186–188; Scharpf, 2009:
93–96).

7. It may be true, however, that for the CDU prime ministers the failure of the
federal convention in 2004 had the attractive side-effect of defeating ambitions
of the SPD policy experts on education to secure more federal influence on
schools and universities. So, there has been a party conflict at play here in a
policy field which is traditionally quite prone to ideological disputes in
Germany (see Wolf, 2006).

8. Mecklenburg-West Pomerania based its no-vote on the argument that the
federal reform would bring negative effects for the small and economically dis-
advantaged *Länder* while also making the federal level less capable of reducing
regional inequalities. The grand coalition of Schleswig-Holstein abstained in the
final *Bundesrat* vote. They had made clear that they were particularly sceptical
about the competitive dynamics arising from the new *Land* competence of regulating the careers, payments and provisions of state civil servants (Laufer and
Münch, 2010: 112).

9. See *Süddeutsche Zeitung*, 4 December 2015, 'Ministerpräsidenten schließen
Finanzpakt' (1).

Disclosure Statement

No potential conflict of interest was reported by the author.

References

Auel, K. (2008), Still no exit from the joint decision trap: the German federal reform(s),
German Politics, Vol.17, No.4, pp.424–439.

Behnke, N. (2015), Stand und Perspektiven der Föderalismusforschung, *Aus Politik und
Zeitgeschichte*, Vol.65, No.28–30, pp.9–16.

Behnke, N. and Benz, A. (2009), The politics of constitutional change between reform
and evolution, *Publius: The Journal of Federalism*, Vol.39, No.2, pp.213–240.

Behnke, N. and Kropp, S. (2016), Marble cake dreaming of layer cake—or: ideology and
reality in the working of federalism, *Regional and Federal Studies*, Vol.26, this issue.

Benz, A. (2005), Kein Ausweg aus der Politikverflechtung? Warum die
Bundesstaatskommission scheiterte, aber nicht scheitern musste, *Politische
Vierteljahresschrift*, Vol.46, No.2, pp.204–214.

Benz, A. (2008), Föderalismusreform in der 'Entflechtungsfalle', in Europäisches Zentrum für Föderalismus-Forschung Tübingen (ed.), *Jahrbuch des Föderalismus 2007. Föderalismus, Subsidiarität und Regionen in Europa*, pp.180–190. Baden-Baden: Nomos.

Benz, A. and Broschek, J. (eds). (2013), *Federal dynamics. Continuity, change, and the varieties of federalism*. Oxford: Oxford University Press.

Bräuninger, T. and Debus, M. (2012), *Parteienwettbewerb in den deutschen Bundesländern*. Wiesbaden: VS Verlag.

Bräuninger, T., et al. (2010), Sachpolitik oder Parteipolitik. Eine Bestimmung des Parteidrucks im Bundesrat mittels bayesianischer Methode, *Politische Vierteljahresschrift*, Vol.51, No.2, pp.223–249.

Burkhart, S. (2008), *Blockierte Politik. Ursachen und Folgen von 'divided government' in Deutschland*. Frankfurt: Campus Verlag.

Deschouwer, K. (2006), Political parties as multi-level organizations, in R. S. Katz and W. Crotty (eds), *Handbook of party politics*, pp.291–300. London: Sage.

Detterbeck, K. (2012), *Multi-level party politics in Western Europe*. Houndmills: Palgrave Macmillan.

Detterbeck, K. and Jeffery, C. (2009), Rediscovering the region: territorial politics and party organizations in Germany, in W. Swenden and B. Maddens (eds), *Territorial party politics in Western Europe*, pp.63–85. Houndmills: Palgrave Macmillan.

Detterbeck, K. and Renzsch, W. (2003), Multi-level electoral competition: the German case, *European Urban and Regional Studies*, Vol.10, No.3, pp.257–269.

De Winter, L., et al. (2006), Introduction: autonomist parties in European politics, in L. De Winter, M. Gómez-Reino, P. Lynch (eds), *Autonomist parties in Europe: identity politics and the revival of the territorial cleavage*, pp.3–34. Barcelona: Institut de Ciènces Politiques i Social.

Filippov, M., Ordeshook, C. and Shvetsova, O. (2004), *Designing federalism. A theory of self-sustainable federal institutions*. Cambridge: Cambridge University Press.

Heinz, D. (2010), Federal reform II in Germany, *Perspectives on Federalism*, Vol.2, No.2, pp.1–14.

Heinz, D. and Hornig, E. (2012), Catch-all politics under stress. Non-territorially defined parties and the quest for symmetry and compromise in territorial reforms, *Central European Journal of Public Policy*, Vol.6, No.1, pp.4–25.

Hepburn, E. (2009), Introduction: re-conceptualizing sub-state mobilization, *Regional and Federal Studies, Special Issue*, Vol.19, No.4–5, pp.477–499.

Hepburn, E. and Detterbeck, K. (2013), Federalism, regionalism and the dynamics of party politics, in J. Loughlin, J. Kincaid and W. Swenden (eds), *Routledge handbook of regionalism and federalism*, pp.76–92. Abingdon: Routledge.

Hough, D. and Koß, M. (2009), Territory and electoral politics in Germany, in W. Swenden and B. Maddens (eds), *Territorial party politics in Western Europe*, pp.47–62. Houndmills: Palgrave Macmillan.

Jeffery, C. (1999a), Party politics and territorial representation in the federal republic of Germany, *West European Politics*, Vol.22, No.2, pp.130–166.

Jeffery, C. (1999b), From cooperative federalism to a 'sinatra doctrine' of the *Länder*, in C. Jeffery (ed.), *Recasting German federalism*, pp.329–342. London: Pinter.

Jeffery, C. (2010), Multi-level party competition in federal and regional states, in H. Enderlein, S. Wälti and M. Zürn (eds), *Handbook on multi-level governance*, pp.136–152. Cheltenham: Edward Elgar.

Jun, U. (2010), Der Bundesrat im föderativen System Deutschlands: Vor und nach der Reform 2006, in K. Schrenk and M. Soldner (eds), *Analyse demokratischer Regierungssysteme*, pp.335–358. Wiesbaden: VS Springer.

Jun, U., et al. (eds). (2008), *Parteien und Parteiensysteme in den deutschen Ländern*. Wiesbaden: VS Verlag.

Kropp, S. (2010), The ubiquity and strategic complexity of grand coalition in the German federal system, *German Politics*, Vol.19, No.3–4, pp.286–311.

Laufer, H. and Münch, U. (2010), *Das föderale System der Bundesrepublik Deutschland*. München: Bayerische Landeszentrale für politische Bildungsarbeit.

Lehmbruch, G. (2000), *Parteienwettbewerb im Bundesstaat. Regelsysteme und Spannungslagen im politischen System der Bundesrepublik Deutschland*. Wiesbaden: Westdeutscher Verlag.

Lenk, T. (2015), Länderfinanzausgleich: Wer blockiert wen? *Wirtschaftsdienst. Zeitschrift für Wirtschaftspolitik*, Vol.95, No.7, pp.445–446.

Leonardy, U. (2004), Federalism and parties in Germany: organizational hinges between constitutional and political structures, in R. Hrbek (ed.), *Parties and federalism. An international comparison*, pp.183–202. Baden-Baden: Nomos.

Lorenz, A. (2011), Constitutional negotiations in federal reforms: interests, *Interaction Orientation and the Prospect of Agreement, Regional and Federal Studies*, Vol.21, No.4–5, pp.407–425.

Mair, P. (2008), The challenge to party government, *West European Politics*, Vol.31, No.1–2, pp.211–234.

Peters, B. G. (2012), *Institutional theory in political science. The new institutionalism*. London: Continuum.

Petersen, T., et al. (2008), Public attitudes towards German federalism: a point of departure for a reform of German (fiscal) federalism? Differences between public opinion and the political debate, *German Politics*, Vol.17, No.4, pp.559–586.

Petersohn, B., et al. (2015), Negotiating territorial change in multinational states: party preferences, negotiating power and the role of the negotiation mode, *Publius: The Journal of Federalism*, Vol.45, No.4, pp.626–652.

Renzsch, W. (1999), Party competition in the German federal state: variations on an old theme, *Regional and Federal Studies*, Vol.9, No.2, pp.180–192.

Renzsch, W. (2010), Federal reform under the grand coalition, *German Politics*, Vol.19, No.3–4, pp.382–392.

Renzsch, W. (2015), Vertagt bis … Zum Scheitern der Bund-Länder-Verhandlungen über eine Neuordnung der bundesstaatlichen Finanzbeziehungen, *Wirtschaftsdienst. Zeitschrift für Wirtschaftspolitik*, Vol.95, No.10, pp.667–670.

Riker, W. (1964), *Federalism. Origin, operation, significance*. Boston: Little, Brown & Co.

Scharpf, F. W. (2005), *No exit from the joint decision trap? Can German federalism reform itself?* Working Paper, No. 05/8. Cologne: Max-Planck-Institut für Gesellschaftsforschung.

Scharpf, F. W. (2009), *Föderalismusreform. Kein Ausweg aus der Politikverflechtungsfalle?* Frankfurt: Campus Verlag.

Scheller, H. (2015), Der 'erschöpfte Föderalstaat'. Reformdebatte und Verfassungsrealität in Deutschland, *Aus Politik und Zeitgeschichte*, Vol.65, No.28–30, pp.17–23.

Stefuriuc, I. (2009), Explaining government formation in multi-level settings: coalition theory revisited, *Evidence from the Spanish Case, Regional and Federal Studies*, Vol.19, No.1, pp.97–116.

Stepan, A. (2001), Toward a new comparative politics of federalism, (multi-)nationalism, and democracy: beyond rikerian federalism, in A. Stepan (ed.), *Arguing comparative politics*, pp.315–361. Oxford: Oxford University Press.

Strom, K. (1990), A behavioral theory of competitive political parties, *American Journal of Political Science*, vol. 34, No. 2, pp.565–598.

Sturm, R. (1999), Party competition and the federal system: the Lehmbruch hypothesis revisited, in C. Jeffery (ed.), *Recasting German federalism*, pp.197–216. London: Pinter.

Sturm, R. (2005), Föderalismusreform: Kein Erkenntnisproblem, warum aber ein Gestaltungs- und Entscheidungsproblem? *Politische Vierteljahresschrift*, Vol.46, No.2, pp.195–203.

Swenden, W. and Maddens, B. (2009), Territorial party politics in Western Europe: a framework for analysis, in W. Swenden and B. Maddens (eds), *Territorial party politics in Western Europe*, pp.1–30. Houndmills: Palgrave Macmillan.

Toubeau, S. and Massetti, E. (2013), The party politics of territorial reforms in Europe, *West European Politics*, Vol.36, No.2, pp.297–316.

Turner, E. and Rowe, C. (2013), Party servants, ideologues or regional representatives? The German *Länder* and the reform of federalism, *West European Politics*, Vol.36, No.2, pp.382–404.

Ware, A. (1996), *Political parties and party systems*. New York: Oxford University Press.

Wolf, F. (2006), Bildungspolitik: Föderale Vielfalt und gesamtstaatliche Vermittlung, in M.G. Schmidt and R. Zohlnhöfer (eds), *Regieren in der Bundesrepublik Deutschland. Innen- und Außenpolitik seit 1949*, pp.219–239. Wiesbaden: VS Verlag.

Marble cake dreaming of layer cake: the merits and pitfalls of disentanglement in German federalism reform

Sabine Kropp and Nathalie Behnke

ABSTRACT
This article explains the zigzag of the stepwise federalism reform in Germany by accessing the theoretical concept of institutional incongruity. It is argued that the existing imbalance between competencies, policy problems and fiscal resources was further exacerbated as actors adopted inconsistent institutional 'layers' during the sequential reform. Two case studies on higher education and unemployment policy reveal that actors finally reverted to joint decision-making and revived ideas of solidarity in order to remedy inconsistent reform results, although 'disentanglement' and competition had been the leitmotivs underlying the first reform step. The article confirms that institutional congruity is hardly attainable in federations. Reform attempts aiming at disentangling responsibilities and fiscal resources encounter insuperable difficulties, because policy issues more than ever transcend the borders of single territorial units and need joint financing. The study concludes by discussing the question whether joint decision-making – compared to dual resp. 'layer-cake' federalism – owns a specific democratic quality.

We modernize the federal system, which in itself contains the imperative to cooperate. ... we realize that we now enter a period in which we need more cooperation ... (German MPs in the plenary debate of 10 October 2014; BT-PlPr. 18/58, at pp.5402, 5394)

1. Introduction

In 2016, Germany is looking back on a decade of stepwise federalism reforms. In comparative research, Germany has been classified as a prototype of cooperative federalism and joint decision-making. Nonetheless, the first reform step (2003–06) was strongly inspired from the ideas and goals of dual federalism, typically represented by the US (Watts, 2006). Hence, it was aimed at disentangling joint tasks, at separating more neatly the competences of the German Länder and the federal level, at strengthening the accountability of all levels of government, and at introducing a number of competitive elements among the Länder. The second reform step in 2009 introduced the debt brake in order to contain the excessive public debts incurred by most Länder and concomitantly established a stability council supervising their budgetary discipline (see Korioth, this issue). As a third step, an encompassing reform of the half a century old fiscal equalization scheme is to be finished until 2019, when the respective laws will expire.[1] Ideally, this step will be accomplished by the grand coalition before the Bundestag elections take place in September 2017.

In the light of obvious shortcomings of cooperative federalism, disentanglement, a clearer assignment of powers to the territorial units and more competition became the central vision of the 2006 reform. Joint decision-making as typical of German federalism had widely been criticized because it typically causes long decision-processes, incrementalism and policy solutions at the lowest common denominator (Scharpf, 1988) due to the high number of veto players involved (Tsebelis, 2000, 2002). Dual federalism seemed to be a compelling vision for restructuring the federal architecture, and its advocates apparently tend to dispose of what are regarded as convincing arguments. Along the boundaries of policies, jurisdictions are clearly split between levels of government. This distinct allocation of jurisdictions provides decision-structures transparent to the citizens, secures accountability of political decision-makers and establishes federal competition driving innovation and which is, accordingly, considered to enhance the citizens' living standards. Furthermore, the need for coordination between levels in policy-making such as protection against negative spill-overs is reduced to an absolute minimum. This keeps transaction costs low and protects citizens from unnecessary taxing by the state. Finally, the idea of competition as opposed to solidarity is attractive to the financially stronger states in a federation as it implies less redistribution.

The observation of the 10-year long process of federalism reform in Germany, however, shows that the idea of dual federalism that guided the first reform step did not materialize in the ongoing everyday federal practice. Rather, we observe more financial and responsibility entanglement than before, with the Länder calling even for more. In accordance, some recent reforms have reversed disentanglement; others established new issues of cooperation. Correspondingly, the citation epigraph at the outset of this article indicates that German political decision-makers are even conjuring up a new stage of federal cooperation.

This article contributes to explaining the peculiar zig-zagging reform path. The German example adds concrete evidence to the insight formulated by Grodzins (1966) in the 1960s, arguing that a pure type of dual federalism never even existed in the first place. Even with regard to the US, he maintained that American federalism in practice resembled more of a marble than a layer cake. Similarly, Hueglin recently questioned the empirical relevance of the US model (2013). Obviously, the very structure and functioning of federal systems require intense coordination between and among levels of government which is widely incompatible with the layer cake ideal of dual federalism. Beyond this observation, the aim of this article is to elaborate the specific mechanism that recurrently shifts the workings and architecture of federal states from layer cake towards marble-cake structures and processes.

This contribution thus provides a theoretical argument for the particular pattern in the three steps of German federalism reform, which started with a major effort at disentanglement, but subsequently retracted basic elements of the initial reform. Typically, stepwise reforms are prone to dilution. Sequential arrangements create specific challenges to reform consistency and robustness over time because political actors, coalitions and majorities change, and new events and crises demand decisions which may deviate from – or even contradict – former solutions. The advantage of stepwise reforms is that they allow for correcting and refining erstwhile decisions. As such, a deviation from the initial step then is not really surprising. Nevertheless, compared to other federations which have initiated and undergone major constitutional reforms in the last two decades (Benz, 2013), the German case features a particular reform path displaying strong topical inconsistencies, even though the group of reform actors remained consistent and external reform drivers did not substantially change. The German example thus represents an extreme case (Gerring, 2008: 653), exemplifying the tension between cooperation and disentanglement and its effects on the dynamics of federal reform.

In developing the argument, the article proceeds as follows: in the next section, based on a brief review of the literature accounting for institutional reform, a mechanism is outlined that supposedly explains the contradictory evidence of the German reform history. In Section 3, this mechanism is exemplified, tracing the zig-zagging paths through the three waves of federalism reform in the fields of higher education and unemployment care. In Section 4, lessons are drawn from the comparative case studies, relating them to the analytic framework as outlined in the introduction to this special issue.

While the research question is clearly a positive one, aiming at providing an explanation for an observed puzzle, the implications of this explanation carry normative weight with respect to whether cooperative federalism is merely a 'second-best' alternative to the superior model of dual federalism, something which is not practically attainable; or whether it does have a specific quality of its own which cannot be attained in dual federalism. While this normative debate on the relative merits of the competing models of federalism is not at the heart of this contribution, the implications of the empirical results for this normative question are: to wit, whether there is a value in and of itself in the practice of entangled multilevel policy-making, and, if so, then cannot be ignored. We thus conclude the analysis in the last section by feeding the results back into the current theoretical debate (see Behnke and Kropp, this issue).

2. The role of institutional incongruity in federal dynamics

There have been numerous attempts to explain the results of the German federalism reforms. Most employ an institutionalist argument, highlighting the reasons for the limited scope of the reforms. These explanatory approaches, however, are unable to account for the specific reform dynamic which shapes the sequence of reform processes. An alternative argument presented in the following paragraphs is based on the notion of institutional incongruity.

Particularly, it was the first stage of federalism reform in Germany that attracted scholarly attention. From an institutionalist perspective, explanations focused on the lack of substantial change in spite of a major reform effort, thereby emphasizing the relative stability of given institutional settings. Researchers highlighted that the reform process revealed the path-dependent development of German federalism (Auel, 2008; Moore and Eppler, 2008). The density of institutions, the existing allocation of powers affording strong veto points, and the high complexity of established rules (Pierson, 2004: 34–37) obviously constrained the institutional designers in their drafting of far-reaching reforms. But even though path dependency can explain the lack of substantial change, it still fails to elucidate why some parts of the already adopted reform were later on replaced.

In a similar vein, the often cited 'joint decision trap' (Scharpf, 1988, 2009) emphasizes the stickiness of entangled federal institutions. More than path dependence, which explores the stability *and* change of institutions (Mahoney and Thelen, 2010), this application of game theory rather predicts the failure of far-reaching reforms.[2] But it tells nothing about the reasons why actors resuscitate federal entanglement after having partially disentangled responsibilities. The same is true for approaches based on rational-choice institutionalism, such as veto-player theory (Tsebelis, 2002). By pointing to scenarios in which party actors align their policy positions with those of competing parties ('absorption rule'), the theory helps explain why reforms are adopted despite given veto rights. However, it cannot clarify why actors dismiss out of hand previous policy positions.

Variants of institutionalism highlighting path dependence, the joint decision trap, or veto-player theory are all useful in explaining the limited scope of the reform. Yet, the real puzzle in the long-term analysis of German federalism reform is the observation that – in spite of a clear ideological orientation towards disentanglement – instances of fiscal and responsibility entanglement were extended or even newly introduced. Within the institutionalist paradigm, we assume that the zig-zagging reform follows an inherent logic, one driven by the institutional incongruity between responsibilities, the scope of the policy problems and financial resources.

The notion of institutional incongruity is originally borrowed from the theory of public finance. Coase (1960) postulated that a clear distribution of property rights was the precondition for contracts to avoid externalities. In fiscal federalism, institutional congruity denotes that territorial authorities are organized in such a manner that the sets of beneficiaries of a decision, of decision-makers and of cost-bearers are congruent (Oates, 2005: 351; Blankart, 2008: 547–549). Only if a territorial authority is also responsible for paying the expenses necessary to fulfil a public task, will the task be fulfilled efficiently and the preferences of the citizens be best accommodated. When tasks are transferred to subnational levels and when transfers into subnational budgets do not cover expenses, resource scarcity may invite financially weak states to shirk responsibility or, indeed, shift the burden by imposing externalities on other entities of the federation (Bednar, 2009: 155).

In economic analysis, the problem of institutional incongruity can be dealt with in two basic ways: either competences are shifted in a manner so that they become congruent with the effects of a decision and match the financial responsibilities. This strategy would in most cases imply a (re-)centralization of responsibilities in order to internalize external effects and to secure a broader financial capacity. The centralizing strategy is typically justified by the vertical fiscal imbalance that exists in all federal architectures; or financial resources are allocated in such a fashion that empowers subnational entities to bear the costs of the public tasks within their jurisdiction. This strategy is commonly used as an argument for increasing the tax autonomy of states or municipalities and aims at reducing the extent of vertical fiscal imbalance. An increase in tax autonomy, however, does not necessarily mitigate the problem of institutional incongruity for it presupposes that the economic strength of an entity allows raising its revenues effectively by levying new or increasing existing tax rates. In federal states where the economic and financial strength of subnational entities varies substantially, an increase in tax levying or tax varying powers is not always an appropriate remedy to cure institutional incongruity. Rather, the financial capacity of the subnational entities is strengthened by (unconditional or conditional) transfers from the federal level or by granting them a larger share of joint taxes.

These two ways to redress institutional incongruity rely exclusively on the toolkit of economic theory and typically provide a static analysis, pointing at inefficiencies or disequilibria in the allocation of jurisdictions and resources (Olson, 1969; Oates, 2005). In practice, however, a perfect mapping (Oates, 2005: 351) of responsibilities, policy effects and resources is hardly attainable, and a feasible alternative to federal cooperation has not as yet been found.[3]

Some tasks, particularly those which increase costs of the modern welfare state, are simply too exorbitant to be shouldered by one federal unit alone. Spill-overs and the multilevel character of numerous policies call for either voluntary federal cooperation or for mandatory joint decision-making, the latter which stipulates cooperation and typically requires qualified majorities or even unanimity. In order to achieve the ever imperfect balance between problems, responsibilities and financial resources, jurisdictions and resources need to be mutually adapted in a continuous process, a route which entails intense coordination and cooperation.

By taking into account the processual nature of creating and redressing institutional incongruity in ongoing processes of constitutional reform, this article broadens the concept's applicability beyond economic theory, thereby linking it to recent theoretical developments of historical institutionalism and highlighting the role of actors and ideas. Political actors take up ideas, because specific concepts seem to respond to current challenges, provide guidance how to solve problems, or warrant legitimacy. Furthermore, we conceive the phenomenon of institutional incongruity in terms of incompatible 'layers' of institutions stemming from different historical or ideational roots.

An argument structurally similar to institutional incongruity was made in historical institutionalist analyses of decentralization processes. Falleti (2005) in her lucid analysis of sequences of decentralization reform in Latin America highlighted the relevance of choosing the 'right' sequence. She pointed out that a transfer of administrative or political competences to sub-national entities hindered rather than promoted the decentralization process, particularly if it was not accompanied by a concomitant transfer of fiscal competences (Falleti, 2005: 329). Beyond mere 'sequences' of reform steps, the concept of 'layers' as historically evolving aspects of institutions (Orren and Skowronek, 1994, 2004; Lieberman, 2002) was applied by Broschek (2011) to constitutional reform processes. By regarding constitutions as 'layered', it is possible to deconstruct the different aspects of the complexities of institutions, explaining the change of one layer as historically contingent, even though it may create frictions and incongruity with another layer stemming from another historical and ideational root.

Based on these theoretical considerations, it is expected that specific sequences will emerge in an analysis of reform processes. Initially, an ideologically grounded deviation from the given institutional setting becomes possible if new ideas find a sufficiently large group of supporters and coincide with the rational self-interest of relevant actors involved in the negotiations. The reform then changes one or several layers of the constitution, thus resulting in a departure from the traditional path. This layering effect can create, however, an institutional incongruity between responsibilities, financial resources of territorial authorities and policy problems. From an economic perspective, then, the actors basically have two possible strategies to remedy this incongruity. They

103

can either redress the distribution of responsibilities or try to enhance their fiscal autonomy in order to collect the resources needed for the new tasks. From a political point of view, however, both strategies have their drawbacks. A shift of competences back to the central level is unattractive for subnational entities because it hampers their self-esteem and autonomy. An increase in tax autonomy risks increasing existing disparities of economic and financial capacity among the subnational entities. Finally, a major financial transfer from the federal to the subnational level does not bode auspiciously for the federal level because it is quite costly; moreover, it is disadvantageous for the subnational entities since it increases their dependence on the federal level. In practice, it is improbable that a 'purely economic' solution can be implemented. Rather, actors will enter new rounds of negotiation, thereby strengthening mutual entanglement, interdependence and coordination and thus effectively undoing the effect of the initial reform.

3. One step forward, one step back – reconstructing the zigzag of federalism reform

The German reform process illustrates the outlined mechanism fairly well. In order to provide more 'grounded' evidence by reconstructing the motives and rationales of the actors involved, two reform cases in the areas of higher education and of unemployment care are analysed. Both of these policy issues belong to the broader field of social policy. In Germany, the logic of the modern welfare state creates intense entanglements – the more so as the constitutional 'postulate of a social state' (art. 20 para. 2 Basic Law) implies general standards and, consequently, strongly interferes with federalism. The cases vividly illustrate the zig-zagging reform path: in both, major reforms were decided in and during the first reform phase (around 2005) and aimed at disentangling more clearly the levels of government. In subsequent years, however, at a sub-constitutional level, those disentanglement reforms were gradually redressed, thereby introducing an even greater financial and competency entanglement than there was before. This mood swing was reinforced by the second constitutional reform in 2009, which introduced the debt brake also for the Länder. The motives and rationale for promoting and supporting subsequent changes and adaptations in legislative processes during a decade of reform are reconstructed in the following through the analysis of parliamentary documents, position papers and expert reports written by practitioners.

3.1. The 'Collaboration Ban' – disentanglement in higher education

Higher education is a prolific policy issue for studying the zigzag of German federalism reform because joint decision-making itself became a contested issue. During negotiations for the first federalism reform, education policy was the 'stepping stone' leading to the failure of the first reform attempt in 2004. The federal government had tried to encroach upon the exclusive responsibilities of the Länder in education policy and thus the Länder, whose autonomy had been considerably strengthened by a ruling of the federal constitutional court in 2004,[4] made their exclusive jurisdiction conditional for any further negotiation. In order to pass the reform in a second attempt in 2006, the federal government had to make far-reaching concessions to the Länder. Bundestag and Bundesrat finally established the so-called cooperation ban in education policy, aiming at disentangling one of the major constitutional 'joint tasks', with the financially strong states of Bavaria, Hesse and Baden-Württemberg being the drivers of this decision. The term 'cooperation ban' is hyperbole, since the reform did not preclude any cooperation between the federal government and the Länder but substantially constrained it. Basically, in art. 91b Basic Law (new version) only the joint responsibility for financing university buildings was abolished in order to enable the Länder to make investment decisions independently from the federal government. The 'Disentanglement Law' of 2007[5] stipulated that until 2019, the Länder are to be compensated for the abolition of the federal financial aid system for university buildings. Thereafter, however, it is unclear how future investments can be secured. Beyond this, cooperation was still allowed in the following instances: scientific research external to universities; construction of research buildings including large devices (laboratories etc.) at universities as well as for projects in science and research (on the premise that all 16 Länder governments agree in the Bundesrat, thus granting each of them the right to veto); and the preparation and conduct of international comparative surveys on the performance of educational systems.

In light of these restrictions, the federal government remained able to set financial incentives and influence the higher education system according to its political goals. With the Initiative for Excellence (2009), the Pact for Research and Innovation (2005) and the Higher Education Pact (2007), large-scale cooperative projects could be launched (Welsh, 2014). Moreover, the federal government was able to steer the debate on educational standards by emphasizing the so-called PISA surveys, that is, international comparative studies evaluating the performance of educational systems according to art. 91b para. 2 Basic Law. A major problem remained the temporality of cooperation projects, as sustainable solutions and long-term planning were seriously hampered by the given legal basis.

While the Länder had momentarily triumphed to have gained exclusive responsibility for education 'from the cradle to the grave', it soon became apparent that the reform was a pyrrhic victory, because any long time financial support of the universities turned out to be unfeasible. Most Länder have little budgetary capacity for covering existing educational tasks or investing in new, innovative ones. Due to the debt brake, the Länder can no longer gen-erate additional revenues by increasing public debts; just few marginal taxes fall under their exclusive jurisdiction (Wieland, 2013: 17, 20). Tuition fees, which had been introduced by a number of Länder after the Federal Consti-tutional Court had abolished a corresponding framework legislation banning fees in 2005,[6] partially balanced this financial scarcity, but were successively abrogated by the Länder parliaments after students' protests had taken place and a people's initiative against fees was launched in Bavaria in 2013.

Higher education provides an illustrative example for free-riding incentives and incongruities inherent to federal systems (Bednar, 2005) because policy issues often transcend the territorial borders of Länder jurisdictions. Intergo-vernmental cooperation is a necessity. One state alone cannot exclusively regulate the students' and scientists' mobility. Financially weak Länder in the German North and the East educate students who often subsequently move to the labour markets in the South, where a higher demand for qualified labour attracts graduates from all regions. As a consequence of this inter-regional migration of qualified labour, the poorer Länder effectively produce a public good to the benefit of the richer ones. Not surprisingly, financially weak Länder governments soon claimed to recalibrate the existing rules, while the stronger ones, such as Hesse, Baden-Württemberg, or Bavaria, refused any extension of federal authority on education policy.[7]

In July 2014, the federal minister of education, Johanna Wanka (Christian Democratic Union [CDU]), finally introduced a constitutional amendment.[8] By offering a package deal, the minister succeeded in avoiding the veto and abstention of those Länder in the Bundesrat which had feared federal encroachment on higher education. As from the end of 2014, the federal gov-ernment covered 65% of the costs for the general students' financial assist-ance (BAFöG; art. 104a Basic Law). The federal government offered to take over the remaining 35% share of the Länder and to terminate mixed finan-cing.[9] As a tandem measure, this offer was linked to the Länder's support of the constitutional revision and declared to expire by the end of 2014.[10] The federal government grants additional 1.17 billion Euros per year to the entirety of the Länder which are free to set their own priorities on pre-school, elementary or secondary education, or university building, with the caveat, however, that universities should receive the lion's share. In order to prevent Länder governments from transferring the money to their general budgets, they were committed to invest it exclusively for education.[11] Yet, the Bundestag's budget committee expressed its mistrust by asking the federal government to monitor the allocation.[12] Indeed, first evaluations reveal that not all Länder have complied with the agreement.[13]

Finally, the 16 Länder governments unanimously adopted the consti-tutional amendment in the Bundesrat.[14] In the Bundestag, the bill was sup-ported by the grand coalition,[15] whereas the opposition abstained from voting.[16] The new article 91b, Basic Law, which replaced the 'cooperation ban', stipulates that the federation and the states are allowed to cooperate in cases of nationwide importance in order to facilitate science, research and teaching.[17] If universities are affected, all 16 Länder must agree. Even though the necessity for the constitutional amendment was uncontested, the opposition criticized that the vague legal term 'nationwide importance', which has to be substantiated by an agreement of the federation and the Länder,[18] somewhat implies that the federal government funds the excellence initiative on a long-lasting basis, while a proposal for a solid basic funding of higher education was tabled indefinitely. Moreover, the unanimity clause was controversially debated, since it gives any state the opportunity to veto projects launched by a majority of the Länder and thus abets problematic package deals. However, unanimity is set in stone as it prevents the federal government's encroachment onto the exclusive state responsibilities.[19] With the package deal, the Länder allowed the federal government to co-finance their tasks in order to overcome financial scarcity, but then in return compensated its increased role by obtaining additional funds not earmarked for certain projects. In other words, the Länder accepted a growing influence of the federal government in higher education by strengthening federal cooperation, but were able to exchange it with a disentanglement of the BAFöG's mixed financing. In fact, this adjustment contributes to reduce incongruity problems and concomitantly increases the financial scope of the Länder.

Evaluating the arguments brought forward in the plenary debates on the 'cooperation ban' and by the Länder governments, it is conspicuous that resource scarcity worked as the primary driver for strengthening entanglement in higher education. The debt brake as the core element of the second reform step, which functioned as a new institutional layer, considerably enforced already existing incongruities between the recently extended state responsibilities and limited fiscal resources. Territorial spill-overs in higher education, by contrast, were occasionally perceived as a problem during the political debate,[20] but in the end played a minor role. When assessing the ideational background of the debate, a significant change comes to the fore. After the leading discourse had been on disentanglement and federal competition for about two decades, the political debate remarkably returned towards the notions of cooperation and social justice.

Tracing the zig-zagging path through the lens of the plenary debates, one encounters three interrelated arguments: firstly, the 'cooperation ban' is predominantly labelled as a 'great mistake',[21] 'nonsense'[22] and a 'meander'.[23] Strikingly, representatives used social justice as a normative yardstick for evaluating policy instruments when arguing in favour of federal cooperation.[24] Balancing inter-regional differences is seen as a necessary condition for equalizing opportunities for individual advancement. Secondly, German politicians across the party camps highlight that institutions should allow for long-term federal cooperation, that there has never been as much cooperation as in the present and that the need for federal cooperation will further increase. Some MPs explicitly conjure up the 'spirit' or 'culture' of cooperation sustainably shaping the German federation as opposed to the US model of dual federalism.[25] Thirdly, although cooperation was generally revitalized as leitmotiv by the Länder and the Bundestag's party groups, party differences are still visible. The CDU/Christian Social Union (CSU) downplayed the negative consequences of the 'cooperation ban' suggesting that the constitutional revision would thus only aim at recalibrating opportunities for cooperation.[26] The Social Democratic Party (SPD) regretted that school policy was excluded from the compromise, but as a party in government supported the bill. In contrast, the parties in opposition, that is, the Green and the Left which, for historical reasons, have weaker federal roots than the CDU/CSU, highlighted the need to overcome scattered regionalism and are more inclined to accept a centralization of tasks which is seen as alternative to federal competition. Altogether, the case of higher education signals a remarkable U-turn. Joint decision-making and cooperation are no longer regarded as obstacles to effective policy-making, but valued as means for balancing incongruities, while avoiding simple centralization.

3.2. 'Hartz IV' – disentanglement in unemployment policy

A second instructive illustration of the emergence of institutional incongruity as a result of institutional layering is provided by the reform of unemployment and social benefits under the heading of 'Hartz IV reform'.[27] Almost simultaneously to the negotiations for the first federalism reform (2003–05), the 'Hartz IV reform' (passed in ordinary legislative procedure in 2003 and entered into force in 2005)[28] laid the foundation for a major financial and organizational joint execution of tasks between the federal and the municipal levels.

The 'Hartz' reforms grew out of a major social democratic reform agenda ('Agenda 2010') in an effort to modernize the German welfare state, to reduce the financial burden for the state and concomitantly to revive the labour market. The fourth labour market reform package ('Hartz IV') united extended unemployment and social benefits into one administrative unit. Before the reform, three distinct benefits had existed: unemployment insurance payments (paid for a limited time, now called unemployment benefits type I and restricted to 18 months); tax paid unemployment benefits for long-term unemployed who received no more insurance payments, and which is paid for by the Federal Labour Agency; and social care paid for by the municipalities.[29] With the reform, the latter two benefits were united to so-called unemployment benefits type II, and were paid for by the Federal

Labour Agency while the municipalities bore the benefits for heat and rent for recipients of type II payments. Under this measure, it was hoped to substantially relieve the financial burden for the municipalities (Hassel and Schiller, 2010: 112; Henneke, 2014: 68), which from the 1990s on had been seriously suffering under the continuously rising expenses for welfare benefits.

The new 'Hartz IV' regulations increased federal entanglement in two respects. Institutionally, they established a new organizational unit at the municipal level, the so-called job centres for administering the new services and payments to the citizens. Those job centres, at least in their standard form, are joint administrations, uniting under one roof a municipal (following the tradition of the municipal responsibility for paying social care) and a federal administration (following the tradition of the federal responsibility for unemployment benefits). This double-hatted administration runs counter to a basic principle for the distribution of tasks in the German federal system which forbids mixed administrations (Remmert, 2008). Financially, because they assigned costly tasks to the municipal level (costs for the municipal part of the personnel and the organization as well as of costs for the heat and rent benefits), they created a considerable and long-lasting financial burden for the municipalities (more specifically for the counties) without providing for an adequate compensation.

Only shortly after the Hartz IV law, the first federalism reform prohibited the direct assignment of tasks from the federal to the municipal level. In such situations when tasks had been assigned directly from the federal to the municipal level – which had occurred frequently before 2005 – the Länder authority of assigning tasks was circumvented, thus quashing the principle of connectivity between the Länder and their municipalities. As a consequence, nobody was directly responsible for paying for those tasks, effectively leaving the municipalities in a situation of helplessness (Henneke, 2006). As a major achievement of the first federalism reform, this regulatory gap was closed by a reformulation of art. 84 para. 1 (7) and art. 85 para. 1 (2) Basic Law which now expresses an explicit ban on direct assignments of tasks from the federal to the municipal level. In this sense, the reform of art. 84 and 85 Basic Law resulted in a clearer distinction between federal and Länder spheres of authority and re-established the protective relationship between the Länder and their municipalities, securing the financial endowment of the latter based on the principle of connectivity.[30] All federal laws, however, that predated the reform and established municipal tasks, retained their validity (art. 125a Basic Law); this also applied to the Hartz IV law.

While the reform had been introduced with the expectation to reduce the municipalities' financial burdens because they no longer had to pay for social welfare benefits, that hope was futile as municipal expenses for social purposes kept rising continuously even after 2005.[31] In this situation of exacerbated institutional incongruity, then, the levels of government had to find creative solutions for closing the municipalities' financial gap, all of which created, however, new instances of fiscal entanglement between the levels of government.

Firstly, even in the first year (2005), the federal level subsidized municipal costs for heat and rent by €3.5 billion. What had initially been intended to be a loan to be repaid later by the municipalities was soon understood to become a recurrent stream of payments by the federal level to support the municipalities who saw no end in containing the rising welfare costs. Since 2005, the municipalities were subsidized by varying degrees, receiving roughly one-third of their costs for heat and rent and a continuously increasing share of their costs for basic social support for the elderly and not fully employed ('Grundsicherung im Alter und bei Erwerbsminderung') (Geißler and Niemann, 2015: 10). Secondly, the Hartz IV reform impacted differently on the Eastern and Western Länder, because the expenses for welfare benefits had been distributed rather unevenly across the territory – the East German Länder had the highest rates of unemployment receivers, but almost no receivers of welfare benefits, whereas the relationship was reversed in the West. Thus the Eastern Länder could profit financially far less from the abolition of municipal welfare payments, but had to incur higher costs for heat and rent. In order to compensate for those uneven consequences of the Hartz IV law, the fiscal equalization law was changed, introducing a new fiscal flow to the Eastern Länder which were compensated by a fixed amount of €1 billion yearly for a period of six years and decreasing amounts from then on (§ 11 section 3a fiscal equalization law, see also Henneke, 2014: 68). Thirdly, in 2011 a new law for strengthening the financial capacity of the municipalities was passed, which increased the share of federal payments for basic social support for the elderly and not fully employed up to 100%.[32] Fourthly, in 2015, a new law raised the federal subsidy from 2015 until 2018 for an additional €5 billion until 2019 according to the revised version of § 46 sec. 5 Social Law Book II, and the federal share of the municipal costs for heat and rent was increased by another €500 million.[33]

As a result, horizontal and vertical financial entanglements in welfare payments were continually tightened. But even the organizational entanglement – the establishment of a mixed administration in the job centres – was confirmed. Actor constellations and interests in this case followed more territorial units than party lines: the counties filed a suit in front of the federal constitutional court against the job centres, arguing that the mixed administration diluted responsibilities. Indeed, the federal constitutional court played – as in the higher education case – an important role in putting pressure on the political actors. It had declared the job centres to be unconstitutional and prompted the federal legislator to remedy this unconstitutionality by 2010.[34] The reaction of the Bundestag was, however, slightly different than what many observers might have expected, as it changed the constitution by inserting a new joint task in Art. 91e.[35] In this decision, party conflicts were largely suspended. In spite of intense protest by municipalities and counties, the federal legislator thus showed that it preferred to provide a constitutional foundation for the continued existence and working of a mixed adminis-tration instead of administratively disentangling the execution of this task by giving it entirely into the hands of the counties.

How can this ideological preference which runs completely contrary to the initial aim of disentanglement be explained? In terms of the new instances of financial entanglement, the answer clearly lies in the problem of institutional incongruity. Public and political debates that accompanied the numerous leg-islative and judicial acts made it very clear that the major concern – across party interests – was constantly how to equip the municipalities with suffi-cient financial means. In terms of institutional entanglement by new joint tasks, the federal level was unwilling to divest itself of the means to control the execution of this important branch of the welfare state. Because social transfer payments amount to the major share of public expenses, they cannot be left to the Länder level alone. Since the municipalities and counties execute welfare laws, the federal level cannot handle it alone either. Conse-quently, a close-knit entanglement is built into the very structure of the modern welfare state.

4. The incongruity of competences and finances – lessons from the comparative case analysis

The mechanisms behind the zig-zagging path in the cases presented support of the general description in Section 2: in the beginning, an overarching coalition of actors aligns along an ideological paradigm, enabling a reform that causes a departure from the given institutional path. In the case of higher education, this reform coalition was mainly formed by liberal and con-servative parties, neoliberal think tanks and donor Länder in the fiscal equal-ization scheme. Problem definitions focused on the ossification of the federal architecture due to the deadlock in the Bundesrat (see Stecker, this issue), on increased economic, political and cultural disparity since unification, and an increasingly regionalized party system (see Detterbeck, this issue). By empha-sizing the values of dual and competitive federalism and by claiming more disentanglement between territorial levels to secure transparency and accountability, an alternative vision of federalism was promoted which offered seemingly attractive answers to the questions 'how much unity and diversity' and 'diversity or unity of what?' Similarly, in unemployment care, the ideas of the 'activating state' and the 'third way' had great appeal far beyond the SPD, because it emphasized corresponding values of autonomy and responsibility.

Subsequently, as a consequence of the reform, the neat separation of leg-islative competences and clear ascription of tasks soon betrayed the expec-tations when it came to everyday policy-making. While responsibilities had been shifted to lower levels of government, this was not accompanied by cor-respondingly enlarged financial means, thus creating a problem of incongru-ity between different institutional layers. In this situation, the European economic, monetary and debt crises overlapped with the existing problem, acting as an external trigger for the second reform step and concomitantly increasing institutional incongruity. On the one hand, costs for the newly gained policy responsibilities in the education and social transfer sectors increased significantly during the crisis; on the other, the tightened economic situation dictated that there is a new paradigm of fiscal austerity and debt ceil-ings, popularizing the debt brake and further restricting the Länder in their options to generate income. In the light of the expiring financial equalization law (end of 2019) and the debt brake's entry coming into force (2020), Länder and municipalities for the third step of federalism reform urgently need a reliable fiscal framework to count on for the coming years. In this situation, the financially weaker Länder – that is, the clear majority – request neither more autonomous fiscal competences nor do they want the federal level take back their responsibilities. Rather, they demand more financial support from the federal budget, thereby stressing the value of solidarity while gra-ciously ignoring that the instances of joint decision-making and co-financing that they had so proudly abolished before were now re-introduced.

As could be shown, triggers for the different reform steps stemmed from changing perceptions of problem constellations – the dysfunctionality of the federal architecture, the European crisis and the constantly rising costs of the welfare state – and were interpreted in analogous ideological para-digms entailing contradictory visions of federalism: first disentanglement, autonomy and competition, then fiscal austerity and conditionality, and finally solidarity and joint responsibility. An overarching vision of the direction in which German federalism ought to develop and which could have linked the contradicting institutional layers of the federal system coherently was obviously lacking (see Benz, this issue). While the content and direction of the reforms zig-zagged along their ideological underpinnings, actor constella-tions did not noticeably change across the reform steps. For all reforms, effec-tively a grand coalition of Christian and Social Democrats, which since 2013 has had to be supported by the Green party which is part of several Länder coalitions, was needed to pass legislation in both chambers. The entirety of the Länder finally supported the throwback to and strengthening of federal entanglement. Altogether, the reform path can be interpreted as rational reac-tions of the involved actors to external circumstances and 'home-made' situ-ations of institutional incongruity resulting from a layered, sequential reform.

5. Concluding discussion

The analysis allows reassessing the quality of entangled federalism. As Grodzins (1966) and Hueglin (2000, 2013) note, entanglement seems to be almost unavoidable in multilevel systems. The economic ideals of institutional congruity, fiscal equivalence (Olson, 1969) and connectivity (see Blankart, 2008: 548) are not feasible under real-life conditions. Particularly, the public tasks of the modern welfare state, and similarly the modern challenges of global environmental problems, terrorism or cyber security, cannot be tackled by single territorial units. Rather, in order to contain negative externalities and to exploit economies of scale and synergetic effects, intense cooperation and coordination as well as joint financing of tasks seem to be the order of the day. These findings also apply for dual federalism, such as Switzerland, where federal cooperation was not coincidentally fixed as a constitutional imperative in 2006, even though the cantons still have the right to deviate from compromises.

Still, the ideals of layer-cake federalism and institutional congruity retain their initial appeal, promising democratic accountability, allocative efficiency and transparency for the citizens. Is the real-life marble-cake federalism thus just a second-best solution to the non-attainable ideal of layer-cake federalism? This article contends that this is not the case. Marble-cake federalism provides a normative quality of its own. One may rightly argue that intergovernmental cooperation also characterizes layer-cake federalism. However, it does make a difference whether cooperation remains voluntary, thereby enabling federal units to pursue their own policies if they do not agree to a common solution, or whether joint decision-making makes cooperation mandatory. While it is true that joint decisions blur responsibilities to the voter and often provide policy solutions reflecting the lowest common denominator, they are, at the same time, more inclusive on the input-side of legitimacy and more sustainable on the output-side.

On the input-side, the concept of joint decision-making, which stipulates that oversized majorities have to be included into the political process, thereby protecting federal units and their citizens from being overruled, shows striking analogies to prominent theories of democracy (Dahl, 1973; Lijphart 1999). These place most emphasis on inclusion, foregrounding the broad representation of citizens which has its own democratic quality. On the output-side, for many policy issues, a concluding solution cannot be found. Problems are difficult to define, targets move, and actors as well as voters' preferences change over time. In such situations, conflicts cannot be ultimately solved by a singular decision but, in the sense of Hueglin's 'treaty federalism' (2000, 2013) or Taylor's 'procedural liberalism' (1992), need to be accommodated in a continued discourse. Joint decision-making provides institutionalized opportunities to keep an issue on the political agenda. It enables actors to continuously process policy problems, albeit it often creates just temporary and small-scale solutions. In other words, even though joint decision-making undoubtedly obscures accountability, decreases transparency, and typically leads to incremental policy-making, it nonetheless possesses a specific quality which is often underestimated but should be weighed against its deficiencies.

Notes

1. See the law on general standards (BGBl. I, 9 Sep 2001, p.2302), the law on fiscal equalization, and the law on continuing the Solidarity Pact (see BGBl. I, 20 Dec 2001, p. 3955).
2. With a critical stance see Benz 2005, 2008.
3. Boundary modifications or 'Functional Overlapping Competing Jurisdictions' (Frey and Eichenberger, 1996) have widely been discussed as possible solutions. Whereas the first option is hard to achieve in Germany due to constitutional hurdles stipulated by art. 29 Basic Law and to reasons of political rationality, the second downgrades the territorial structuring of federalism and can partially be realized at best.
4. See decision of the Federal Constitutional Court on the 'junior professors', 2 BvF 1/03, 2 BvF 2/02, 27 July 2004.
5. BGBl. I, 2098, 2102.
6. See decision of the Federal Constitutional Court 2 BvF 1/03, 26 Jan 2005.
7. See http://www.stuttgarter-nachrichten.de/inhalt.bildungsbereich-abschaffung-des-kooperationsverbotes.9e358d03-8ca7-458f-a740-78c64ba3e94c.html; http://www.spiegel.de/unispiegel/studium/bildungsfoederalismus-das-kooperationsverbot-kippelt-a-814584.html (accessed 5 Aug 2015).
8. BT-Drs. 18/2710.
9. See the draft bill, BT-Drs. 18/2663; BT-PlPr. 18/57.
10. BT-PlPr. 18/57.
11. See BT-Drs. 18/3359; response of the federal government to the minor interpellation of the Left party.
12. See BT-PlPr. 18/66, at p.6231.
13. See http://www.deutschlandfunk.de/hochschulpolitik-frei-gewordene-gelder-von-laendern-nicht.680.de.html?dram:article_id=320375 (accessed 5 Aug 2015).
14. BR-Drs. 570/14, decision on the amendment of the Basic Law (art. 91b).
15. Originally, the SPD had proposed to include school financing and advocated a new Art. 104c Basic Law in order to realize durable federal financing.
16. BT-PlPr. 18/66, at p.6237.
17. Draft bill of the federal government, BT-Drs. 18/2710; BR-Drs. 323/14.
18. See BT-Drs. 18/2710, at p.7.
19. Standing committee for education, research and technological impact assessment, recommendation for decision and report, see BT-Drs. 18/3141, at pp.10, 11, 13; BT-PlPr. 18/26, at p.2044.
20. See the statement of the minister president of Saxony-Anhalt *Rainer Haseloff*, http://www.welt.de/print/die_welt/article128361059/Haseloff-dringt-auf-neuen-Finanzausgleich.html (accessed 31 July 2014).
21. BT-PlPr. 18/58, at pp.5390, 5400.
22. BT-PlPr. 18/66, at p.6231.

23. BT-PlPr. 18/66, at p.6228.
24. See, for instance, BT-PlPr. 18/58; BT-PlPr. 18/66; BT-PlPr. 18/57.
25. See, for instance, BT-PlPr. 18/66, at p.6277.
26. See BT-PlPr. 18/58, at pp.5384, 5402.
27. The reform was nicknamed 'Hartz IV', because Peter Hartz, a businessman, chaired a governmental reform commission 'modern services for the labour market' established in 2002. The commission produced a series of reform proposals for modernizing social policy. The largest and politically most controversial fourth reform proposal concerned the social law books no. II and XII with the initiative to join unemployment benefits and social security payments.
28. Fourth Law for Modern Services at the Labour, BGBl. I, pp.2954–2955 of 24.12.2003.
29. The term 'municipalities' is used as an umbrella term for different territorial units at the lowest level of government, including cities, boroughs and counties. It is the counties, however, who administer and pay for unemployment benefits.
30. Furthermore, by establishing the right of the Länder to deviate in their regulation of administrative units and procedures from federal laws (art. 84 para. 1 (2 and 3) – this provision parallels the concomitant regulations on deviation rights in legislation in art. 72), the reform of the article also aimed at reducing the number of consent laws in the Bundesrat.
31. In 2004, the municipalities had total expenses above €32 billion for social benefits, which amounted to above 20% of their budgets, and in 2015 nearly €50 billion, amounting to more than 24% of their budgets, see Geißler and Niemann (2015: 22–23).
32. Social payments 'Grundsicherung im Alter und bei Erwerbsminderung' were to be paid to 45% by the federal level (€1.2 billion) in 2012 (BT-Drs. 17/7402).
33. Law on the promotion of investments in municipalities with low fiscal capacity and to relieve the Länder and municipalities when accommodating asylum seekers, BT-Drs. 18/4975 of 20 May 2015.
34. Sentence of the federal constitutional court of 20.12.2007 (2 BvR 2433/04, 2 BvR 2434/04).
35. BT-Drs. 17/1554, entering into force on 21 July 2010.

Acknowledgements

We would like to thank the reviewers for their constructive comments on this paper.

Disclosure statement

No potential conflict of interest was reported by the authors.

References

Auel, K. (2008), Still no exit from the joint decision trap: the German federal reform(s), *German Politics*, Vol.17, No.4, pp.424–439.
Bednar, J. (2005), Federalism as a public good, *Constitutional Political Economy*, Vol.16, No.2, pp.189–205.
Bednar, J. (2009), *The robust federation. Principles of design*. Cambridge: Cambridge University Press.

Benz, A. (2005), Kein Ausweg aus der Politikverflechtungsfalle? Warum die Bundesstaatskommission scheiterte, aber nicht scheitern musste, *Politische Vierteljahresschrift*, Vol.46, No.2, pp.204–214.

Benz, A. (2008), From joint decision traps to over-regulated federalism – adverse effects of a successful constitutional reform, *German Politics*, Vol.17, No.4, pp.440–456.

Benz, A. (2013), Balancing rigidity and flexibility: constitutional change in federal systems, *West European Politics*, Vol.36, No.4, pp.726–749.

Blankart, C.B. (2008), *Öffentliche Finanzen in der Demokratie* (7 ed). München: Vahlen.

Broschek, J. (2011), Conceptualizing and theorizing constitutional change in federal systems: insights from historical institutionalism, *Regional and Federal Studies*, Vol.24, No.4-5, pp.539–559.

Coase, R.H. (1960), The problem of social cost, *Law and Economics*, Vol.3, October, pp.1–44.

Dahl, R.A. (1973), *Polyarchy: Participation and Opposition*. New Haven, London: Yale University Press.

Falleti, T.G. (2005), A sequential theory of decentralization: Latin American cases in comparative perspective, *American Political Science Review*, Vol.99, No.3, pp.327–346.

Frey, B.S. and Eichenberger, R. (1996), FOCJ: competitive governments für Europe, *International Review of Law and Economics*, Vol.16, No.3, pp.315–327.

Geißler, R. and Niemann, F.-S. (2015), *Kommunale Sozialausgaben – wie der Bund sinnvoll helfen kann*. Gütersloh: Bertelsmann-Stiftung.

Gerring, J. (2008), Case selection for case study analysis: qualitative and quantitative techniques, in J. Box-Steffensmeier, H.E. Brady and D. Collier (eds), *Oxford Handbook of Political Methodology*, pp.645–684. New York: Oxford University Press.

Grodzins, M. (1966), *The American System: A new View of Government in the United States*. New Brunswick, NJ: Transaction Publishers.

Hassel, A. and Schiller, C. (2010), Sozialpolitik im finanzföderalismus – Hartz IV als Antwort auf die Krise der Kommunalfinanzen, *Politische Vierteljahresschrift*, Vol.51, No.1, pp.95–117.

Henneke, H.-G. (2006), Die Kommunen in der Föderalismusreform, *Deutsches Verwaltungsblatt*, Vol.121, No.14, pp.867–871.

Henneke, H.-G. (2014), Neuordnung der Aufgaben und der zugehörigen Finanzströme: Beispiele rund ums SGB II & XII, in M. Junkernheinrich and J. Lange (eds), *Föderale Finanzen. Auf dem langen Weg zu Einer Reform*, pp.65–78. Loccum: Evangelische Akademie Loccum.

Hueglin, T. (2000), From constitutional to treaty federalism: a comparative perspective, *Publius: The Journal of Federalism*, Vol.30, No.4, pp.137–153.

Hueglin, T. (2013), Treaty federalism as a model of policy making: comparing Canada and the European Union, *Canadian Public Administration*, Vol.56, No.2, pp.185–202.

Lieberman, R.C. (2002), Ideas, institutions, and political order: explaining political change, *American Political Science Review*, Vol.96, No.4, pp.697–712.

Lijphart, A. (1999), *Patterns of Democracy: Government Forms and Performance in Thirty-six Countries*. New Haven: Yale University Press.

Mahoney, J. and Thelen, K. (2010), *Explaining Institutional Change. Ambiguity, Agency, and Power*. Cambridge: Cambridge University Press.

Moore, C. and Eppler, A. (2008), Disentangling double politikverflechtung? The implications of the federal reforms for bund – länder relations on Europe, *German Politics*, Vol.17, No.4, pp.488–508.

Oates, W.E. (2005), Towards a second-generation theory of fiscal federalism, *International Tax and Public Finance*, Vol.12, No.4, pp.349–373.

Olson, M. Jr. (1969), The principle of "fiscal equivalence": the division of responsibilities among different levels of government, *American Economic Review*, Vol.59, No.2, pp.479–487.

Orren, K. and Skowronek, S. (1994), Beyond the iconography of order: notes for a "new institutionalism", in L.C. Dodd and C. Jillson (eds), *The Dynamics of American Politics*, pp.311–330. Boulder, CO: Westview Press.

Orren, K. and Skowronek, S. (2004), *The Search for American Political Development*. Cambridge: Cambridge University Press.

Pierson, P. (2004), *Politics in Time. History, Institutions, and Social Analysis*. Princeton, NJ: Princeton University Press.

Remmert, B. (2008), Rechtliche Grundlagen der Zusammenarbeit zwischen Bund und Ländern im bereich der Verwaltung, in H. Scheller and J. Schmid (eds), *Föderale Politikgestaltung im Deutschen Bundesstaat*, pp.36–49. Baden-Baden: Nomos.

Scharpf, F.W. (1988), The joint-decision trap: lessons from German federalism and European integration, *Public Administration*, Vol.66, No.3, pp.239–278.

Scharpf, F.W. (2009), *Föderalismusreform. Kein Ausweg aus der Politikverflechtungsfalle?* Frankfurt/New York: Campus.

Taylor, C. (1992), *Multiculturalism and the "Politics of Recognition"*. Princeton, NJ: Princeton University Press.

Tsebelis, G. (2000), Veto players and institutional analysis, *Governance*, Vol.13, No.4, pp.441–474.

Tsebelis, G. (2002), *Veto Players: How Political Institutions Work*. New York/Princeton, NJ: Russell Sage Foundation/Princeton University Press.

Watts, R.L. (2006), *Comparing Federal Systems*. Montreal: McGill-Queen's University Press.

Welsh, H.A. (2014), Education, federalism and the 2013 bundestag elections, *German Politics*, Vol.23, No.4, pp.400–414.

Wieland, J. (2013), *Neuordnung der Finanzverfassung nach Auslaufen des Solidarpakts II und Wirksamwerden der Schuldenbremse*. Speyer: Deutsche Universität für Verwaltungswissenschaften.

A Path to Balanced Budgets of Bund and Länder? The New Shape of the 'Debt Brake' and the 'Stability Council'

Stefan Korioth

ABSTRACT

This paper analyses the implementation of new debt rules and the function of the new Stabilitätsrat since its establishment in 2011. The new rules are explained and the effect of the new limit for public debt is examined. Furthermore, the composition, tasks and procedures of the Stabilitätsrat are described and evaluated. Finally, its activity is judged with individual examples. As a result, it is shown that for the new rules of Art. 109 para. 3, Art. 115 and Art. 143d GG to be successful, a normative commitment and corresponding political discipline not to incur new debts is required. The Stabilitätsrat alone is insufficient as an institutional framework to encourage budgetary discipline. Abolishing the Stabilitätsrat would be a first step in giving back control to politics in regard to debt and in dispelling the illusion that technocratic determination of the possibility to take new debt could end the debt problem.

1. Introduction: Constitutional Law as Frame

The function of the provisions of the Grundgesetz (Basic Law, Constitution of the Federal Republic of Germany, GG) concerning the organization of the state is understood as a mechanism for providing a framework for political processes. They have been understood as such for a long time—binding in their overall restrained limits and guidelines for action, but with leeway for politics within this framework.[1] Following that line in 1986, the Bundesverfassungsgericht (Federal Constitutional Court) set standards for the Länderfinanzausgleich (financial compensation between the German states ['Länder']): "The normative determinations of the financial constitution are partially [...] not as detailed as is characteristic for regulations concerning the state-citizen-relationship. They prefer to use unspecific terms and therefore create margins for evaluation and discretion [...]" (Bundesverfassungsgericht,

BVerfGE 72, 330 (390) [translation *the author*]). In the past two decades, this basic understanding of the constitution as a framework has been left unacknowledged and has been disregarded multiple times by the legislative body responsible for constitutional amendments. This has also had an impact on financial constitutional law. The implementation of new debt rules and the existence of the new Stabilitätsrat for five years[2] give reason for this paper to explain the new rules (Section 2), to examine the effect of the new limit for public debt up until now (Section 3), to describe and evaluate the composition, tasks and procedures of the Stabilitätsrat (Section 4) as well as to judge its activity in its first sessions between April 2010 and May 2014 with individual examples (Section 5).

What is the basis of this assessment? Since the new regime has been enacted by way of constitutional amendment, it is not in itself unconstitutional: it meets the limited substantive criteria for constitutional reform set up by Art. 79 para 3 GG. The critical assessment therefore is conceptional and comparative: Will the new regime be better able to help reduce sovereign debt than the old one or than other possible models? Or might it even be counterproductive by distracting from the actual problems? While the article is written from a constitutional lawyer's perspective, its main thesis is a political one: The article stresses that constitutional budgetary rules can only be implemented by a strong political will. The problems are not about the legal design of a debt brake, but about adamantly avoiding new debt and reducing current debt.

2. Constitutional Debt Rules in Germany

While the regulation of debt limits is a notable constitutional provision which is consistent with the German tradition, the second stage of the Föderalismusreform in 2009 introduced new debt rules into the constitution (Art. 109 para. 3, Art. 115, Art. 143d GG). These rules include the new limits for new debts of Bund and Länder, the regulatory content of which is highly detailed, far from being a frame and conceptually questionable.

There were three main reasons for the political decision to take the step for reform. Firstly, the legislator amending the constitution pointed to problems with the former debt rule (Art. 115 GG), introduced in 1969, under which public debt climbed from 20% to 70% of gross domestic product.[3] The conclusion drawn in 2009 was quite simple: the rule was wrong, politics had no chance to avoid more public debt. This was evidently short-sighted. The old rule had a clear design, but the needs of the welfare state during the 1970s and German reunification were paid with new debt. A frank evaluation of the old rule would have concluded that its failure was due to lack of political discipline.

A debt brake is the legal part of the problems—voters and politicians voting for and using the brake are the main prerequisites for successfully avoiding new debt. Secondly, the legislator wanted to implement the European Stability Treaty (Art. 126 para. 2 AEUV) by inserting a stricter and more explicit formula into German constitutional law. Thirdly, the Great Coalition forming the Bund's government from 2005 to 2009, had promised 'reforms' in all relevant political areas and during 2008–2009 it was under pressure to fulfil this—so the analysis of the actual need for certain reforms was neglected.

Despite significant exceptions, the core message is: As of 2020 (compare Art. 143d para. 1 GG), there will be no new debt on either level. This promise, though in itself not new,[4] has now been implemented in the form of a highly detailed legal norm of the highest rank, which has been devised for both Bund and Länder. The implementation of this legal promise is, for the following reason, not without risk: An increased mass of self-imposed legally and, more notably, constitutionally binding provisions is only reasonable and credible as long as the relative bodies bound by these provisions can and will adhere to them.[5] They are not credible if political stakeholders repeatedly violate those rules due to economic and political constraints. In case of repeated violations, law, constitutional law, and political stakeholders and their institutions become damaged with lasting effect. This might be one of the reasons for the fact that the constitution amending legislature has, in the meantime, delayed the implementation of these new debt rules. These are now due to come into full effect in the year 2020.

1. The main features of the new public debt rules are outlined below. Art. 109 para. 2 GG declares the debt limits set forth by EU law (Art. 126 TFEU, Treaty on the Functioning of the European Union) as national constitutional obligations which Bund and Länder are obliged to fulfil together. The limits on new debt that apply directly to Bund and Länder can be found in Art. 109 para. 3 GG.[6] According to Art. 109 para. 3 (1) GG, the annual budgets of Bund and Länder must, "in principle", be balanced without new debt. The phrase "in principle" demands special attention: its use directs focus on the exceptions. These are set forth by the Grundgesetz in the following, linguistically convoluted sentences. Prior to this perpetuation the constitution declares something counterfactual: The Bund complies with the ban on new debt, if its net new indebtedness does not exceed 0.35% of the nominal gross domestic product in the relevant year (Art. 109 para. 3 (4) GG). This currently stands at 10 billion euros. In consequence, new debt within this limit does not affect the balanced budget. This process is subject to the euphemism: "substantive balanced budget". The second peculiarity follows: As of 2020, the Länder are not permitted new debt up to this limit without justification (Art. 109 para. 3 (5), Art. 143d para. 1 GG) —the inconsistency is evident:[7] The Bund may incur structural debt even

though it has all relevant means of adjusting income sources. In contrast to this, the Länder are not allowed to take on further debt even though they have practically no possibility of adjusting their own income.

The following sentences of Art. 109 para. 3 GG contain exceptions—in this case for Bund and Länder—to the ban on new debt. However, these exceptions are so loosely formulated that they give rise to doubt about the restrictive function of the new debt rules in critical cases. Firstly, Bund and Länder "may introduce rules intended to take into account, symmetrically in times of upswing and downswing, the effects of market developments that deviate from normal conditions" (Art. 109 para. 3 (2) Alt. 1 GG). In terms of style and content, this norm is unfit for constitutional use. However, if one is not deterred by its unfavourable wording, one will identify the old exception in this norm, namely the previous concession to accrue new debt in case of a disturbance in the macroeconomic balance.[8] In this exceptional case there is neither an absolute limit nor an obligation to implement a repayment scheme. The Bund substantiates this exception for accruing new debt in cases of cyclical market developments in Art. 115 para. 2 GG and in the "Act regarding Art. 115 GG". However, this is achieved through complex procedures for production output gaps which leave plenty of room for imaginative interpretation. The second exception applies to natural disasters, the third, following the improper and disputed term of European Union Law, to "unusual emergency situations beyond governmental control and substantially harmful to the state's financial capacity". Should an emergency situation of financial relevance arise, this could prove to be a precursor for conflict. This would especially be the case if, for example, a worldwide financial crisis or a great number of refugees seeking asylum were to constitute an emergency in these terms.[9] For the last two exceptions, a reimbursement scheme is mandatory (Art. 109 para. 3 (3) GG). However, the Grundgesetz does not proffer any specifications as to how the scheme should be construed or whether it has to be implemented in statutory form. As a result, the exceptions allow for a significantly broader span for new debt compared to the old regulations. Neither old nor new rules factor in the problem of existing debt, despite it being highly relevant due to the overall debt of 2050 billion euros in all public budgets.[10] Overall the normative design of the new rules already raises doubts as to whether it can adequately regulate new debt while preventing this debt from becoming excessive.

2. The second part of the Föderalismusreform II demands as much attention as the first. The high degree of detail in the amendment to the constitution concerning new debt is accompanied by numerous verbose provisions with unclear normative content. For example, the debt rules in Art. 109 and 115 GG are accompanied by a procedural norm in Art. 109a GG. If one were to read this text with the usual expectation of finding a legal norm stating prerequisites and legal consequences, one would be

surprised and, most likely, startled. The Grundgesetz is known for its strict nor-mativity and its high claim for validity in comparison to other historical and international situations. With this in mind, it delivers grounds for surprise in the form of Art. 109a GG, which provides for the implementation of a panel[11] designated to 'monitor' the budgets of Bund and Länder and sets up 'principles' for critical developments, but does not provide said panel with decisive powers. The panel is called 'Stabilitätsrat' ('Stability Council'). The word 'stability' sounds strong and dependable; the term 'council' sounds venerable and reputable. The reader will be startled because the wording of Art. 109a GG gives an insight into the reason for creating this panel. The current state of public finances is, in the light of Art. 109a GG, visibly unstable and threatens to become worse despite the new debt brake promising a contrary effect. The first question about this council is why mutual monitoring and control of Bund and Länder will be necessary at all in a future in which new debt is precluded by the implementation of Art. 109 para. 3 GG, and what it can change about financial crises. Why is the strong self-commitment not to take on new debt as of 2020 (the year the new rules will also come into full effect for the Länder) not sufficient? In addition, the term 'Haushaltsnotlage' (budgetary emergency), which has been defined as a legal term by the Bundesverfassungsgericht, is being used at the constitutional level for the first time. Constitutional specifications do not however cease to exist. Why does the constitution speak of emergen-cies even though it simultaneously attempts to prevent them through the implementation of new debt rules? Is the Stabilitätsrat therefore part of a (useful) crisis management between the promise of no new debt and the dif-ficult reality? Or, is crisis considered a normality and is the Stabilitätsrat only part of a legal regime designed to ensure that causes can be identified in case the promise of no new debt is broken?

3. An Interim Result for the New Debt Rules

A comprehensive practical test for the new so-called debt brake has not yet taken place. This is primarily due to two factors.

Firstly, it will only be in full effect for the Bund in 2016, and for the Länder as of the fiscal year 2020 (Art. 143d para. 1 GG). The explanatory statements to the Föderalismusreform 2009 explain this strange and unprecedented amendment to the constitution as a "provision for the future" which requires long transition periods. These are necessary for the change to the new, alleg-edly stricter, rules. These explanations have been unconvincing from the very beginning.[12] Looking at the wide exceptions to the rule of no new debt, which is, as outlined above, is not even strictly regulated for the Bund, the transition could have been handled within two to three years. The underlying reason for delaying these new regulations from coming into full effect by a decade may in fact be uncertainty from a political point of view as to whether the public promise of balanced budgets without new debt could actually be kept. In 2009, the suggestion was made to postpone the answer to this unpleasant question until the year 2020.

The second reason why it is currently only possible to partially evaluate the efficiency of the new rules is related to the financial crisis in 2008 and 2009. After weathering this crisis, tax income in Germany has unexpectedly been rising constantly and profoundly in all areas since 2010. The overall tax income has risen from 524 billion euros (in 2009) to 643.6 billion euros (in 2014). It should not come as a surprise that in this situation the Bund could easily reach an approximately balanced budget ("Schwarze Null"). As regards the Länder, there are great differences: While some are doing well, others are facing severe financial crises which continue despite increased income. From the perspective of 2015, it can be expected that, as of 2020, some of the Länder will find budget management without new debt either impossible, or only achievable with gargantuan efforts on their part. As well as Bremen and Saarland, this could apply to North Rhine-Westphalia, Rhine-land-Palatinate and other Länder that are struggling with low tax income. In these Länder, interim solutions are already being visibly put into action, e.g. new fiscal leeway is achieved by outsourcing from the core budget or by creative changes to the debt brake of the Grundgesetz for the constitutions of the Länder (as seen in Rhineland-Palatinate[13]). This fiscal leeway should have been inhibited according to the phrasing and intention of Art. 109 para. 3 GG. In addition, for medium-term forecasts, significant fiscal risks have to be taken into account, even if these may not necessarily become a reality. For all territorial communities, the danger of future economic decline and consequently lower tax income cannot be ruled out. The currently low interest burden due to historically low interest rates in the capital markets may rise in response to higher interest rates. The Bund will probably have to fulfil obligations undertaken during the European public debt crises (in particular within the European Stability Mechanism). Due to demographic changes, social security systems will need higher subsidies from the budget of the Bund (compare Art. 120 para. 1 (4) GG). Those subsidies currently amount to around 85 billion euros per year. Then again, there is a positive effect of the new debt rules: The general (and factually hardly appropriate) reference to the "constraints of the debt brake" is currently capable of decreasing demands for higher expenditures and lower taxes in federal as well as in state politics.

Overall, only a few statements can be made about the efficiency of the new debt brake. Some general experiences—historical, comparative legal situations and on a supranational level within the European Union—about constitutional or statutory attempts to implement and enforce effective debt rules must however also be remembered. These experiences show that, for a limitation to public debt, the crucial factor is the corresponding political will, not the law, which is surprisingly weak in taking control in this area. Despite its simple and clear-cut concept, the former German debt brake of 1969 was not effective. It basically prohibited new debt. Exceptions to this rule were that new debt was permitted in times of economic growth up to the amount of simultaneous public investments, as well as in the case of a disturbance of the macroeconomic balance (Art. 115 para. 1 GG of 1969).[14] There were definitely lapses in the attention to detail in the old law. This can be seen in the lack of a definition of public investments, the lack of an obligation for reimbursement and the exception for the Bund's separate assets. However, these were not the main reasons for the debt brake's lack of effectiveness. The reason was the inability of politics to respect the limits and to counter with expensive tasks and demands for higher spending. On a European level, there are detailed rules for the permitted new debt for member states (Art. 126 TFEU), which are partially consistent with the new German rules. Experiences have been and are negative. In times of crisis and against states that are in crisis, these rules are not being applied. Furthermore, the original criteria (maximum permitted new debt of 3% of the GDP; a maximum public debt of 60% of the GDP in each member state) have been mitigated by means of secondary legislation. In dramatic terms: It is not about the legal design of a debt brake, but about adamantly not taking on new debt and reducing current debt. In other words, how a debt brake is constructed, whether it is broken or adhered to, is of secondary importance. Any debt brake can be adhered to or broken. In Germany in 2009, it would have been sufficient to observe strictly the implementations of the old law rather than implementing new law.[15] The new rules of Art. 109 para. 3, Art. 115 and Art. 143d GG will not be successful because of the implementation of a new normative commandment. The success in their implementation will only be realized with and due to corresponding political discipline. The old problem will stay the same.

4. Development and Characteristics of the Stabilitätsrat

1. The history of the Stabilitätsrat begins with the first rulings of the Bundesverfassungsgericht about budgetary emergencies (Haushaltsnotlagen) in some Länder. In 1986 and 1992, Bremen and Saarland, which already had high levels of debt in the 1980s, were the subjects (BVerfGE 72, 330ff.; 86, 148ff.). Following economic considerations, the court developed criteria that have been used as indications for a budgetary emergency or an extreme budgetary emergency. The court's findings determined that both Länder found themselves in a state of extreme budgetary emergency and needed help to be able to get out of this vicious circle. Based on the principle of federalism of Art. 20 para. 1 GG, it found that the possibilities to act

according to Art. 106, 107 GG had to be utilized. In particular, the vertical allocation of funds (Bundesergänzungszuweisungen) according to Art. 107 para. 2 (3) GG had to be applied as an exception for a limited time. According to the court, the Länder, due to their political autonomy, were to be held responsible for the "budgetary consequences" caused by their self-determined political decisions. However, there might be "exceptions due to the principle of state federalism if support through supplementary allocations is irrefutably demanded due to the budgetary situation of a state and there is no other viable solution (Art. 104a para. 4 GG)" (BVerfGE 72, 330 (405), translation S.K.).

> Should the legislature take exceptional burdens from a budgetary emergency within the federal supplementary allocations into account, this can only be done to the extent that equates to the function of the federal supplementary allocations within the financial compensation as its final stage. (BVerfGE 86, 148 (261), translation S.K.)

In spite of this the Bundesverfassungsgericht has recommended procedural rules for the first time:

> First and foremost, it is of the utmost necessity and urgency to define common obligations and procedural rules for the federation and the states that counteract the development of a budgetary emergency and that are capable of reducing an existent budgetary emergency. [...] Possible provisions could, for example, be principles about federal and state obligations to respect [...] limits defined by certain key financial figures within their budget planning, for example at financing through new debt and the total debt level. In addition the obligation could be implemented to set up a (mandatory) restructuring scheme to lead the budget management back to normal if the limits are exceeded. (BVerfGE 86, 148 (266ff.), translation S.K.)

On this basis, Saarland and Bremen received rehabilitation aid (§ 11 (6) Financial Compensation Act old version) from 1995 to 2005. However the court's references to the prevention of emergencies faded away without any reaction from the legislature.

When the court had to deal with an alleged budgetary emergency in Berlin in 2006 (BVerfGE 116, 327ff.), it had to acknowledge that the aid granted to the two smallest Länder had had practically no effect.[16] This was one of the influential factors in the court's decision to change its judicature. The court excluded the problem of budgetary emergencies from the scope of Art. 106 and 107 GG. It only confirmed that the budgetary circumstances in highly indebted Berlin were under strain. This financial situation, though fraught with debt, did not conform to the classification of a federal state of emergency (bundesstaatlicher Notstand), the definition of which was left largely indeterminate, and therefore could not justify claims for financial aid. Following this instance, the court repeated its demand for prevention rules in reference to its decision in 1992.

In addition, a serious weakness of the current law is the lack of necessary procedural and substantive rules for primary action as to how to deal with areas within the federal state which either currently or, later, could potentially require reorganization [...] Until now, it has not even been possible to coordinate the different budget systems, despite the principle of consistent formal structure of budget plans as prescribed by sub-constitutional law (§§ 10, 11 Budget Principles Act, §§ 13, 14 Federal Budget Act and similar state law). This coordination aims at gaining transparent comparative information about the budget policy in each case by simple key figures of the budget without the necessity for prior statistical adjustments. Also, the tasks and authority of the financial planning council—limited to discussions and suggestions about budget discipline—according to § 51a Budget Principles Act only refer to obligations within the European Economic and Monetary Union. It is only in recent times that there have been signs of political consensus, which, at least at the so-called Föderalismusreform, have given grounds to an urgent need to discuss basic reforms to the financial relationship between Bund and Länder. In doing so, fundamentally new [...] concepts for the prevention of budgetary emergencies and for coping with them have to be thoroughly evaluated [...]. The principle of federalism necessitates such efforts due to the currently [2006] unsatisfactory legal situation.[17]

This decision from 2006 was completely convincing in the sense that it precluded claims of distressed Länder for rehabilitation aid according to Art. 20 para. 1, 107 para. 2 (3) GG with only one exception. This exception, the federal state of emergency, was formulated very restrictively: Following the court's wording, the occurrence of such exceptional situation is either impossible, or it would lead to the other Länder and the Bund being practically unable to provide aid.[18] It is part of the autonomy of the Länder to fulfil both their legal obligations and their self-assumed tasks with funds provided by the financial compensation in the four stages outlined in Art. 106 and 107 GG. The distribution of funds is not aligned correctly and needs to be readjusted through the vertical distribution of turnover tax (Art. 106 para. 3 and para. 4 GG) if a large number of Länder prove no longer to be capable of independently fulfilling their tasks. Problems in only some of the Länder indicate an arguably problematic structure of their expenditure, not of their income and not at all of a consistently poor financial situation of all Länder. However, it remains unclear why the Bundesverfassungsgericht combines its interpretation of substantive law, which it articulates in such a way as to make its content evident and to prevent misinterpretation, with procedural requirements concerning prevention.[19] With respect to the principle of autonomy and the individual responsibility for debt taken, who was to inform, warn or be warned about what and why? Is it not enough to state that debt cannot be socialized? Does this statement not set sufficient incentives for reasonable budget policy? That being said, having the Länder warn each other or reminding each other of their promises will hardly do any harm, unless this leads to the Länder disguising their financial problems by means of new and creative forms of budget design as a consequence, or they begin to blame the lack of sufficient warnings as the source of budgetary problems in this context.

In the Föderalismusreform II, the constitution-amending legislature has not taken up the Bundesverfassungsgericht's clear request for a comprehensive discussion and—if necessary—a comprehensive reform of the financial relationship within the federal state. The focus was put on new debt rules which were also with regard to the Bundesverfassungsgericht's budgetary emergency decision of 2006 not really a federal issue. In addition to this, the application of Art. 109a GG[20] has made mutual monitoring obligatory. These actions set priorities in the wrong areas. The focus was put on secondary issues.

2. The Stabilitätsrat is not a constitutional body.[21] It is a joint political body of Bund and Länder that is alien to the system[22] of separated constitutional scopes of Bund and Länder as stipulated by the Grundgesetz. Council sessions are held at least twice a year, usually in May and at the beginning of December. The constitution does not declare the council and its members independent.[23] According to § 1 para. 1 Stabilitätsrat Act, the council members comprise the ministers for finance of the Bund and the Länder as well as the Federal Minister for Economic Affairs and Energy.[24] Decisions need the consent of the Federal Minister for Finance and of two-thirds of the Länder. For a 'decision' about an individual Land, the concerned Land is not entitled to a vote. If a decision is about the Bund, the resolution needs to be approved by a two-thirds majority of all members. The parliaments' lack of involvement corresponds to the system of coordination by the executive branch within German federalism, but sets narrow limits for the competences of the Stabilitätsrat: Its resolutions do not necessarily interfere with the budgetary power of the Bundestag (German Parliament) or of the parliaments of the Länder. According to § 7 Stabilitätsrat Act, the Stabilitätsrat is supported by an 'advisory board' consisting of independent members when controlling whether the limit for structural financial deficits of all public budgets have been observed. This was implemented by legislation regarding the European Fiscal Compact of 2012.

3. "Avoiding budgetary emergencies" is the primary task of the Stabilitätsrat (Art. 109a para. 1 GG, § 1 para. 1 (1) Stabilitätsrat Act).[25] In addition to this, Art. 109a para. 1 no. 1 to 3 GG, §§ 3 to 5 Stabilitätsrat Act provide three consecutive scopes of action: ongoing control of budget management for Bund and Länder; setting indicative criteria and key figures for forthcoming budgetary emergencies;[26] and arranging restructuring programmes. This also includes the control over the consolidation obligations of Länder that currently receive aid (Art. 143d para. 2 GG, § 2 Consolidation Aid Act). According to §§ 51, 52 Budget Principles Act, the Stabilitätsrat also took over the task of the Finanzplanungsrat (Financial Planning Council) to coordinate the budget planning of the Bund and Länder. In all its decisions, the Stabilitätsrat enjoys a

margin of appreciation. The grounds for this emanate from the political composition of the council and from the fact that the council itself has to set the key figures used to assess budgets.

All of that applies only to budgets of public territorial communities and separate assets that are not legally independent. Legal entities with their own budgets, including social security agencies and municipalities, are not taken into account as Art. 109a para. 1 GG only refers to "budget management of Bund and Länder" (Heun, 2010: Art. 109a para. 20, 24). The provision concerning "restructuring procedures" (§ 5 Stabilitätsrat Act) is especially informative about the Stabilitätsrat's possibilities in the area of its core task. In the case of a forthcoming budgetary emergency, the Stabilitätsrat 'agrees' with the concerned Land or with the Bund on a restructuring programme (paragraph 1) which takes course over five years. However, the legal nature of this programme remains unclear. Despite the implementation of this procedure, an agreement can only be reached with the consent of the territorial community concerned. Once a programme has been agreed on, the respective Land or the Bund have to send back semi-annual reports (paragraph 2). If the restructuring measures are unsuitable or insufficient, the Stabilitätsrat can 'request' 'intensified' restructuring measures. This request can be repeated numerous times if necessary (paragraph 3). Prescription § 5 para. 4 Stabilitätsrat Act documents the lack of power in critical cases:

> After the restructuring programme, the Stabilitätsrat evaluates the budgetary situation of the Bund or the Land. In the case of a forthcoming budgetary emergency despite the full implementation of the restructuring programme, the Stabilitätsrat agrees on a new restructuring programme with the Bund or the Land.

This legal provision reinforces doubts about whether the acts of observing, informing and evaluating can solve or even help to solve a financial crisis. The legislature does not appear to do so. Taking the law at its word, multiple new restructuring programmes are possible—provided that the catastrophe that should have been prevented by the observations and agreements has not yet occurred.

The only enforceable legal obligation between the Bund and each Land is the obligation to collaborate and to inform each other reciprocally.[27] Both obligations are necessary for the Stabilitätsrat to fulfil its other tasks prescribed by the new legislation regarding the European Fiscal Compact: According to § 51 para. 2 Budget Principles Act, the council has to observe, whether the "structural deficit limit for all public budgets" is kept. Länder that receive consolidation aid have the additional obligation to adhere to the corresponding requirements. If this is not the case, the Land will receive a warning from the Stabilitätsrat. As a consequence, the Land will not receive aid for that year. In "justified exceptions", the

Stabilitätsrat can declare exceeding the limits as "irrelevant" (§ 2 para. 2 Consolidation Aid Act). So far there has not been a case in which aid has been omitted.

5. Present Experience with the Stabilitätsrat

How has the Stabilitätsrat used these possibilities for consulting and evaluating in its first nine sessions between 2010 and 2014? This can be evaluated by looking at the eighth and ninth sessions.[28] The session of May 2014 is especially informative as, on this occasion, the advisory board to the Stabilitätsrat gave its first session statement.

The first sessions of the Stabilitätsrat were not spectacular. The representatives mutually assured each other of being on the right track to balanced and sustainable budgets. Also, they confirmed that the group of Länder bound to fulfil their specific consolidation obligations according to Art. 143d para. 2 GG, § 2 Consolidation Aid Act from 2011 to 2019 satisfied those obligations. The Stabilitätsrat took note of the progress reports submitted by the 'new' Länder (area of former East Germany) and by Berlin, as well as of the Federal Government's statement to these reports. The first critical point was reached in the eighth session on 5 December 2013, which concerned Bremen. The Stabilitätsrat found about Bremen's restructuring procedure:

> The Stabilitätsrat takes note of the restructuring report submitted by the Land Bremen on September 15th 2013. It acknowledges that the Land has taken further restructuring measures since the last update of the programme one year ago. However, when measured against the monitored overall development of income and expenditures, these measures do not lead to a sufficient relief of Bremen's budget. The enhancement of consolidation efforts put forward by the Stabilitätsrat in May does not as of yet deserve recognition. The Stabilitätsrat is of the opinion that the continual downscaling of the safety gap [between projected net borrowing and its arithmetical upper limit that results from the reduction plan until 2019], to be implemented between the years of 2014 to 2016, is putting the success of the restructuring programme at risk. For this reason the Stabilitätsrat has decided to request Bremen to strengthen its consolidation efforts.[29]

Bremen had already rejected criticism and the request in a statement about the draft for the decision on 26 November 2013. According to this statement, Bremen complied with the agreed restructuring programme, the projected safety gap was sufficient and, furthermore, not part of the original restructuring agreement between the Land and the Stabilitätsrat. In an interesting turn of events, the projected security gap increased in the updated restructuring programme of 2014 following this controversy. The reasons for this were not expenditure savings or other measures taken by Bremen, but, in the evaluating board's words:

The reasons for this were [...] significantly better framework conditions as seen in higher tax income, lower interest spending, and additional reimbursements through the gradual absorption of the costs for basic income of the elderly and of persons with reduced earning capacity by the Bund. Bremen has been able to avail of this for budget consolidation in the past year.[30]

In plain English, Bremen had done practically nothing (or had not been able to do anything), the improvements were caused solely by higher tax income. This interim result of the consolidation measures until 2019 could and even should have been a cause of concern for the Stabilitätsrat. It meant that any deterioration of the framework conditions which was possible at any time would have had a drastic effect on Bremen. The reason was that restructuring measures that could be influenced by the Land had not yet, or not sufficiently, been taken. Therefore, time was lost for the annual reduction of net borrowing as determined until 2019. The Stabilitätsrat was of a different opinion. On 28 May 2014 it decided:

The Stabilitätsrat has taken note of the restructuring report submitted by the Land Bremen on 30th April 2014. It appreciates that the Land has largely implemented the measures as announced and that it has complied with the net borrowing limit in 2013 as set forth by the restructuring agreement with clear distance. In its decision of 5th December 2013 the Stabilitätsrat requested Bremen to strengthen its restructuring measures. The Stabilitätsrat welcomes that first measures in this regard have been taken in the course of terminating the system of global savings by the City of Bremerhaven and that further steps have been instigated by the programme for a 'reorganization of tasks 2014/15' as decided by the Senate of Bremen in March 2014.[31]

Taking into account the statement of the advisory board to the Stabilitätsrat in regard to compliance with the upper limit for the structural financial deficit of all public budgets according to § 51 para. 2 Budget Principles Act, serious doubts arise about the Stabilitätsrat's evaluation of Bremen's financial path. The advisory board—correctly—points out that there are short- and medium-term risks for the overall public budget.

The projection [for the structural general public deficit according to § 51 para. 2 Budget Principles Act] is based on undisturbed macroeconomic development under very good framework conditions for public finance. Risks are caused inter alia by unresolved debt crises in other countries and by uncertain geopolitical developments. In addition, the consequences of economic measures such as child care subsidies ('Betreuungsgeld'), implementation of a minimum wage, and extended pension fund payments are hard to estimate [...][32]

In other words, the restructuring plan for Bremen will only work if there are no disturbances in the further development. It represents the upper limit of optimism that is still justifiable.

What is the (legal) consequence of those clearance certificates handed out by the Stabilitätsrat if tax income suddenly declines (as happened for example in 2009), if expenditures rise and if especially Bremen (and perhaps also other crisis-endangered Länder such as Saarland and Berlin) are not able to meet the ambitious fiscal goals? Using Saarland as an example, Matthias Woisin puts forward the theory that the "consulting-continuity" of positive assessments of the restructuring measures forces the Stabilitätsrat, and therefore Bund and Länder, "into responsibility" "if the path of restructuring goes astray. In this case, the affected Land can demand financial aid by Bund and Länder even more emphatically." (Woisin, 2014: 184 [translation *the author*]). This result is correct. However, It cannot be solely based on the Stabilitätsrat's assessments. Since this council can only observe, evaluate and advise, but is not able to impose sanctions, its actions cannot incur obligations to support if risks are negligently disregarded or not estimated. This would also contradict the jurisprudence of the Bundesverfassungsgericht, which rejects socialization of debt. The deep running and newly established reason for the obligation to support that primarily binds the Bund, but also the Länder is substantive law, namely Art. 109 para. 3 GG. Contrary to the principle of budgetary autonomy, the Grundgesetz places the obligation on the Länder to structurally balance their budgets without new debt as of 2020, with pre-emptive effects on budget planning in the prior decade (Art. 143d para. 1 GG). At the same time, it does not leave the Länder scope for making their own decisions in the area of income or public activities that are determined by federal law. In light of this, the Bund has taken on a new obligation with respect to the Länder. If a Land does not meet the goal set forth by the Grundgesetz for 2020, the Bund will become the party primarily obliged to resolve this emergency situation by means of financial aid. The conditions of this security bond only take effect as long as the Land can prove it has made use of all available measures and that the Stabilitätsrat regards its financial status as positive.

6. Conclusions

The assessment of both the debt brake and the Stability Council exemplifies an important and often-neglected danger inherent in constitutional promises with regard to public finance: Neither the insertion of new rules, nor the creation of new institutions can by itself guarantee that public debt is reduced. On the contrary, constitutional hyperactivity may distract from solving the actual problems, create new grounds of justification for not taking the right steps and even set wrong incentives for short-sighted measures.

These dangers inherent in the promise contained in Art. 109 para. 3 GG become most visible with regard to the Stability Council. Here, they are exacerbated by the Stabilitätsrat's status of having its own tasks while not having the authority to take action. For Bund and Länder, one can only hope that reality will not have its revenge in 2020 and that the constitutional promise will not be broken. The Stabilitätsrat's ritual could have consequences. It could provide grounds for differential reasoning when it comes to distributing responsibility and accountability. If the Stabilitätsrat's duties and conclusions have been conceived to "pre-emptively" reduce the risk of "solidary liability of Bund and Länder",[33] then it needs to change its practice in areas assessment and consultancy without delay. Only the advisory board of the Stabilitätsrat currently seems to have a grasp on reality in this regard. In its first statement from 21 May 2014, it found deficits of totalling 8.2 billion euros in eight Länder for the year of 2013, including 2.3 billion euros in North Rhine-Westphalia, 1.8 billion euros in Hessen and 1.3 billion euros in Hamburg. The advisory board estimates that the determined requirements for consolidation have reached a significant scale in some Länder. There are five more years to go until 2020.

The insufficient institutional framework of the Stabilitätsrat and its present actions provide reasons for thinking about the consequences for legal policy. On the one hand, it would be possible to strengthen the authority of the Stabilitätsrat and give it the power to influence budgets. But this would be a strange option in the light of federal constitutional principles guaranteeing the state character ('Staatsqualität') of the Länder.[34] Budgetary autonomy is an important part of this and protected by Art. 109 para. 1 GG. Furthermore, budgetary autonomy has an important role in the parliamentary system of the Bund and all of the Länder.[35] Even by amending the constitution it would therefore be impossible to impose sanctions on a Land by the other Länder and the Bund. Another less intensive proposal, made by the Miniter-präsidenten of the Länder in December 2015, is to give the Stability Council power to control the implementations of the debt brake. This minor change would require an amendment of Art. 109a GG. On the other hand, the Stabilitätsrat could be abolished. This second option should be considered seriously. Providing the Stabilitätsrat with a higher level of authority would further restrict the Länder's hand in helping to mould the federal structure. However, abolishing the Stabilitätsrat would be a first step in giving back control to politics in regard to debt and in dispelling the illusion that technocratic determination of the possibility to take on new debt could end the debt problem. At present, constitutional law is denatured in two respects: On the one hand, it is used to stipulate detailed obligations for politics while leaving numerous exceptions untouched (as seen in Art. 109 para. 3 GG). On the other hand, it institutionalizes consultancy without any consequences (as seen in Art. 109a GG).

Notes

1. About financial constitution BVerfGE (Decisions of the German Federal Constitutional Court) 67, 256 (288); 105, 185 (103): "self-contained framework and procedural order". Wieland, 1988: 410ff.; Korioth, 1997: 72ff.; Korioth, 2011: 207ff.

2. A first appraisal was written within the *Jahrbuch für öffentliche Finanzen* (year-book for public finance) by Hildebrandt, 2011: 369ff. See also Henneke, 2010: 313ff. A comprehensive overview—unfortunately without an evaluation of the Stabilitätsrat's actions—Thye, 2014.

3. BT-Drs. (Bundestags-Drucksache) 16/12410, 5.

4. The popular saying of an 'introduction' of a debt brake in 2009 is wrong. The Grundgesetz already included limits for the Bund's new debts in its version from 1949 (Art. 115 GG [1949]). Those limits were fundamentally redesigned in 1969 in accordance with the fiscal theory of overall control of the economy by public budgets, especially through countercyclical fiscal policy (Art. 115 GG [1969]). The constitutions of the Länder followed this guideline for the Länders' budgets. Therefore, the debt regulations as implemented in 2009 are the third try at a constitutional debt brake under the Grundgesetz.

5. The constitutional legislature's self-doubt is documented by the first norm of the new public debt law. Art. 109 (3) (1) GG: "The budgets of the Federation and the Länder shall in principle be balanced without revenue from credits." It is all about the term "in principle", which in fact has no place in a constitutional wording.

6. See Koemm, 2011 for a comprehensive account; additionally, Selmer, 2009: 1255ff.; Korioth, 2009a: 729ff., 2009b: 389ff.; Neidhardt, 2010.

7. Some want to derive the concept of the new Art. 109 para. 3 GG in the light of Art. 79 para. 3 GG as being repugnant to the constitution from this: Fassbender, 2009: 737ff.; for discussion Koemm, 2011: 243ff., 306ff.

8. Heintzen, 2012b: 14:

> This [...] exception comes close to the old regulation that new debt was allowed to exceed the sum of the estimated expenditures for investments in case of a disturbance of the macroeconomic balance. However, it is made clear that public borrowing in times of economic downswing has to symmetrically correspond to public debt repayment in times of upswing, so that at the end of an economic cycle, there in principle has to be at least a zero. [translation S.K.].

9. See Wieland, 2011: 242; Kube, 2014: Art. 109 para. 206; Heintzen, 2012a: 14.

10. About current considerations regarding a past-burden-fund: Bovenschulte et al., 2013: 2ff.

11. The Stabilitätsrat replaces the former "Finanzplanungsrat" (Financial Planning Committee) which had in addition to the—largely without consequences—coordination of the Bund's and the Länder's financial planning (§ 51 Budget Principles Act old version, since 1969) since 2002 the task to give "recommendations about budgetary discipline" and its "restoration" (§ 51a Budget Principles Act old version).

12. Differing opinion by Heintzen, 2012b: 14.

13. Art. 117 para. 1 no. 2b Constitution of Rhineland-Palatinate allows—contrary to Art. 109 para. 3 GG—new debt "in compensation [...] of an adjustment, which is limited to a maximum of four years, to a structural change in the situation of income and expenditures which is based on legal norms and is not attributable to the state." [translation S.K.].

14. The Bundesverfassungsgericht comprehensively explained these requirements for politics in two rulings without finding followers: BVerfGE 79, 311ff.; 119, 96ff.

15. Compare the dissenting opinion of judges Di Fabio and Mellinghof of 2007 to BVerfGE 119, 96 (155): "An uncontrolled descent of public fiscal and budgetary

management cannot so much be slowed down by demands from legal policy for better brakes, but first and foremost by making use of the existing brakes." [translation S.K.]. See also Waldhoff and Dieterich, 2009: 97ff.

16. This confirmed an old and prevalent experience: Public budgets of democratic states can neither be recapitalized by warnings nor by financial aid of others. The only way to manage this is autonomous restructuring carried out by means of individual initiative.

17. BVerfGE 116, 327 (393ff.) [translation S.K.]. See Rossi, 2007: 394ff.; Buscher, 2010: 185ff.

18. Cf. Rossi, 2007: 395; Kemmler, 2009: 552.

19. For critique already Korioth, 2007: 182ff.; Korioth, 2011b: 45ff.

20. The draft bill for the second stage of the Föderalismusreform in regard to Art. 109a GG particularly refers to the Bundesverfassungsgericht's jurisprudence, BT-Drs. 16/12410, pg. 12.

21. Therefore it is not capable of being a party of, for example, the proceedings between federal organs (Organstreit Proceedings) according to Art. 93 para. 1 no. 1 GG, Heun, 2010: Art. 109c para. 36; Thye, 2014: 54ff.

22. There are no constitutional concerns based on Art. 79 para. 3 GG: The Stabilitäts-rat is an institutional equivalent to the common tasks of mutual budget moni-toring, cf. Heun, 2010: Art. 109a para. 8 f.; Thye, 2014: 41ff.

23. Sieckmann, 2014: Art. 109a para. 5, against Heintzen, 2012a: Art. 109a para. 5, who wants to derive the independence and the freedom from instructions from the task of the Stabilitätsrat to monitor. However, deducing the right to independent action from the task is not sufficient. The composition of the Sta-bilitätsrat shows its originally political function and integration within which independence would be dysfunctional. Differentiating Heun, 2010: Art. 109a para. 11, who concedes independence to the Stabilitätsrat, but not to its members.

24. With well-founded reasoning, the legislature did not follow proposals as partially submitted to implement a panel of experts unconnected to political processes. Panels of experts do not have democratic legitimacy. Therefore, they may not decide upon anything that could have legal consequences; they are not bound by duty, but their statements tend not to have any relevance, especially if they criticize politics. See also Kirchhof, 2010: Art. 109a para. 14, 18: "Rather than this, the Stabilitätsrat analyses, assesses, and demands; however, it exer-cises state authority through information, warnings, and transfer of knowledge and therefore needs democratic legitimacy." [translation S.K.].

25. In addition, the Stabilitätsrat has to discuss the annual progress report 'Develop-ment East' from the eastern Länder, § 11 para. 3 Financial Compensation Act. Finally, the Stabilitätsrat monitors—implemented by legislation about the Euro-pean Fiscal Compact in 2012—whether the upper limit for structural financial deficits of all public budgets as permitted by European regulations is observed (§ 51 para. 2 Budget Principles Act, §§ 6, 7 Stabilitätsrat Act).

26. Concerning the key figures determined by the Stabilitätsrat (fiscal balance, credit financing ratio, interest tax rate, debt level and a standardized projection of the medium-term budget development) Hildebrandt, 2011: 372ff. with critical summary: The key figures are inconsistent, too generous and display a lack of stringent reasoning as to why their threshold should indicate critical budgetary situations or budgetary emergencies. For a comprehensive evaluation see also Thye, 2014: 145ff. With the conclusion (p. 168): "Severe deficiencies in the

system of key figures and thresholds." [translation S.K.]. From a legal point of view, there is the additional problem of whether and to what extent the legislature was allowed to delegate the power to determine thresholds to the Stabilitätsrat. This is only permitted insofar as a breach of the key figures' critical limits does not immediately lead to legal consequences.

27. Kube, 2014: Art. 109a para. 46, 52; Sieckmann, 2014: Art. 109a para. 19. Differently—and contradicting the wording of Art. 109a GG—the reasoning in the preparatory works to the Föderalismusreform, BT-Drs. 16/12410, pg. 12: Affected territorial communities are "obliged [...] to agree on a corresponding restructuring programme with the Stabilitätsrat" [translation S.K.].
28. Decision, consultation materials and protocols can be found on the Stabilitätsrat's website. Publicity is demanded by Art. 109a para. 2 GG. It shall make public control possible and exercise pressure on territorial communities with a bad budgetary situation if necessary (cf. BT-Drs. 16/12400, pp. 7, 18). Both have hardly worked so far. In the media, there are at most brief remarks about the Stabilitätsrat's sessions.
29. Decision of the Stabilitätsrat on agenda item 3 (Bremen), 8th Session on 5 December 2013 [translation S.K.].
30. Agenda item 3 of the Stabilitätsrat's 9th session on 28 May 2014, restructuring programme 2012 to 2016 of the Land Bremen. Assessment of the restructuring report (April 2014) by the advisory board, 22 May 2014, p. 1 [translation S.K.].
31. Decision of the Stabilitätsrat about agenda item 3 (Bremen), 9th session on 28 May 2014 [translation S.K.].
32. First statement of the advisory board to the Stabilitätsrat of 21 May 2014, p. 1 [translation S.K.].
33. Cf. Heun, 2010: Art. 109a para 37 [translation S.K.].
34. BVerfGE 34, 9 (20).
35. See BVerfGE 129, 124ff.; 130, 318.

Disclosure Statement

No potential conflict of interest was reported by the author.

References

Bovenschulte, A., Hickel, R. and Sieling, C. (2009), Ein Fonds zur Tilgung der Altschulden der Länder und Kommunen—den Finanzföderalismus solidarisch und nachhaltig gestalten, *Weiterdenken. Diskussionsimpulse des Julius-Leber-Forums der Friedrich-Ebert-Stiftung*, Vol.2/2013, pp.1–8.
Buscher, D. (2010), *Der Bundesstaat in Zeiten der Finanzkrise*. Berlin: Duncker & Humblot.
Fassbender, B. (2009), Eigenstaatlichkeit und Verschuldungsfähigkeit der Länder, *Neue Zeitschrift für Verwaltungsrecht*, Vol.2009, pp.737–741.
Heintzen, M. (2012a), Art. 109, 109a, 109f, in P. Kunig and I. von Münch (eds), *Kommentar zum Grundgesetz*, Vol.II, 6th ed., pp.1181–1217 Munich: C.H. Beck.
Heintzen, M. (2012b), *Das neue deutsche Staatsschuldenrecht in der Bewährungsprobe*. Berlin: De Gruyter.
Henneke, H.-G. (2010), Gemeinschaftsorgan Stabilitätsrat, *Niedersächsische Verwaltungsblätter*, Vol.2010, pp.313–317.
Heun, W. (2010), Art. 109, 109a, in H. Dreier (ed.), *Grundgesetz-Kommentar*, 2nd ed., Supplementum 2010, pp.160–208. Tübingen: Mohr Siebeck.

Hildebrandt, A. (2011), Ein Jahr Stabilitätsrat—erste Ergebnisse und ihre Bewertung, *Jahrbuch für öffentliche Finanzen*, Vol.2011, pp.369–384.

Kemmler, I. (2009), Schuldenbremse und Benchmarking im Bundesstaat, *Die Öffentliche Verwaltung*, Vol.2009, pp.549–557.

Kirchhof, G. (2010), Art. 109a, in H. von Mangoldt, F. Klein and C. Starck, *Kommentar zum Grundgesetz*, Vol.3, 6th ed., pp.1491–1499. Munich: Vahlen.

Koemm, M. (2011), *Eine Bremse für die Staatsverschuldung*. Tübingen: Mohr Siebeck.

Korioth, S. (1997), *Der Finanzausgleich zwischen Bund und Ländern*. Tübingen: Mohr Siebeck.

Korioth, S. (2007), Haushaltsnotlagen der Länder: Eigenverantwortung statt Finanzausgleich, *Wirtschaftsdienst*, Vol.87, pp.182–188.

Korioth, S. (2009a), Das neue Staatsschuldenrecht—zur zweiten Stufe der Föderalismusreform, *Juristenzeitung*, Vol.2009, pp.729–737.

Korioth, S. (2009b), Die neuen Schuldenregeln für Bund und Länder und das Jahr 2020, *Jahrbuch für öffentliche Finanzen*, Vol.2009, pp.389–416.

Korioth, S. (2011a), Finanzverfassung—Ausdruck separierter "Finanzfunktion", Rahmenordnung der zentralen staatlichen Steuerungsressource oder Sammlung politischer Kompromisse?, in T. Vesting and S. Korioth (eds), *Der Eigenwert des Verfassungsrechts*, pp.207–220 Tübingen: Mohr Siebeck.

Korioth, S. (2011b), Staatsbankrott im deutschen Föderalsystem—Instrumente innerhalb und außerhalb des Finanzausgleichs, in K. von Lewinski (ed.), *Staatsbankrott als Rechtsfrage*, pp.45–58 Baden-Baden: Nomos.

Kube, H. (2014), Art. 109 f, Art. 109, 109a, in T. Maunz and G. Dürig (eds), *Kommentar zum Grundgesetz*, 72nd delivery, pp.1–108, 1–38. Munich: C.H. Beck.

Neidhardt, H. (2010), *Staatsverschuldung und Verfassung. Geltungsanspruch, Kontrolle und Reform staatlicher Verschuldungsgrenzen*. Tübingen: Mohr-Siebeck.

Rossi, M. (2007), Verschuldungsautonomie und Entschuldungsverantwortung, *Juristenzeitung*, Vol.2007, pp.394–402.

Selmer, P. (2009), Die Föderalismusreform II—ein verfassungsrechtliches monstrum simile, *Neue Zeitschrift für Verwaltungsrecht*, Vol.2009, pp.1255–1262.

Sieckmann, H. (2014), Art. 109a, in M. Sachs (ed, pp.2331–2335.), *Kommentar zum Grundgesetz*, 7th ed. München: C.H. Beck.

Thye, M. (2014), *Der Stabilitätsrat*. Tübingen: Mohr Siebeck.

Waldhoff, C. and Dieterich, P. (2009), Die Föderalismusreform II—Instrumente zur Bewältigung der staatlichen Finanzkrise oder verfassungsrechtliches Placebo?, *Zeitschrift für Gesetzgebung*, Vol.2009, pp.97–122.

Wieland, J. (1988), Die verfassungsrechtliche Rahmenordnung des Finanzausgleichs, *Jura*, Vol.1988, pp.410–419.

Wieland, J. (2011), Soziale Nachhaltigkeit und Finanzverfassung, in W. Kahl (ed.), *Nachhaltige Finanzstrukturen im Bundesstaat*, pp.229–245 Tübingen: Mohr Siebeck.

Woisin, M. (2014), Länderbericht Saarland, *Jahrbuch für öffentliche Finanzen*, Vol.2014, pp.181–191.

Gradual Constitutional Change and Federal Dynamics – German Federalism Reform in Historical Perspective

Arthur Benz

ABSTRACT

In order to understand reform in German federalism, this article applies the framework of "dynamic institutionalism". It explains change as a result of a particular pattern of constitutional policy emerging in a sequential evolution of institutions and responding to changing state–society relations. Historical legacies found expression in negotiations predominated by bargaining among governments, guided by legalist approaches of lawyers and court decisions and influenced by specialists in public administration. In this context, societal change affected the agenda but had limited impact on processes and outcomes. In consequence, the reform ended with many detailed constitutional amendments not amounting to substantial change. In a comparative perspective, German federalism may have its strengths, but its reform should not be regarded as a role model for other federations. Instead, it exemplifies the problematic consequences of a constitutional policy not sufficiently separated from normal intergovernmental policy-making and strongly embedded in a self-enforcing evolution of institutions.

1. Introduction

Compared to other reform projects in federal states (Behnke and Benz, 2009; Benz and Knüpling, 2012; Grotz and Poier, 2012; Benz, 2016) and to the high expectations raised in public, German reform of federalism ended with limited constitutional or institutional change. On balance, two constitutional amendments prepared by Federal-*Länder* commissions ended with contradictory outcomes, those decentralizing and centralizing powers, those separating powers and sharing them and those increasing and constraining the autonomy of federal and *Länder* governments. A meaningful reform of fiscal federalism failed, and negotiations of the necessary renovation of fiscal equalization is likely to lead to a gradual change at best. A guiding idea of federalism has not surfaced during the reform process, which, to a considerable extent, was driven by specific administrative interests and addressed particular policy issues rather than pressing constitutional problems.

These changes of the federal constitution resulted from a process of joint decision-making, and this explains the incrementalism in policy-making. However, as reforms in other federations (e.g. Switzerland; Freiburghaus, 2012) and significant change in other policy fields in Germany (e.g. Förster and Klenk, 2012; Mierzejewski, 2015) indicate, the institutional constraints of joint decision-making can be circumvented if veto-players delegate the task of negotiating a reform proposal to actors or arenas separated from the arena of decision-making (Benz, 2013). This opportunity has not been used in Germany. Despite all intentions to "modernize" federalism, politics of constitutional reform right from the beginning excluded all issues which could lead to an effective change in the allocation of powers or fiscal resources since no government should end up on the losing side. Thus, representatives of the federal and *Länder* government deliberately turned an ambitious reform project into a process of gradual constitutional evolution without a clear direction. In the end, responsible politicians sold constitutional amendments as significant improvements, while in fact they only revised rules of the existing federal constitution without touching upon the normative principles or institutional structures. Not by coincidence, members of the reform commissions took decisions of the Federal Constitutional Court, that is, interpretations of existing rules, as instructions for a reform, whereas they ignored innovative suggestions by experts. Public hearings had merely symbolic purposes, interest intermediation remained fruitless and opinions of experts were construed so as to confirm positions of individual policy-makers.

This article aims to explain why federalism reform in Germany proceeded in this way. The analysis is based on the framework of dynamic institutionalism (Benz and Broschek, 2013). It combines historical institutionalism with theories centred on societal conditions and policy-making. Institutional change is explained as a result of historical legacies, external factors, and strategic action of policy-makers, with the relative impact of these conditions reflecting unique features of a political system. As will be explained in the following sections, the reform of German federalism was embedded in an institutional framework reflecting ideas, rules and patterns of interactions that emerged and where shaped during sequences of state formation since the sixteenth century. They reveal a continuous search for balancing unity and diversity, and this balance has remained a basic aim of German constitutional politics. In the course of this history, negotiated agreements among delegates of governments and the constitutional law emerged as principle devices for settling conflicts and balancing powers. Intergovernmental negotiations supported by a strong administration and governance under the rule of law turned out as institutionally entrenched patterns of politics that shaped recent reform of German federalism. Moreover, as the theoretical framework points out, agendas and conflicts among political actors were influenced by interest inter-mediation and party politics reflecting state–society relations. As I will outline in Section 3, these relations had contradicting effects since they supported uniform policies across the federation and expressed regional diversity. During the reform process of the last decade, they influenced the agenda but did not generate effective pressure for substantial change. In fact, the set-up of policy-making and politics of federalism reform reflected the lega-cies of institutional development, as explained in Section 4. It was the inter-play of established executive, if not administrative, cooperation between federal and *Länder* governments and the interaction of intergovernmental bargaining and decisions of the Federal Constitutional Court that determined constitutional politics. These routines of intergovernmental policy-making made constitutional amendments possible, but they proved inadequate in coming to an effective reform, while the legalistic approach, supported by administration, lawyers and the constitutional court, led to detailed amend-ments constraining the flexibility of federalism. Nonetheless, German federal-ism is not destined to end up in the joint decision trap. In the final section, some insights from comparative research point out how this trap can be avoided.

2. Historical Legacy: Institutional Evolution between Unity and Diversity

Federal states constitute complex structures of dividing and sharing powers, linked to particular types of (democratic) government. Thus they have to be conceived as multi-dimensional institutionalization of power. The different dimensions may develop simultaneously, but usually they are shaped through a sequence of development. Historical sequences often cause contra-dictory institutionalizations harmonized by patterns of political practice or by ideas (or ideologies) concealing the tensions entrenched in institutions (Benz and Broschek, 2013).

To understand the structures and operation of German federalism, the his-torical background is particularly important, as scholars such as Gerhard Lehmbruch have pointed out (Lehmbruch, 2002, 2015). However, historical accounts often overemphasize the integrating effects of cooperative federal-ism and the accommodation of diversity by agreements. According to an interpretation of German state history predominating for a long time, the late birth of the nation state reflected a decline of the federal order stemming from the feudal era. Scholars who have focused on the simultaneous creation of the federation and the nation state by German unification in 1870 have overemphasized the unitary nature of politics and policy-making (Abromeit, 1992: 33–36). In doing so, they have tended to cover only one dimension of development and disregard different streams of evolution producing contradictory institutions. Meanwhile, historians have corrected this narrative and unmasked it as being influenced by normative state theories of the nineteenth century (Schilling, 1989; Whaley, 2011; Stollberg-Rilinger, 2013). In fact, German history reveals "a prolonged tension between unity and diversity, between the search for cohesion and the fact of fragmentation" (Sheehan, 1981: 22). The institutional framework of German federalism was – and still is – characterized by a dualism between unity and diversity in the ideational framework, by decentralized building of states with significant administrative capacities and integration of the federation through law, and by political practices combining intergovernmental cooperation and political competition.

Back to the old German *Reich* federalism balanced centrifugal and centripetal forces, on the one hand in rather complicated structures of politics, and on the other hand supported by a culture reflecting diversity and uniformity. This culture and the institutions responded to the conflicting exigencies and challenges which emerged in the early sixteenth century when Germany was an empire with changing borders and consisted of a multitude of diverse territories and corporations (Imperial Estates). The character of the confederation was shaped by attempts of an institutional reform determined as much to advance integration as to prevent disintegration. While reforms mainly failed, they did signify first perceptions of an identity of the Empire (Schmidt, 1999), although they did not prevent political and administrative decentralization to continue. Moreover, expanding trade relations and the Reformation affected the evolution of the federation. Economic developments increased the role of administration, but also found expression in city leagues organizing trade. While still remaining decentralized, both administration and trade contributed to the development of administrative networks and German as a uniform language (Whaley, 2011/I: 52–53). Similar dual effects unfolded during the Reformation. On the one hand, it divided Germany by cultural terms, when the Imperial Diet decided that each ruler of a territory should determine the religious denomination of his subjects. On the other hand, Luther's translation of the Bible into German and the Protestant practice of holding services in the language of the common people was a further step towards linguistic unification. This interplay of uniformity and diversity continued to characterize the cultural and ideational dimension of German federalism during later centuries.

The same holds true for the structure of government. The Reformation divided the German confederation at a time when state building set off. This process of institutionalization of power changed feudal relationships into a territorially based political organization. Moreover, power was both legitimized and limited by law, while at the same time becoming more effective by an extending administrative staff. In Germany, the territorial organization of government remained fragmented. This fact obstructed a concentration of power by the Emperor, but also of state building in general. Effective state capacities and administration did not evolve before the eighteenth century, and they mainly developed in the *Länder*. In contrast, since the birth of the German confederation, constitutional law was primarily a matter of the Reich and formed a framework holding the territories together. The Imperial Court founded in 1495 turned into a fundamental institution of governance by law and demonstrated substantial integrative power. Decisions of the Imperial Diet or through peace treaties contributed to determine the law and to settle conflicts by legal reasoning. Thus, Germany became one of those places in Europe where the idea of rule of law gained ground (Fukuyama, 2011: 245–275). Consequently, the state was conceived as a legal institution. Since at least the nineteenth century, this legal order of the state was deemed to integrate not only society but also constituent units of the federation (Dyson, 1980: 122–123).

These contradicting developments of ideas and institutions, some of which fostered unity while others sustained diversity, called for patterns of politics and policy-making appropriate to overcome tensions and frictions. They gave rise to the practice of negotiation and governing by consensus, a practice which has characterized German cooperative federalism throughout its history. What needs to be emphasized here is that since the Peace of Westphalia, negotiations became the task of delegates of rulers and later, increasingly, of delegates supported by administrative staff or by civil servants themselves. In line with these traditions, the culturally and institutionally differentiated constituent units of the German federation became more and more integrated by a dense network of administrative relationships. Involved actors pursued the interests of their government concerning power and cultural aspects, but they also aimed at fulfilling specific tasks of their departments. In any case, as civil servants in a bureaucracy, they followed the rule of law. These inter-administrative relations proved highly effective for accommodating diversity and unity.

During the nineteenth century, nationalism, power politics between European states, central state building, democratization, party politics and social policy prevailed as centralizing forces relating to ideas, institutions and patterns of policy-making (Nipperdey, 1986: 80–88). Yet the German nation state remained a federation; it did not turn into a unitary or centralized state. Regional cultures survived or were reinforced, since governments of medium-sized *Länder* engaged in educational and cultural policies in order to maintain loyalties of their citizens in the face of growing nationalism (Umbach, 1999; Green, 2001). *Länder* governments kept significant powers, not the least of which were in the executive sphere and related to public infrastructure, thus allowing them to pursue a policy of modernization on their own. In this context, administrative networks of the *Länder* gained in importance. Even the organization of public social insurance, which the central government under Bismarck founded during the 1880s in order to promote nation building (Manow, 2005: 226), reflected a federal structure existing until the present. Rather than national loyalties, the main integrative force was the rule of law, which found expression in theories perceiving the state as a coherent legal order. Accordingly, state theories reflecting on the reality of a federal system, or on the problem of divided sovereignty, emphasized the need for federal comity, unity and integration instead of diversity (Oeter, 1998: 74–87).

The real reason for Bismarck's social policy was the rise of political parties, in particular the Socialists. Founded in the second half of the nineteenth century, they gained power in the directly elected federal parliament. Although the evolving party system was affected by regional diversity (Urwin, 1982), it mainly reflected the societal cleavages of industrialization and the duality of the class conflict. From about 1890, the parliament turned into the centre of politics at the federal level, and after 1918, the Weimar constitution added the parliamentary system to federal institutions of government. Emphasizing the state as a legal order, German constitutional lawyers never adopted the idea of the sovereignty of parliament. Nonetheless, scholars saw parliamentary democracy to be in conflict with federalism. Some of them, such as Otto Hintze and Georg Jellinek, perceived federalism as an obstacle against democratization (Ritter, 2005: 30), while others emphasized the mutual interference of both institutional dimensions limiting effectiveness of governance and democratic legitimacy. In fact, party competition in the parliamentary arena affected intergovernmental negotiations between federal and *Länder* governments (Lehmbruch, 1976). In the Weimar Republic, the council of *Länder* governments ("Reichsrat") lost its veto rights, but party conflicts nevertheless shaped the relations between federal and *Länder* governments. In the Federal Republic, governments supported by competing parties have had to negotiate agreements in order to avoid a *Bundesrat* veto in federal legislation. This tension between competitive and cooperative modes has significantly constrained German politics. However, administrative intergovernmental relations have contributed to lessen these tensions. In cases of political conflicts, governments and parties in parliament can reframe the agenda. More often than not, they have defined matters as constitutional issues to be decided either by cross-party agreements or by the constitutional court. Thus, they have circumvented open party competition threatening to block legislation, while at the same time avoiding the blame for joint decisions or declaring them as inevitable.

Therefore, historical development in Germany did not simply generate unitary or cooperative federalism. It generated a federal system which, considering its multi-dimensional structures, is distinguished mainly by three particular institutional features: First, in order to balance the demands of uniformity and territorial diversity, governments of different levels coordinate their policies, often by applying shared powers. Linked to parliamentary governments, intergovernmental coordination interferes with competitive party politics (Lehmbruch, 2000). Second, intergovernmental relations are supported by continuing interaction or networks linking administrations of the different jurisdictions. Although they may include federal administration, they still constitute a strong element of decentralization (Benz, 2001). Third, the impact of the law and legal reasoning contributes to integrating decentralized administrative policy-making and moderating party conflicts. This does not imply that the law and decisions of the constitutional court promote centralization. Rather they balance powers and make conflicts manageable by depoliticizing issues. These three basic institutional features determined the reform of federalism, which seemed to respond to changes in state–society relations, but actually was hardly affected by them.

3. Federalism and Changing State–Society Relations

Beyond the historical development of institutions evolving in particular sequences and resulting in path-dependence, state–society relations drive the dynamics of federal systems. Following Hirschman (1970), the impact of societal change on territorial structures of a federal government can be explained by three social mechanisms contributing to the constitution or dissolution of boundaries. These mechanisms are exit and entry, that is, mobility of actors across borders, reconfiguration of loyalties towards communities and voice, that is, the creation and restructuring of political organizations to pursue collective interests. Limited mobility, strong loyalties to regional or local communities and decentralized organizations of parties and interest groups generate forces towards decentralization.

In Germany, these social forces appear to work in an opposite direction and instead strengthen the central government. In view of the integrated party system, the homogeneity of German society and the centralized organization of societal interests (Katzenstein, 1987), scholars disputed the federal character of German government (Wheare, 1963; Abromeit, 1992). Moreover, the German welfare state seemed to make federalism obsolete, along the lines of what Harold Laski in 1939 predicted as a global trend (Laski, 2005 [1939]). Indeed, social policies of the federal government turned out as an integrating force. However, societal conditions of German federalism and changes in state–society relations have been more variegated than comparative studies have suggested.

During the first decades after the Second World War, mobility transformed West German society, not least due to the arrival of refugees from Eastern Europe and later the immigration of so-called guest workers. Moreover, because of their limited fiscal autonomy, *Länder* governments lacked the instruments to prevent firms from moving to locations outside their territory or attracting private corporations or taxpayers. However, like institutional structures of the state, economic structures developed in a path-dependent manner. Although the German economy went through deep structural change affecting particularly old industrial areas, regional "clusters", which had been created with the support of *Länder* governments during the nineteenth century, persisted and still constitute a diverse economic landscape (Herrigel, 1996). Beyond transaction costs, positive external effects generated by networks of industries as well as public investments and public utilities slowed down the exit and entry mechanisms in the economy. During the 1980s, regionalization of the economy revitalized the role of *Länder* in economic policy (Benz et al., 2000) and induced decentralist trends when *Länder* governments discovered the new economic regionalism (Keating, 1998).

Compared to multi-national federations, allegiances of citizens to *Länder* governments have always remained limited. Until the nineteenth century, the *Länder* provided the basic orientation framework for citizens. This changed due to different processes of realignment, such as social change in the area of industrialization, the destruction by wars or the dissolution of local or regional milieus in the modernizing of society. Meanwhile, scholars have discovered that there are multiple loyalties of German citizens to different levels of political communities or governments (Sturm et al., 2011). Moreover, research has uncovered particular political cultures in different parts of the country (Mannewitz, 2015). Presumably, this does not appear as a new phenomenon, if we take into consideration the continuous interplay of uniformity and diversity in political culture. Rather than a mechanism causing centralization and uniformity, this reconfiguration of social communities favours federalized structures of politics and government, including contradicting claims inherent in multiple loyalties.

Finally, political structuring of society also reveals a differentiated pattern. Special interest groups have established strong centralized organizations, although they tend to maintain subdivisions in the *Länder*. They usually call for federal legislation and uniform implementation of the law in the policy areas they are addressing in their political activities. At a glance, the same holds true for political parties. There is no doubt that German federalism has been held together by an integrated party system (Filippov et al., 2004: 211–213). However, in many analyses an important characteristic feature has been neglected. The two "mainstream parties", the Christian Democrats and the Social Democrats forming the core of the integrated party system, differ in their organization and degree of vertical integration (Detterbeck, 2011: 254–256), their concept of federalism and their role in intergovernmental and constitutional politics and policy-making.

For a long time, the Social Democratic Party (SPD) represented the vertically integrated party typical for the German party system. Although its organization being divided in central, regional and local levels, it tried to pursue a uniform policy through all divisions, corresponding to the party's policy preferences. In the negotiations on the West German constitution, for example, the Social Democrats made the case for a strong federal government. In the early decades of the Federal Republic, they supported uniform policies implementing the principle of social equality and the expansion of the welfare state. Consequently, the party tended to favour federal policies. This changed during the 1970s, when the Social Democrats discovered ideas of new regional economics and the relevance of decentralized social service for maintaining the welfare state (Münch, 1997). During the 1980s, after it had lost its majority in the federal parliament, the party profited from election successes in *Länder* governments. These developments led to a certain regionalization in political orientations and power structures, but the SPD still remained an integrated party in the federal system.

The conservative Christian Democrats, the Christian Democratic Union (CDU) and the Christian Social Union (CSU), supported federalism and decentralization during constitutional negotiations on the Basic Law, whereas they contributed to a centralist trend with social policies as majority parties until 1969. Within its organization, the CDU allowed considerable autonomy for its regional subdivisions. The *Länder* level in the party gained even more power when the Social Democrats, in a coalition with the Liberals, formed the federal government from 1969 to 1982. Even after that period, representatives of the *Länder* strongly influenced party politics. The role of the Bavarian CSU reinforces the federalized character of the conservative party camp. Although an independent party, it forms a continuing coalition with its "sister party" CDU at the federal level. Not only is the CSU a regional party, rooted in a single *Land*, it also exerts particular influence on federal politics via this specific partnership with the CDU, a federally organized, but "state-wide party". The agreement to form a joint party group in the *Bundestag*, which is regularly renewed after general elections (CDU-CSU, 2013), gives the CSU a veto power in matters concerning Bavaria and federalism in general. It goes without saying that this has significant repercussions on constitutional policy.

Thus, state–society relations in Germany reflect the dualism between unity and diversity. This is manifested in economic structures and processes determined by a common market but also in specific territorial conditions for production, in multiple loyalties of citizens to federal, regional and local communities, and in a party system which on the one hand is federalized and vertically integrated but includes an element of regionalist politics and asymmetry in favour of Bavaria on the other hand. These relations have changed over time. Since German unification, regional differentiation has been reinforced in all three dimensions. Despite continuing mobility between East and West Germany and despite efforts of federal and *Länder* governments to stimulate growth in the new *Länder*, economic structures have diverged. Notwithstanding the expression of East German citizens to be part of one nation, German society – though increasingly shaped by immigrants from many parts of the world – is still divided in regional political cultures (Mannewitz, 2015: 334–367). Despite the transfer of West German party organizations after the collapse of the Wall, party constellations differ in East German *Länder*, and the differences between the *Länder* in general have also increased (Bräuninger and Debus, 2012). To an increasing extent, regional subdivisions of state-wide parties pursue somewhat different policies compared to the federal party (Detterbeck and Renzsch, 2003).

Increasing diversity in economic, social and political structures changed the conditions for multi-level coordination in German federalism. Against this background, federal and *Länder* governments decided to reform German federalism and launched their project for a constitutional reform. Nevertheless, they draw different conclusions for the agenda. In line with regionalist trends in politics and society, *Länder* governments and their parliaments demanded a decentralization of powers. The federal government, however, acted from a different perspective. Confronted by obstacles in joint decision-making due to the growing assertiveness of *Länder* governments with heterogeneous interests, it aimed at constraining the veto powers of the *Bundesrat* (see Stecker, forthcoming). Moreover, although the need for a reform of federalism was widely discussed in public, the reform process was isolated from society by an institutional setting which reflected the historical legacies of German federalism. After more than a decade of reform policy – still unfinished – the basic features of German federalism have hardly changed, and as far as change can be noted, it led to detailed regulation which undermined the former flexibility of the German federal system.

4. Constitutional Policy between Politics, Administration and Constitutional Law

There is no need to tell the story of German reform of federalism in detail since several publications provide an insight into processes and outcomes (Breske, 2008; Moore et al., 2008; Scharpf, 2009; Sattler, 2012). In order to explain patterns of constitutional policy chosen by governments and their effects, it is sufficient to characterize the three distinct stages of reform and then to summarize the results. As I will demonstrate, reform policy was clearly influenced by the three integrative forces entrenched in institutions of German federalism, namely intergovernmental political negotiations, administrative policymaking and the law interpreted and preserved by the constitutional court. There are reasons to assume that these integrative forces counteracted the potential intensity of conflicts caused by changing state–society relations, that is, increasing economic disparities, emerging regional cultures and territorial divides inside the party system. However, they did so by ruling out significant changes in the distribution of power and fiscal resources. While the established patterns of politics facilitated decisions on constitutional amendments, they constrained the scope of the reform, thwarted potential innovations and allowed only gradual adjustments or rules.

As regards structures and procedures, the three stages of reform policy in German federalism conformed to the traditional pattern of joint decision-making, but they varied in some important details. While at the beginning, federal and *Länder* governments seemed to be willing to significantly modernize German federalism in public discourses, the executive clearly controlled the process in later stages.

The first "Joint Commission of the *Bundestag* and the *Bundesrat*" (2003–04) included representatives from the federal parliament and the *Bundesrat*, the latter standing for the 16 *Länder* governments. Resembling a joint committee of the federal legislature, the commission de facto institutionalized the inter-play between party politics and intergovernmental relations in German federalism. Party groups and the *Länder* governments prepared plenary sessions of the commission in separate meetings. Furthermore, the federal government and the *Länder* governments used the support of their administration for ana-lysing problems or elaborating proposals for constitutional amendments. While at the federal level, expertise was submitted by special departments of the executive, the *Länder* government resorted to generalists in the Land ministries who provided knowledge in constitutional law. In addition, the commission invited 12 experts from the academic sector, among them 8 lawyers, some of whom had political experience as former ministers in the federal government. To a considerable extent, participation of these experts prevented negotiations in the commission from being dominated by party political or intergovernmental bargaining right from the outset. Yet for this very reason, leaders of party groups and governments suspected that they would lose control of the process. Therefore, they reduced the influence of experts when they formed sub-committees on specific issues and excluded most experts from them. Representatives from national parliaments and local governments participated in the process as consultative members. Thus, they were in a position to issue their opinion but did not have an impact on bargaining processes. The commission was embedded in an emer-ging public discourse, since several public or private organizations held con-ferences on particular issues of the reform. Furthermore, interest associations and individual citizens submitted opinions to the commission. However, there are no indications that these communications mattered. Neither did they alter the character of negotiations between parties and governments nor did they affect outcomes.

In general, bargaining actors cannot find a consensus on a redistribution of powers or fiscal resources. Therefore, the commission had to make a package deal. It started its work on the premise that constitutional amendments should not modify the allocation of financial resources between governments. Accordingly, after a hearing of the experts on this issue, members of the commission decided that most matters concerning fiscal federalism be left off the agenda. In accordance to the demands of the federal government, the commission found a compromise on modified rules defining veto powers of the *Bundesrat*, but agreed on significant concessions to the *Länder* governments. In final bargaining processes, the federal government also accepted a decentralization of legislative powers. Actually, it was not the commission which achieved this result. Instead, the federal executive submitted proposals for decentralization of legislative powers, apparently under pressure from the Federal Constitutional Court (Scharpf, 2009: 96). In several decisions since 2000, the court had reinterpreted the conditions for federal legislation in matters falling under the rules of concurrent legislation. For particular issues, it had denied the right of the federal government to legislate. In view of the risk of further decentralization of powers and a fragmentation of the law, the federal government recognized the need for an amendment of the constitution. In consequence, the federal administration elaborated proposals for transferring legislative powers to the *Länder*, after the Federal Ministry of Justice had sent a request to the other federal ministries. When the commission nevertheless failed to find an agreement, a small group of party leaders negotiated the final compromise. This bargaining process continued after the 2005 federal elections, when the Christian Democrats and the Social Democrats formed a coalition government.

The constitutional amendment passed in June 2006 modified the distribution of legislative powers and the conditions for a veto right of the *Bundesrat* in federal legislation. With the right to regulate university education and to determine the remuneration of their civil servants, as well as the decentralization of several additional matters, the *Länder* parliaments gained significant powers (Dose and Reus, forthcoming). The federal government did not achieve its goals although the number of laws subject to a *Bundesrat* veto has decreased since the reform. Meanwhile, the detailed regulation of powers and intergovernmental relations aiming at separating responsibilities turned out to be an obstacle to effective governance (Benz, 2008). Moreover, the non-reform of fiscal federalism was soon felt as a serious deficit and one which a second reform commission had to address.

This interplay of political bargaining, administrative negotiations and court decisions recurred in the second stage of the reform (2007–09). In the second joint commission of the *Bundestag* and the *Bundesrat*, academic experts were not invited to participate as members of the commission, which started to work by organizing two hearings on fiscal and administrative issues. Topics to be addressed demonstrated the impact of administrations. The agenda resulted from a compilation of questions collected by federal and *Länder* departments. The questionnaires sent out to experts comprised about 500 more or less detailed issues. Moreover, the Federal Constitutional Court gave an impetus on its own to the reform process, after the *Land* Berlin had instituted legal proceedings against the federal government claiming fiscal support to overcome an alleged budget crisis. In its judgement, the court denied the existence of such a crisis, but required legal provisions to prevent *Länder* governments from running into such a situation. The commission took this as a clear order to amend the constitutional rules on deficit spending and to find an early warning mechanism in budget policy.

As in the first commission, representatives of federal and *Länder* governments excluded all issues requiring decisions with redistributive effects. Certainly, they discussed all aspects of fiscal federalism, including a reallocation of taxation powers. In the end, however, they only found compromises on some administrative issues and on a new debt rule. Moreover, they suggested setting up a "Stability Council" responsible for supervising budget policy of the federal and *Länder* governments (Korioth, 2016). A group of administrative experts prepared detailed criteria and proceedings, which the commission and the legislature ultimately endorsed (Heinz, 2016). As a result, the second reform of federalism implemented the request of the Federal Constitutional Court by increasing the legal constraints for fiscal policy and by introducing an evaluation process for individual budgets. In contrast with the aim of separating powers the first commission clearly focused on, the second reform introduced new joint tasks (Seckelmann, 2009).

When in 2013 another Grand Coalition government was formed at the federal level, the parties agreed to initiate negotiations between the federal and *Länder* governments on a reform of fiscal equalization and, in addition, to establish a new commission (Coalition Treaty, 2013: 95). The latter should have again addressed issues of fiscal federalism in general, including the allocation of revenues and expenditures. In fact, this commission never materialized. Instead, intergovernmental negotiations started which focused on fiscal equalization, in view of the term limit of the current law which will expire at the end of 2019.

These negotiations followed the traditional pattern of executive federalism in Germany. Prepared by experts of the responsible departments, ministers of finance of the federal and *Länder* governments met in private to discuss proposals to reform fiscal equalization. Again, legal proceedings overshadowed the negotiations, after the governments of Bavaria and Hesse decided to submit the matter to the Federal Constitutional Court. So far, the court has not dealt with the case, leaving instead the search for an agreement to politics. In this process, a number of experts commissioned by the *Länder* governments and party groups presented concepts for a renewal of fiscal equalization (Geißler et al., 2015, contributions by Eichel et al., Behnke, Lenk, Geißler, Färber and Scheller). Yet the impact of these proposals seems to be limited. Negotiations among ministers aimed at package deals, which turned out as quite difficult although the federal government conceded talking about extending tax sharing. The federal minister of finance tabled a paper elaborated together with the mayor of Hamburg, while the Bavarian government issued its own proposal to abolish horizontal equalization. Both suggestions provoked resistance from *Länder* governments which expect to lose revenues, according to their calculations. Several meetings of Land premiers with the federal chancellor ended without result. Finally, the former agreed on a package deal, yet without the assent of the federal government, which, according to this proposal, should bear an additional billion Euros to compensate losses of *Länder*, in addition to the 8 billion the federal minister of finance had already conceded.[1] So far the bargaining process continues. Given the state of the reform, it is safe to predict that change will be limited.

The three stages of reform policy in German federalism combine into a particular sequence. Unintended by policy-makers, it developed when parties and governments reacted to disappointing or problematic outcomes of reform processes by starting a new round of negotiations. Throughout this sequence, the pattern of intergovernmental policy-making in an interplay between political executives, administrative actors and the constitutional court gained more and more ground. The first reform commission can be interpreted as being an attempt to institute a new arena of constitutional policy although it never opened up of the legislative process to deliberation with new actors and civil society. The second commission seemed to continue the first reform approach, but actually insulated the legislative and intergovernmental arena against external influence. In the third stage, governments returned to the traditional intergovernmental mode, which will be followed by the formal legislative proceedings. Like the actors involved, the issues addressed were reduced from one stage to the next, although the problems of federalism remained the same. Whereas the narrowing of the actor constellation would be appropriate if the reform proceeded in consequential steps from negotiating constitutional principles and rules, followed by implementation of the revised constitution in specific laws (as observable in Swiss reform of federalism; Benz, 2016: 70–77), this logic has not guided the course of federalism reform in Germany. Rather the process can be explained by failures to solve problems in previous stages when important issues had been postponed. In addition, the sequences demonstrated increasing efforts of policy-makers to contain the intensity of conflicts, by turning to the well-established procedures of German federalism.

Concerning fundamental problems of fiscal federalism, these efforts were doomed to fail for at least three reasons. First, when fiscal federalism in general and fiscal equalization in particular reappeared on the agenda, redistributive issues came to predominate. Regardless of the difficulty to deal with such issues in joint decision-making, they turned out as highly complicated under the constraining effects of previous reforms (like limitations of federal grants and constitutional regulation of balanced budgets). These conflicts even affected negotiations among specialists in administrations and divided them according to the position of their *Land* in fiscal relations. Second, the veto power of the Bavarian government increasingly affected negotiations at the political level. Consequently, compromises inside the Christian-Democratic party camp, and in consequence between parties, became more problematic, although fiscal equalization usually is not a decisive matter of party politics. Third, concerning fiscal equalization, constitutional amendments and court decisions have led to a detailed regulation that leaves hardly any room for further interpretations. Therefore, guidelines by a decision of the Federal Constitutional Court are unlikely to facilitate a settlement of these conflicts.

5. Why History Matters, and how Significant Change Nevertheless is Possible

In reforms of federal constitutions, actors from different levels of government and different institutions are involved, often with the power to veto amendments. For this reason, success or failure result from policy-making in interlocked arenas (Benz and Broschek, 2013: 379–382). In the multi-dimensional institutional setting of federalism, actors participating in the process are subject to different logics of collective action, and different conditions constrain their strategic actions. Intergovernmental bargaining, party competition, administrative problem solving and legal reasoning shape negotiations and decision-making processes to a varying extent.

Joint decision-making constitutes a particular type of this multi-level policy which typically applies to reforms of federalism, not only in Germany but also in many other federations where actors from the different levels need to come to an agreement and parliaments have to ratify negotiated amendment bills (Benz, 2013, 2016). In the German case, the historical evolution outlined above has generated and cemented a particular pattern of joint decision-making. Beyond political bargaining among federal and *Länder* governments influenced by territorial interests and party politics, specialized administrations influence negotiations, and actors regularly follow the guidelines of the law and its interpretation by the constitutional court. This particular combination of modes of interaction allows achieving agreements despite confrontation of parties or redistributive conflicts between governments which usually are ratified in legislative procedures. However, these decisions rarely produce significant changes of the constitution; rather they end up with changes in details.

This kind of constitutional policy has its costs. As indicated above, the different stages of federalism reform have brought about contradictory results. They have been guided neither by a coherent idea nor a reform strategy. Ten years of reform policy have revealed more of a muddling through than modernization of German federalism. In processes of intergovernmental bargaining and under the influence of special administrations and the Federal

Constitutional Court, amendments of the Basic Law led to a growing density of constitutional regulation of how federalism works. The prevailing legal framing implying that powers have to be clearly defined by law as well as the interplay between joint decision-making and legal proceedings contributed to this development. Detailed regulation reduces the flexibility of power structures, which is essential for maintaining a "robust federation" (Bednar, 2009). Federal and *Länder* governments still respond to new challenges in a flexible way, but more often than not, they have to find approaches to circumvent constraining rules in policy-making. For instance, the first reform of federalism introduced a so-called ban on cooperation between federal and *Länder* governments. In practice, this rule turned out as inconvenient and has been undermined in practice. In labour market policy, the Federal Constitutional Court compelled governments to legalize their cooperation by introducing a new joint task. In education, the ban on cooperation was partly lifted by the 2009 amendment (Kropp and Behnke, forthcoming). Yet discussions about the practical problems continue, although they have not led to a search for appropriate modes of coordination. Hence, the alternation of political practice and constitutional regulation is likely to persist, with problematic effects for the stabilizing function of the constitution and for the operation of federalism.

The shaky foundation of cooperative federalism has further consequences. Apparently, German federalism is confronted with redistributive issues, but the usual modes of intergovernmental policy-making and court proceedings are inappropriate for legitimizing redistributive decisions. In general, governments use norms of distributive justice established in the 1950s, and they try to avoid significant modification of the allocation of resources to territories. However, the long story of fiscal equalization demonstrates the limits of incremental adjustment, particularly in view of the new constraints of the debt rule and budget control.

For these reasons, there are ample indications that German federalism is becoming more and more rigid and that the continuity of evolution is turning into a burden of path-dependence. After 10 years of reforms determined to revive federalism and strengthen powers of *Länder* governments, federalism has in fact been weakened. Not only did joint decision-making trump steps towards decentralization, in reality the balance of power has shifted to the centre while most *Länder* governments have shown no willingness to take responsibility for autonomous policies. Constitutional amendments did not cope with the challenges of increasing economic and social diversity and the need for policy coordination under the condition of diversity. Lacking a concept for designing a modern federal constitution, reform has turned into an incoherent regulation of details.

In view of these problematic developments, two questions need to be addressed: First, why are historical legacies in German federalism rather strong and find expression in particular patterns of constitutional policy-making? Second, given the path-dependence of institutions and patterns of policy-making, how can these constraints be circumvented?

Regarding the first question, the persisting influence of administration and law seems to provide a convincing answer. Intergovernmental networks of administrations survive changes in governments and party constellations. They became established practice, in some policy fields they are institutionalized in joint tasks, and they have proved resistant against attempts of governments to trim the number of meetings or committees (Zimmer, 2010). The German *Rechtsstaat* implying a strong role of the Federal Constitutional Court and reflected in a dominance of lawyers in constitutional policy and reform commissions can be considered as manifestation of German state tradition. The pattern of constitutional policy described above conforms to these historical legacies.

Under these conditions, changes of state–society relations had minor effects. Reform of German federalism as well as the debate about federalism in general found little public attention. Among interest groups, those representing economic interests raised their voice and instigated discussion on federalism. During the last three decades, decentralization and subsidiarity were emphasized to counter the presumed trend towards centralization or joint decision-making. Since the turn of the century, the Bavarian CSU became a strong protagonist of these aims (Ziblatt, 2002). Yet unlike multi-national federations, Germany was never subject to societal movements challenging the existing structure of federalism, not least since changes in society had ambivalent effects in terms of unity and diversity. Finally, the problems of federalism have been defined by experts and governments. Beyond that, federalism remained a matter of academic discourses, and its reform was controlled by governments and their administration.

Finally, while rigidity of policy-making and blockades of significant reforms has been criticized by experts and in the media, the preservation of the constitution in general and federalism in particular has been considered a basic value in the German political system. For this reason, patterns of politics and policy-making limiting the scope of constitutional change may serve the political and administrative elites interested in maintaining control over reform processes, and there is hardly any debate about alternatives. This signifies that the political elites and the wider public have approved the legacies of history as safeguards against far-reaching constitutional change, the consequences of which are uncertain. So far, Germans seem to live with the contradiction that they prefer the conservative effects of political structures, while at the same time blaming exactly these structures for causing governance deficits.

Although the gradual evolution conforms to the logics of the existing patterns of policy-making in the German federal system, the consequence of historical evolution reinforced by the state-centred development of federalism is not entirely determined by history or societal conditions. The path-dependency of history affects institutionalized and emergent patterns of constitutional policy, but politics can certainly establish other patterns if it separates "constitutional choice" from "collective choice" (Ostrom, 2005: 62–64). Instead of using well-established routines of policy-making, governments could design specific arrangements of constitutional policy, in particular arrangements concerning the processes of negotiations on amendment bills. With the reform commission established in 2003, federal and *Länder* governments did not create appropriate structures allowing policy-makers reflect on federalism at a distance from political and administrative procedures and habits. When they realized that they might lose control over the process, they resorted to the traditional patterns of joint decision-making. However, as comparative studies show (Benz, 2013, 2016), significant changes can only be achieved if those in power differentiate constitutional and normal politics and policy-making, and if they decide on reform under a veil of ignorance regarding the results of a constitutional change. Moreover, innovative proposals can only surface in loosely coupled arenas of policy-making reflecting a plurality of actors. An appropriate sequential organization of the process and a division of arenas of negotiation allowing actors from various backgrounds to elaborate their opinions can create a communicative process countervailing bargaining processes in intergovernmental or party political confrontation. Instead of taking advantage of these opportunities, German reformers merely pursued politics as usual.

6. Conclusion

From a comparative perspective, Germany stands as a model of a stable federal system. Moreover, policy-making appears to be highly effective and legitimate. The German government has proved able to respond to the challenges of recent crises and has a reputation of guaranteeing good governance. Therefore, the problems of federalism outlined above should not be exaggerated. However, compared to other cases of constitutional reform in federal systems, the last ten years of German endeavours to modernize federalism cannot be taken as a good example.

Federal systems are permanently changing, and their dynamics are driven by different mechanisms built into the architecture of any particular federation. Continuity and change appear in historical evolution, the sequential creation of institutions and its often contradictory effects on politics and policy-making, they are triggered by changing state–society relations, and finally result from institutional reforms and adjustments. To produce significant change, reforms should either be supported by pressure from society or should be negotiated in arenas of constitutional policy separated from patterns of policy-making resulting from path-dependent historical evolution. As has been shown, German reform policy remained embedded in the well-established routines of policy-making, allowing gradual adjustment but not significant change of structures. In consequence, reformers run into the trap of path-dependence of institutional change. They did not implement an appropriate design for effective constitutional policy, a policy turning federal dynamics from a self-enforcing process into a process of an intended change. In a comparative perspective, reform of German federalism demonstrates *ex negativo* that constitutional policy at a distance from normal politics is a prerequisite to make federalism reflective.

Note

1. http://senatspressestelle.bremen.de/sixcms/detail.php?id=157180 (last accessed 26/01/2016).

Disclosure statement

No potential conflict of interest was reported by the author.

References

Abromeit, H. (1992), *Der verkappte Einheitsstaat*. Opladen: Leske + Budrich.
Bednar, J. (2009), *The robust federation: principles of design*. New York, NY: Cambridge University Press.
Behnke, N. and Benz, A. (eds) (2009), *Federalism and constitutional change* ("Publius. *The Journal of Federalism*" Special Issue Vol.39, No.2). Oxford: Oxford University Press.
Benz, A. (2001), Interadministrative relations in the federal system, in K. König, H. Siedentopf (eds), *Public administration in Germany*. Baden-Baden: Nomos.
Benz, A. (2008), From joint decision traps to over-regulated federalism: Adverse effects of a successful constitutional reform, *German Politics*, Vol.17, No.4, pp.440–456.
Benz, A. (2013), Balancing rigidity and flexibility: constitutional dynamics in federal systems, *West European Politics*, Vol.36, No.4, pp.726–749.
Benz, A. (2016), *Constitutional policy in multilevel government. The art of keeping the balance*. Oxford: Oxford University Press.
Benz, A. and Broschek, J. (2013), Conclusion. Theorizing federal dynamics, in A. Benz and J. Broschek (eds), *Federal dynamics: Continuity, change, and the varieties of federalism*. Oxford: Oxford University Press.
Benz, A., et al. (2000), *Regionalisation. Theory, practice and prospects in Germany*. Stockholm: Fritzes.
Benz, A. and Knüpling, F. (2012), Federalism and constitutional change, lessons from comparison, in A. Benz and F. Knüpling (eds), *Changing federal constitutions. Lessons from international comparison*. Opladen: Barbara Budrich Publishers.
Bräuninger, T. and Debus, M. (2012), *Parteienwettbewerb in den deutschen Bundesländern*. Wiesbaden: VS Verlag.
Breske, G. (2008), *Die Landesparlamente in der Föderalismusreform: Eine Analyse der Positionsfindung und Positionsdurchsetzung*. Saarbrücken: Vdm Verlag Dr. Müller.

CDU-CSU. (2013), *Vereinbarung über die Fortführung der Fraktionsgemeinschaft zwischen CDU und CSU für die 18. Wahlperiode des Deutschen Bundestages*. Available at https://www.cducsu.de/themen/innen-recht-sport-und-ehrenamt/fortfuehrung-der-fraktionsgemeinschaft (accessed 9 January 2016).

Coalition Treaty. (2013), *Deutschlands Zukunft gestalten*. Koalitionsvertrag zwischen CDU, CSU und SPD 18. Legislaturperiode. Available at http://www.bundesregierung.de/Content/DE/_Anlagen/2013/2013-12-17-koalitionsvertrag.pdf?__blob=publicationFile&v=2 (accessed 15 September 2015).

Detterbeck, K. (2011), Party careers in federal systems. Vertical linkages within Austrian, German, Canadian and Australian parties, *Regional and Federal Studies*, Vol.21, No.2, pp.245–270.

Detterbeck, K. and Renzsch, W. (2003), Multi-level electoral competition: the German case, *European Urban and Regional Studies*, Vol.10, No.3, pp.257–269.

Dose, N. and Reus, I. (forthcoming), The effect of reformed legislative competences on Länder policymaking: Determinants of fragmentation and uniformity, *Regional and Federal Studies*, Vol.26, No.4.

Dyson, K. (1980), *The state tradition in Western Europe*. Oxford: Martin Robertson.

Filippov, M., et al. (2004), *Designing federalism: A theory of self-sustainable federal institutions*. New York, NY: Cambridge University Press.

Förster, C. and Klenk, J. (2012), Innovationskraft trotz Vetospieler: Bildungspolitische Reformen im deutschen Föderalismus, *WSI-Mitteilungen* No.6, pp.412–418.

Freiburghaus, D. (2012), Swiss federalism, fiscal equalisation reform and the reallocation of tasks, in A. Benz and F. Knüpling (eds), *Changing federal constitutions. Lessons from international comparison*. Opladen: Barbara Budrich Publishers.

Fukuyama, F. (2011), *The origins of political order*. New York, NY: Farrar, Straus and Giroux.

Geißler, et al. (eds) (2015), *Das Teilen beherrschen. Analysen zur Reform des Finanzausgleichs 2019*. Baden-Baden: Nomos.

Green, A. (2001), *Fatherlands. State-Building and nationhood in nineteenth-century Germany*. Cambridge: Cambridge University Press.

Grotz, F. and Poier, K. (2012), Between joint project, institutional bargaining and symbolic politics: initiatives for federalism reform in Germany, Austria and Switzerland. *Zeitschrift für Vergleichende Politikwissenschaft*, Vol.6, No.1, pp.77–101.

Heinz, D. (2016), Haushaltspolitik, in A. Benz, J. Detemple and D. Heinz (eds), *Varianten und Dynamiken der Politikverflechtung*. Baden-Baden: Nomos.

Herrigel, G. (1996), *Industrial constructions: The sources of German industrial power*. Cambridge: Cambridge University Press.

Hirschman, A.O. (1970), *Exit, voice and loyalty. Responses to decline in firms, organizations, and states*. Cambridge, MA: Harvard University Press.

Katzenstein, P.J. (1987), *Policy and politics in West Germany: the growth of a semi-sovereign state*. Philadelphia: Temple University Press.

Keating, M. (1998), *The new regionalism in Western Europe. Territorial restructuring and political change*. Northampton: Edward Elgar.

Korioth, S. (2016), A path to balanced budgets of bund and länder? The new shape of the 'Debt Brake' and the 'Stability Council', *Regional & Federal Studies*. doi:10.1080/13597566.2016.1214130.

Kropp, S. and Behnke, N. (forthcoming), Marble cake dreaming of layer cake - the merits and pitfalls of disentanglement in German federalism reform, *Regional and Federal Studies*, Vol.26, No.4.

Laski, H. (2005 [1939]), The obsolence of federalism, in D. Karmis and N. Wayne (eds), *Theories of federalism. A Reader.* New York, NY: Palgrave Macmillan.

Lehmbruch, G. (1976), *Parteienwettbewerb im Bundesstaat.* (1st ed.). Stuttgart: Kohlhammer.

Lehmbruch, G. (2000), *Parteienwettbewerb im Bundesstaat. Regelsysteme und Spannungslagen im Politischen System der Bundesrepublik Deutschland.* (3rd ed.). Wiesbaden: Westdeutschre Verlag.

Lehmbruch, G. (2002), Der unitarische Bundesstaat in Deutschland: Pfadabhängigkeit und Wandel, in A. Benz and G. Lehmbruch (eds), *Föderalismus. Analysen in entwicklungsgeschichtlicher und vergleichender Perspektive.* Wiesbaden: Westdeutscher Verlag.

Lehmbruch, G. (2015), Der Entwicklungspfad des deutschen Bundesstaats: Weichenstellungen und Krisen, in G. Ambrosius, C. Heinrich-Franke and C. Neutsch (eds), *Föderale Systeme: Kaiserreich – Donaumonarchie – Europäische Union.* Baden-Baden: Nomos.

Mannewitz, T. (2015), *Politische Kultur und demokratischer Verfassungsstaat. Ein subnationaler Vergleich zwei Jahrzehnte nach der deutschen Wiedervereinigung.* Baden-Baden: Nomos.

Manow, P. (2005), Germany: cooperative federalism and the overgrazing of the fiscal commons, in H. Obinger, S. Leibfried and F.G. Castles (eds), *Federalism and welfare State. New world and European experiences.* Cambridge: Cambridge University Press.

Mierzejewski, A. (2015), Paradigm shift: the reform of the German Public Pension System in 2001, *Journal of Policy History*, Vol.27, No.4, pp.695–721.

Moore, C., et al. (eds) (2008), *German Federalism in Transition?* (Special issue of *German Politics* Vol.17, No.4). London: Routledge.

Münch, U. (1997), *Sozialpolitik und Föderalismus: Zur Dynamik der Aufgabenverteilung im sozialen Bundesstaat.* Opladen: Leske + Budrich.

Nipperdey, T. (1986), Der Föderalismus in der deutschen Geschichte, in T. Nipperdey (ed), *Nachdenken über die deutsche Geschichte.* München: Beck.

Oeter, S. (1998), *Integration und Subsidiarität im deutschen Bundesstaatsrecht.* Tübingen: Mohr Siebeck.

Ostrom, E. (2005), *Understanding institutional diversity.* Princeton, NJ: Princeton University Press.

Ritter, G.A. (2005), *Föderalismus und Parlamentarismus in Deutschland in Geschichte und Gegenwart.* München: Beck.

Sattler, A. (2012), *Deliberativer Föderalismus: Analyse der Beratungen zur Modernisierung der Bund-Länder-Finanzbeziehungen.* Baden-Baden: Nomos.

Scharpf, F.W. (2009), *Föderalismusreform. Kein Ausweg aus der Politikverflechtungsfalle?* Frankfurt a.M.: Campus.

Schilling, H. (1989), *Höfe und Allianzen. Deutschland 1648-1763.* Berlin: Siedler Verlag.

Schmidt, G. (1999), *Geschichte des Alten Reiches. Staat und Nation in der Frühen Neuzeit 1495-1806.* München: Beck.

Seckelmann, M. (2009), "Renaissance" der Gemeinschaftsaufgaben in der Föderalismusreform II? *Die Öffentliche Verwaltung*, Vol.62, No.18, pp.747–757.

Sheehan, J. (1981), What is German history? Reflections on the role of the nation in German history and historiography, *The Journal of Modern History*, Vol.53, No.1, pp.2–23.

Stecker, C. (forthcoming), The effects of federalism reform on the legislative process in Germany, *Regional and Federal Studies*, Vol.26, No.4.

Stollberg-Rilinger, B. (2013), *Das Heilige Römische Reich Deutscher Nation. Vom Ende des Mittelalters bis 1806.* (5th ed.). München: Beck.

Sturm, R., et al. (2011), Citizenship im unitarischen Bundesstaat. *Politische Vierteljahresschrift*, Vol.52, No.2, pp.163–194.

Umbach, M. (1999), Reich, Region und Föderalismus als Denkfiguren in der Frühen und der Späten Neuzeit, in D. Langewiesche and G. Schmidt (eds), *Die Föderative Nation: Deutschlandbilder von der Reformation bis zum Ersten Weltkrieg*. München: Oldenbourg.

Urwin, D.W. (1982), Germany: from geographical expression to regional accommodation, in S. Rokkan and D.W. Urwin (eds), *The politics of territorial identity: Studies in European Regionalism*. London: Sage.

Whaley, J. (2011), *Germany and the holy roman empire (2 Volumes)*. Oxford: Oxford University Press.

Wheare, K.C. (1963), *Federal government*. (4th ed.). New York, NY: Oxford University Press.

Ziblatt, D. (2002), Recasting German federalism? The politics of fiscal decentralization in post-unification Germany, *Politische Vierteljahresschrift*, Vol.43, No.4, pp.624–652.

Zimmer, C. (2010), Politikkoordination im deutschen Bundesstaat: Wandel in den Arbeitsstrukturen?, *Zeitschrift für Parlamentsfragen*, Vol.41, No.3, pp.677–692.

How differently actors cope with demanding constitutional amendment rules: two types of constitutional politics in federal democracies

Astrid Lorenz

ABSTRACT
The article seeks to explore why a high formal hurdle for constitutional amendments (constitutional rigidity) as it is present in Germany does not automatically lead to a lower number of amendments when compared with low rigidity countries and why Germany's amendment rate is so much higher than that of some other federations. It theorizes that the frequency of interactions between stable, interdependent actors influences their willingness to compromise. Thus analyses of constitutional politics must expand the focus to longer time-horizons and to the parliamentary and federal context. Case studies on constitutional politics in two parliamentary federations, Germany and Canada, confirm that actors cope differently with the problem of multiple veto players in constitutional politics. In the long run, two distinct patterns of constitutional politics have emerged.

Introduction

The past federal reforms in Germany were laden with greater ambitions than most of the earlier amendments of its Basic Law. However, constitutional changes are not rare moments in Germany. Its constitutional amendment rate of 0.91 indicates that a new amendment to the federal Basic Law is passed nearly each year. Against the background of conventional institutionalism and veto player theory, this is more than surprising because federations are typically marked by a higher complexity of veto actors than unitary states. In Germany, amendments need the consent of a supermajority (two-thirds) of all Bundestag members and additionally a supermajority (two-thirds of the votes) in the upper house. Such high hurdles for decision-making should limit constitutional activism. Have the institutional restrictions not worked as theoretically expected?

To answer this question, the article starts with a broader look at all democracies. Similar to the German case, the federal character of a political system and a high constitutional rigidity do not prevent a high degree of constitutional activism. However, de facto two groups of federal democracies exist with either a very high or a very low amendment rate. Based on this contra-intuitive fact and the methodological problems to investigate constitutional politics by quantitative cross-country analyses alone, the article pleads for more comparative case studies and within-case comparisons as well as for expanding purely institutionalist approaches by more actor-centred elements. Both could contribute to explaining the different effect of institutional arrangements in a more comprehensive way. As a proposition, the section outlines a preliminary approach, which comprises assumptions that are agreed on by rationalist and sociological approaches.

The following part deals with constitutional politics in Canada and Germany. It legitimizes the selection of these cases by describing their similarities and differences in light of the proposed approach. Both countries are federal parliamentary democracies with a high constitutional rigidity but diverge concerning the frequency of constitutional amendments. The study then explores in the long-term perspective how actors have shaped constitutional politics in each country. It finds that the interaction style in Canada is more competitive, corresponding to institutionalist reasoning, while political actors in Germany have developed a more collaborative style of interactions using diverse practices of conflict management that have obstructed the effect of formal constitutional amendment restrictions. The final section summarizes the empirical observations in light of the general question and makes suggestions for future research.

Theorizing institutional restrictions on constitutional politics

Constitutional dynamics are a sign that federal unions and other systems are capable of adapting to changing contexts (Bednar, 2013). However, irrespectively of a growing interest in constitutional politics, there is still a lack of empirical knowledge about causes and patterns of constitutional amendments. Moreover, the findings of empirical studies are often puzzling and contradict conventional institutionalist expectations.

This can be best demonstrated for the possible effect of the federal character of a system on constitutional politics. Conventional institutionalist wisdom suggests that the typically higher diversity of interests and veto players in federations (as compared to unitary states) prevents frequent constitutional amendments because it lowers the prospect of reaching broad compromises usually necessary for adopting amendments. Interestingly, the mean constitutional amendment rate of federations was nearly twice as high as in unitary states during the time period of 1945–2005 (Figure 1). At the same time, there is a high within-group variation of federal democracies.

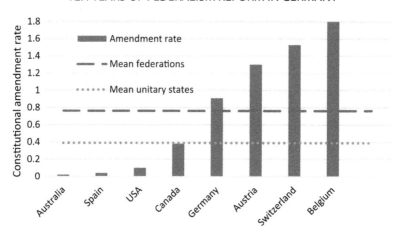

Figure 1. Constitutional amendment rates in federal democracies, 1945–2000.

Notes: Based on own calculations. The individual time spans for each country vary because of the selection rule outlined in Lorenz (2005). The data for Belgium refer to the period from May 1993 (when it became federal) to 2005.

More precisely, there is one group of federations with very rare constitutional amendments and another with frequent amendments.

Obviously, constitutional politics work differently in federations. While the reform-blocking effect of more complex and diverse institutional arrangements seems to be present in some countries, it is absent in those responsible for the high mean amendment rate of federations.

A similar empirical puzzle was observed for the effects of constitutional rigidity. The pro-intuitive assumption is that higher formal majority requirements to pass constitutional amendments dampen the frequency of getting constitutional amendment proposals adopted (Lutz, 1994; Elster, 2000: 102). However, in empirical tests using different rigidity measures, the constitutional rigidity failed to explain the variation of amendments rates (Ferejohn, 1997; Lorenz, 2005; Closa, 2012; Ginsburg and Melton, 2014).

For the particular group of federations, there is also no consistent picture. For the time period 1945–2005, the highest amendment rate of federations was present in Austria (1.3) with its comparably low constitutional rigidity (3 according to the Lorenz index) and the lowest amendment rate (0.1) was recorded in the USA which has the second highest rigidity (9.0). In Belgium, however, the highest constitutional rigidity of all federal democracies (9.5) went along with the highest amendments rate (1.82). In Switzerland, the amendment rate remained nearly the same (1.53–1.4) although the constitutional rigidity decreased significantly from 4.0 to 7.0 after a constitutional revision in 2000. The other cases rank between these observations.

While any variable which failed to explain an overall empirical pattern still might be important to explain particular cases or situations, depending on the context, we face problems investigating this by quantitative cross-country comparisons. Federation is an analytical category "founded upon the notion of a liberal democratic constitutional state" (Burgess 2006, 98) and as we know, the logic of political action differs significantly in democracies and non-democratic systems. If we take that seriously, we must focus our analyses of constitutional politics on *democratic* federations in order to produce meaningful results.[1] But their number is small, as we see in Figure 1, and at the same time, their institutional design and context conditions are more heterogeneous than that of unitary states. For Spain it is even contested whether it is federal or not.

Given the puzzling empirical findings of quantitative analyses of constitutional politics in (federal) democracies and their methodological problems, it seems essential to draw two conclusions that form the starting point of the following study. First, we must probably expand the explanatory focus from a narrow institutionalist perspective to more actor-centred neo-institutionalist approaches to understand how veto players actually cope with constitutional texts and institutional restrictions. Second, we must also use comparative case studies and within-case comparisons as methodological tools for a more complex theory-building. Both is done in the present paper with the aim of understanding how constitutional politics differ in those federal democracies which adopt many constitutional amendments irrespectively of their high complexity of actors and in those which are marked by a low amendment rate.

The analytical approach is driven by the idea that we should not reject the logic of theorizing institutional restrictions completely but instead try to include just one additional aspect: How often do constitutional veto players meet in situations where they need the other veto players' consent? Such an expanded analysis must cover the history of interactions in constitutional politics but also day-to-day federal practices. Where actors are experienced in cooperating across party lines and levels of government, it should not be so difficult and costly for them to also reach constitutional agreements even when these require higher majorities. Thus the general parliamentary and federal framework might be more important for explaining constitutional amendments rates than the particular constraints as imposed by constitutional amendment procedures.

This approach can fruitfully combine assumptions made by institutionalist, sociological and rationalist theories, as will be sketched out in the following.

In general, we can expect that actors in democracies accept constitutional arrangements as rules of the game—be it because any deviation causes costs and because complementary safeguards of the constitution prevent violations of the rules (North, 1990; Filippov et al., 2004; Bednar, 2013), be it because actors are socialized by the system (March and Olsen, 1989: 39ff.). Sociologist strands of theory assume that even when constitutional arrangements were introduced instrumentally to realize certain political goals, they can become part of the actors' complex of values. Thus the logic of a constitution affects habits, attitudes and acceptances (Livingston, 1952: 91–92). Rationalist approaches also acknowledge that a web of rather persistent "interpretative norms, canons, and practices" emerges around the constitution (Ferejohn et al., 2001: 10). Accordingly, constitutional settings, for example, the federal framework, should affect actors' perceptions and strategic behaviour, as well as the pattern of their interactions (Scharpf, 1997; Colino, 2010).

However, actors are not merely norm addressees. They probably seek for strategies to reach their goals within the general parliamentary and federal arrangement, which always leaves room for various possibilities to act and to decide (Lehmbruch, 2000: 14, 17). They can also use strategies to circumvent institutional restrictions as long as this does not undermine the functioning of the whole institutional system and they can try to alter the constitution. In this sense, constitutional arrangements are in the meantime causal factors for structuring human behaviour and the outcome of the reflected actions of purposeful and socialized actors. In the rationalist version of this idea, actors "respond to a set of institutions that are themselves intended to be incentive-compatible" (Filippov et al., 2004: 38).

What happens when the frequency of interactions increases in which veto players need the others' consent? Scholars of different strands of research found arguments why this constellation makes cooperation more probable. Game theoretical experiments have shown that even for purposeful actors, a combination of generosity and reciprocity may produce better long-term gains when the (few) interaction partners are stable (Axelrod, 1984). It was shown that routines of interaction decrease transaction costs (North, 1990). Therefore, policy proposals must provide lower gains to become profitable when the interaction partners are stable. Repeated interactions allow also for tit-for-tat games, log rolls and sequential conflict resolution to accommodate others' interests. Even for actors who always intentionally use only those tools to solve problems, which they have already used successfully in the past for saving costs (Bednar, 2013), a higher frequency of joint decision-making of same actors should increase the prospect of agreement.

Sociologists highlight that among actors who repeatedly make joint decisions, patterns of reciprocity, trust, maybe a sense of community but surely internal practices of conflict-management emerge. More frequent discussions improve the chance that actors develop common perceptions of issues, norms and problems which also facilitate joint decision-making. The appropriateness of interaction practices may not be questioned (March and Olsen, 1989: 39ff.). Ginsburg and Melton (2014: 12) suppose that national collectives of actors share a specific "set of attitudes about the desirability of amendment, independent of the substantive issue under consideration and the degree of pressure for change" which they call "amendment culture". Their operationalization of amendment culture as a country's previous constitution's amendment rate (Ginsburg and Melton, 2014: 19) ignores attitudes and focuses alone on (previous) action, but the approach corresponds to the key argument above about repeated joint decisions.

In their quantitative analysis of constitutional amendment rates, Ginsburg and Melton (2014: 22) found that out of a number of institutionalist and other variables, the only consistently significant predictor was the previous constitution's amendment rate. But other features of the broader federal and parliamentary context can also lead to more or less routines of joint decision-making. Such practices of cooperation or conflict might produce "behavioural spill-overs" to constitutional politics (cf. Bednar, 2013: 291; Bednar et al., 2012).

In all federations, the federal level and the federal units share some competences and are marked by interdependencies which can foster cooperation routines. However, some countries tend more to the dual federation type (USA, Australia, Canada), others to a functional separation of powers (Germany, Austria, Switzerland and Spain; Thorlakson, 2009: 165). The provinces' capacity to veto legislation in the federal government's area of jurisdiction also varies. Where the provinces participate in legislation outside their exclusive jurisdiction, a permanent risk of delays and stalemate can cause a need to develop negotiation routines. Such routines might be absent or weaker in federations where the federal government's and the provincial legislation are made by completely different actors.

When we talk about constitutional politics in federations, then parties play a key role (Burgess, 2006: 150). Governments interpret through their parties' lenses, what the interests of the federation or of their province are. Party structures are able to link the various policy-making levels when they umbrella different positions (Riker, 1964; Lehmbruch, 2000; Filippov et al., 2004; Erk and Swenden, 2010: 10). The other way round, asymmetric and vertically disintegrated party systems can obstruct cooperation across levels of government (Riker, 1964; Elazar, 1987: 178–179; Filippov et al., 2004). Elazar mentioned Canada as an example because of the propensity of regional parties and the internal division of federal parties along provincial lines. In such systems, it is probably more complicated and costly to develop cooperation routines among decision-makers across the levels and provinces.

The type of parliamentarism can also foster or hamper cooperation. In systems where the government typically cannot rely on an own party majority in parliament, it must establish coalitions or other forms of cross-party cooperation to realize own legislative majorities. That trains the routines to make concessions and facilitates the emergence of trust. Where both is absent, collaboration must probably be legitimized by clear gains from the concrete project because it is unsure when the next collaboration will take place. Lijphart has shown that the concentration (or fragmentation) of executive power correlates strongly with the number of parliamentary parties, the executive dominance, executive-interest groups relations and electoral rules. According to his study, these and other inter-correlations produce patterns of systematically higher (consensus democracies) or lower (majoritarian democracies) willingness to cooperate across party lines.

In sum, the presented approach rests on the idea that actors are embedded in the incentive structure of their general federal and parliamentary environment and routines as established by previous interactions (cf. Rodden, 2004: 491). Practices of coalition-building, a symmetry of actors in federal government's ordinary legislation and federal constitutional politics or other factors can foster the willingness to cooperate irrespective of the institutional restrictions and of the expected policy gains. Under such conditions narrow institutionalist models and veto player theory (Tsebelis, 2000) might lose their explanatory power.

Case studies: Canada and Germany

As it was already said, the few number of federal democracies and their high diversity curtail the applicability of quantitative cross-country analyses. Therefore, case studies are used to get a deeper impression of how the mentioned factors are interconnected. Canada and Germany are good cases for such a comparison because they display similarities in institutional design (e.g. democracy, parliamentary systems, rather high constitutional rigidity) and context (e.g. size, longer federal roots) but are dissimilar concerning their constitutional politics. Germany has a high constitutional amendment rate and Canada a low one. Yet in both cases, we find a number of constitutional amendment bills, which decreases the risk of misinterpretations.

Both Germany and Canada belong to the democracies with the highest formal restrictions for constitutional amendments. Germany ranks at place 29 (with a rigidity value of 6), Canada at place 31.5 (with a value of 7) when 39 democracies are compared (Lorenz, 2005). Moreover, in both countries the provinces can veto all (Germany) or most (Canada) constitutional amendments in that a certain share of them must consent in the upper federal chamber (Germany) or individually (Canada). Canada is also an interesting case because its constitution entrenched multiple routes of constitutional amendment with different participants and thus varying degrees of symmetry between federal government's ordinary law-making and federal constitutional politics.

The federal structure of both countries includes spheres of autonomous provincial jurisdiction, for example, concerning education, a large number of federal jurisdiction and also areas with shared jurisdiction. In both Canada and Germany, a strong "executive federalism" is present for coordinating legislative and administrative matters. Federal–provincial relations have evolved rather similarly with regular formal meetings between federal and provincial ministers and their respective civil servants (Burgess, 2006: 138).

However, the provincial veto rights in ordinary federal legislation outside the exclusive spheres of provincial jurisdiction diverge.

Both countries are parliamentary systems in which parties are key organizations for recruiting members of the executive and mobilizing support for governmental legislative projects. But Canada has a much lower score than Germany at Lijphart's executive-party dimension of democracy indicating, *inter alia*, a higher concentration of executive power and higher executive dominance (Lijphart, 2012). The more unitary, centralized government resulting from simple majoritarian procedures is typical for Westminster systems with a clear majority party. In Germany, coalition governments dominate at the federal as well as the provincial level.

Are these differences relevant for conflict management in constitutional politics? The following case studies start with describing each model of parliamentary democracy and law-making, focusing on the federal level of government. After that, the main characteristics of federal constitutional politics are analysed in long-term perspective. This analysis covers the subjects that were tabled to be re-regulated in the constitution, their initiators, the interaction style and success rates. The study is based on existing scholarly literature about Canadian and German constitutional politics but it also includes own analyses of primary sources.

A mix of competitive and collaborative constitutional politics in Canada

In Canada, the provincial governing majorities have traditionally a low veto capacity in legislation outside the domain of exclusive provincial jurisdiction. In the area of federal government's jurisdiction, the federal House of Commons and the Senate are key veto players. The federal governments regularly interact with the provincial executives for legal and administrative coordination and for avoiding or resolving struggles on competences before courts, especially in areas of shared competences, but they are not formally obliged to do so. In contrast, federal constitutional amendments in many areas must be approved not only by the federal parliament but also by seven provinces representing at least half of Canada's population, in specific cases even by all ten provinces.

The Canadian houses of parliament enjoy nearly the same formal rights to adopt or veto federal ordinary legislation. However, the Senate is less politicized than the lower chamber, partly because of its precarious and publicly contested legitimation. Each province and territory shares a certain—not really representative—number of seats. The members are appointed after nomination by the Canadian prime minister(s) who traditionally nominates fellow party members. The executive is linked to the upper chamber by the Leader of the Government in the Senate and the most senators are also members of their party's caucus, but they are not dependent on anyone's will after appointment until they retire at the age of 75. Traditionally the Senate abstains from vetoing legislative acts.

In the federal lower chamber, the governing party tends to enjoy a larger majority than its German counterpart because of the diverging electoral system. Party discipline is rather strong. There are regional parties in the House of Commons but they are weak. Coalitions have not yet been formed at the federal level. Therefore, no or limited obligations to compromise with other parties exist in the federal parliament's ordinary legislation.

When the first amendments of the Canadian federal constitutional foundation took place, the Ottawa governments did not ask the provinces for their consent. But at the beginning of the twentieth century, these insisted on own rights. Disputes began to rank around their status and veto rights in the amending procedure which had not been formalized yet. They gave their consent to a modification of subsidies paid to them (Russell, 2010: 23) but in the meantime insisted on maximum positions in the dispute around the amending formula. This even prevented Canada from getting full sovereignty from Britain. Since 1931, Canada has been independent regarding ordinary legislation but London remained to have the final say in several issues, for example, constitutional amendments. In this situation, the federal government assigned itself the formal right to alter some constitutional documents (Russell, 2004).

By the 1960s the First Ministers' Conference became the central process of managing Canadian federalism. However, regular constitutional conflicts resurfaced around the federal–provincial relationship, the rights of all or particular provinces or the Senate which could not be solved. The governments were not willing to make concessions and started to "explore the environment for additional resources, either to strengthen their bargaining power within executive federalism or to bypass it altogether" (Cairns, 1985: 112). The rare constitutional amendments that were adopted until 1982 with the provinces' consent referred to the allocation of jurisdiction over unemployment insurance and old-age pensions between the federal and provincial level, to the provision of a compulsory retirement age for judges appointed by the federal government to the provincial superior courts, to the addition of new provinces or to other rather technical issues (Russell, 2010: 23).

The federal governments attempted several times to solve the constitutional conflicts in rounds of "mega-constitutional politics" (Russell, 2004; 2010). In these rounds, Quebec often formulated maximum positions, but the other provinces' governments also presented quite far-reaching deviating positions. That also led to conflicts between provincial executives and federal governments that were composed by the same parties. Some provincial governments put strong pressure on MPs of their own party elected in the respective province to oppose proposals made by their federal government

(Cairns, 1985). Although the provincial premiers were very powerful within the provincial framework and directed all legislating in the province (Baier, 2012: 182), they also continued to activate additional veto players that were not entrenched in the constitution to put pressure on the federal government.

Some agreements were reached for getting full sovereignty by the way of "patriating" the constitution in 1982. *Inter alia*, a Charter of Rights and Freedoms and a pattern of four amendment procedures were established: Amendments in relation to the executive government of Canada or the Senate and House of Commons can be adopted by the federal parliament, amendments that affect the matters of one or some province(s) need the additional consent of that province(s). Other amendments require the additional assent of either seven provinces representing at least 50% of the Canadian population or—in only five matters—of all provinces. The last mentioned procedures gave the provinces an explicit veto right which they fought for long.

However, constitutional negotiations went on because many problems still remained unresolved and because Quebec's parliament rejected the patriation package. In 1987, after long negotiations among the executives, the Meech Lake Accord was agreed on by the First ministers. It comprised several constitutional amendments concerning, *inter alia*, the competence allocation and the Senate. We see here that with repeated negotiations among stable, interdependent partners, agreements became possible. However, the Accord failed to be implemented because it later did not get unanimous assent by the provinces. That confirms the theoretical assumptions concerning an expansion of veto players.

Afterwards, the federal government continued to negotiate these issues with the provincial governments and even more societal participants, especially aboriginal groups. The topics became much broader with the allocation of federal and provincial competences, the Senate, the House of Commons, the recruitment of Supreme Court judges, the establishment of social rights and others. The agreements included amendments of nearly all parts of the constitution and were formalized in the Charlottetown Accord. However, this accord was then put to a first countrywide (consultative) referendum on constitutional matters. A high share of the electorate used this exceptional chance to articulate its general will, thus "acting as a constitutionally sovereign people" (Russell, 2004: 190). Many voters in Quebec thought that the amendments "gave Quebec too little, whereas the vote against it in the rest of Canada was led by those who thought it gave Quebec too much" (Russell, 2010: 35). The referendum was defeated in most provinces and this marked the end of mega-constitutional politics.

Analyses of constitutional politics in Canada mention various reasons for the breakdown of constitutional compromises, among them situational, institutional and more structural. It is often mentioned that Quebec opposed virtually all final compromises because of its particular understanding of Canada as a binational political society formed by itself and the rest of Canada. That implied an explicit veto right for Quebec in federal constitutional politics (Burgess, 2006, 114). Canadian governments' strategy to protect individual citizen rights and to recognize aboriginal rights and self-government was seen as an anglophone policy designed to reduce Quebec's legitimate claims to be a founding national partner of the Canadian federation to a "merely ethnic phenomenon" (Burgess, 2006: 121–122). Economic and financial disparities, the party composition of federal and provincial governments and other factors also influenced Canadian constitutional politics.

However, constitutional politics in all countries are influenced by complex factors and plural interests. The more relevant factor seems that the Canadian veto players perceived constitutional politics as an extraordinary field of federal jurisdiction where the provinces and later the people finally succeeded to have a direct say and the federal government is only a "primus inter pares" (cf. Baier, 2012). Not only Quebec was eager to save and use this right to enforce own interests, *inter alia*, by establishing additional veto actors that were supposed to support them (Cairns, 1985).

Of the 36 Constitution Act amendment bills which were introduced in the Canadian parliament from 1994 to 2015,[2] only those were adopted that required an agreement among the House of Commons and the Senate, or which required the additional consent of a single province. None had to be adopted by other provinces as well. During these 22 years, Conservative federal governments (2006 until 2015) were much more active than governments led by other parties. Half of the 10 federal government amendment bills referred to the election of Senators as well as to their tenure and retirement age. An almost identical share of bills referred to the number of members of the House of Commons and the representation of the provinces therein as well as to the readjustment of electoral boundaries. The liberal government introduced only one bill aimed at assigning the newly created territory of Nunavut mandates in the House of Commons and in the Senate.

Oppositional constitutional amendment proposals referred mostly to majority requirements for adopting certain bills and amending clauses in the bill of rights, to the number of members of the House, the representation of the provinces therein, the legislative period as well as budget and spending limit. Additionally, there were proposals regarding the protection of property rights. Oppositional private member bills introduced in the Senate all referred to Senate issues: the modes of electing its Speaker and Deputy Speaker, the voting procedure in the Senate and the provision that candidates to the Senate must own certain property and land. The rare initiatives that were started by single provinces referred mostly to schooling in that province.

As it is typical for ordinary law-making in the Canadian federal parliament, government bills had a much higher success rate. This resulted in biased constitutional amendments dealing mainly with single province matters and state-organizational issues at the federal level but not or seldom with rights or with the allocation of federal–provincial competences. The prevalence of state-organizational issues had already been noticeable for the extensive Canadian constitutional reform attempts that took place between 1985 and 1992.

In 1996, the Canadian government tried to make the tableau of negotiation partners in constitutional politics clearer. The federal parliament then adopted an Act respecting Constitutional amendments which provides that a bill for a constitutional amendment which later requires the assent of seven provinces should obtain the consent of certain provinces (including Quebec) and other provinces representing the majority of two regions' population before it is tabled in Parliament. This guarantee, engineered as a reaction to a narrowly defeated secession referendum in Quebec, can facilitate the emergence of trust and iterative negotiation rounds among those who are explicitly stated. However, establishing explicit veto rights for some provinces risks neutralizing others' potential veto power. Thus it also reduces trust among those provinces which are not explicitly stated. Moreover, the extraordinary pattern of federal constitutional politics remains, perpetuating "instability and unpredictability" as main characteristics (Cairns, 1985: 134) of Canadian federal constitutional politics.

Because of the competitive interaction style of at least some participants in Canadian constitutional politics, many crucial problems are still politically unresolved, including the status of Quebec, the role of the Senate or regional representation at the federal level (Erk and Swenden, 2010: 4). Moreover, practices of conflict resolution below the constitutional level have become "the principal instruments for reforming the Canadian federation" (Lazar and McLean, 2000: 148). The Canadian governments made agreements with the provinces and territories, for example, in 1999 a Social Union Framework Agreement, and established new practices intended to compel their successors to comply. That includes, for example, the appointment of Senators. The other key player for changing the constitution without amending the constitutional documents was the Supreme Court which identified, *inter alia*, unwritten constitutional principles concerning the right of provinces to secede unilaterally and concerning the proper constitutional amendment procedure for Senate reforms (Albert, 2015).

Collaborative constitutional politics in Germany

Unlike Canada, the restrictions for federal ordinary legislation and constitutional politics in Germany are rather symmetric. The participants clearly overlap. According to the federal constitution, it is the explicit purpose of the German Bundesrat to represent the provinces' interests in federal lawmaking. In many legislative matters which fall outside the areas of exclusive provincial jurisdiction, the Bundestag is nevertheless obliged to obtain an agreement with the provinces because the Bundesrat can veto them. In other areas of federal legislation, the Bundesrat can veto but may be overridden by the Bundestag. Here, vetoes that were passed by an ordinary majority of the provincial votes can be overridden by a majority of all Bundestag members and vetoes that were passed by two-thirds of the provincial votes can be rejected by a two-thirds majority in the Bundestag representing at least the majority of the Bundestag members. Constitutional amendments need, as it was already mentioned, a support by two-thirds of the Bundestag members and two-thirds of the Bundesrat votes.

The typical format of the executive in Germany is a coalition. Therefore, cross-party compromises are a prerequisite for governance and law-making. Complex practices of intra-coalition conflict management via rules, coordination, bargaining and trust-building measures have emerged which also include the coalition factions in parliament. This is also true for the Länder. Since the provinces are obliged to cast unified votes in the Bundesrat, Land parties negotiate before coalition-building how the executive will behave in the Bundesrat.

The provinces' number of votes in the German Bundesrat is more closely based on their size of population than in the Canadian Senate. The chamber is composed by representatives of the provinces' executives whose decision-making is fully dependent on their government's party composition, declared will and period of office. Thus elected provincial majorities have a direct say on federal ordinary and constitutional legislation and their behaviour is more coordinated within the parties than that of the non-elected[3] Canadian senators. The German federal and provincial party organizations have rather similar positions in many policy fields. This is relevant since diverging party majorities in the chambers of parliament have become a frequent constellation. Often political demands of the Bundestag opposition are supported by provincial executives in the Bundesrat which are composed by the same party.

In face of the often diverging majorities in Bundestag and Bundesrat and the latter's right to veto a high share of federal legislation, the federal governments must frequently negotiate with opposing provincial executives prior to formal decision-making in the Bundesrat. Indirectly, they often also negotiate with parts of the Bundestag opposition when its political demands are supported by province executives in the Bundesrat. Moreover, they are informally linked with those provinces whose executives are composed by the same parties to improve the ground for own legislative projects. Over the course of time, a permanent stable negotiation 'infrastructure' has emerged.

The pattern of federal constitutional politics in Germany is very similar to what was described for ordinary legislation. Often the actors actually do not clearly differentiate between ordinary and constitutional legislation. Many amendment proposals appear as minor side-elements of bills focusing in their main part on regular policy measures. This especially refers to bills which are tabled by the government side. The packages are justified by the argument that the subjects are narrowly interconnected and therefore must be discussed together. In such cases, constitutional amendments are dealt with as merely 'technical' preconditions for realizing policy goals. Many other amendments were just devoted to "tidying up political administrative processes in order to facilitate policy-making and co-ordination" (Banting and Simeon, 1985: 12). As a result, constitutional amendment proposals are, in many cases, not top-level issues with core elements negotiated by the prime minister (as in Canada) or high-ranking officials. Instead they are often perceived as pieces of ordinary legislation which are mainly (albeit not exclusively) discussed by political experts without public interest.

This pattern is also strengthened by the sheer number of constitutional amendment proposals and their topics. From 1949 until 2015, 253 bills to amend the federal constitution were tabled in Germany.[4] They were introduced by federal governments, by government factions, by opposition parties, by inter-factional groups and by the Bundesrat. That the government factions (unlike Canada) introduce own bills is a tradition in the Bundestag where nevertheless all such bills are coordinated with the executive and within the coalition.

German government proposals for constitutional amendments mostly referred to taxes, judiciary, legislation and finance. There was some variation caused by party programmes of the governmental parties setting different priorities. The subjects of other government bills overlapped with bills of government parties in parliament. They were related to international topics, public administration staff, privatization, or territorial issues. For other issues of constitutional amendment bills, we observe an overlapping interest of all parliamentary factions, that is, no government–opposition split. These issues were either related to the parliament's competencies (such as legislative procedure, petitions or election of the federal president), or society-related topics (such as anti-discrimination measures, direct democracy or education), or they referred to basic rights and duties (e.g. property rights, military service or right of asylum). Rights and society-related topics (e.g. social rights, data protection, *in vitro* fertilization, abortion, environmental and animal protection) were mainly the domain of amendment proposals made by the opposition. Amendment initiatives of the upper federal chamber referred mainly to the federal legislative competences and procedure, domestic security (which affects states' competencies), federal issues and provincial judiciary.

As in the Canadian case, the German actors' constitutional interests overlapped in some points, but unlike Canada, these issues were the distribution of competences in federal legislation, finance and budget as well as taxes. All the mentioned types of actors (governments, governmental and opposition parties, Bundesrat) made proposals referring to these issues. Although they differed concerning the proposed policies, it was only possible to find agreements for topics that were interesting for many actors. Accordingly, inter-factional initiatives, that typically fix compromises that were reached among key players, referred to finance, legislative procedure and competencies (see also Lorenz, 2007). Here, the federal government was willing to make concessions to the Länder and to the opposition to have constitutional amendments adopted. As a matter of routine, proposals that were solely in the interest of the opposition were not adopted.

Just as expected, the cooperative federalism pattern strongly influenced constitutional politics. It made it possible that the number of constitutional amendments per year was higher with an increased share of 'oppositional' Land votes in the Bundesrat. From 1958 to 1961 and in the 1990s, for instance, many amendments were passed although the party constellation in the Bundesrat was very uncomfortable from the federal government's perspective. Of all constitutional amendment bills that were introduced by the federal government side and which were not adopted, only two failed to be passed by an uncooperative Bundesrat (1951 and 1995). In the meantime, we observe a certain self-restraint on the federal governments' side. They did not use comfortable party majorities in the Bundesrat (for instance in the 1980s) for pushing through more constitutional amendments (Lorenz, 2007).

The ability to build grand federal coalitions (unlike in Canada) was also a driver of constitutional change because it made it easier to mobilize sufficiently large majorities in the Bundestag and Bundesrat. In the periods of such grand coalitions (1966–69, 2005–09, since 2013), the number of constitutional amendments per year was 2.6 times higher than in the rest of the time (1.9 compared to 0.7). However, this was mainly due to the 12 amendments passed under the first grand coalition from 1966 to 1969. Under the later grand coalitions, 1.5 (2005–09) and 0.3 amendments (in the actual legislative period) were adopted per year. This is not very different from other coalitions. In general, coalitions are a good precondition to compromise across levels because the federal minor coalition party can bridge differences to third parties with which it coalesces at the Länder level.

In many cases, the topics of the constitutional amendments have been discussed over decades and on the basis of many competing constitutional amendment bills introduced by the parties. Those collective actors who had the final say on the amendments were all included in the negotiations in rather stable constellation. Over the course of time, they often arrived at common general perceptions across the government–opposition line and across Länder and levels. We can observe this, for example, for the question how federal–provincial relations should be designed and which problems and advantages arise from alternative arrangements. Even when the preferences changed, they changed into the same direction across parties and Länder, thus making the federal reforms of the last decade possible.

Besides this, belonging to the same coalition or the prospect of meeting repeatedly again in future federal law-making, although in varying majority constellations, made the actors think that there is no exit option. (The Canadian case demonstrates that this is a misperception because even with 'no'-votes, the federation will somehow survive.) They calculate gains not on the basis of a certain bill only but on the basis of overall gains. Moreover, executives fear stalemate. That facilitated the options for cross-policy package deals, side payments and tit for tat (Benz, 2003). Negotiations under such conditions can also fail, as the talks prior to the federal reforms in Germany indicate (Scharpf, 2005), but the interaction style is more collaborative than that of some Canadian veto players.

As in Canada, society- and basic rights-related proposals for constitutional amendments have mostly been rejected. That is not only caused by the fact that such bills were mainly introduced by the Bundestag opposition. Proposals relating to rights tend to produce deeper conflicts among the parties inside coalitions and parliament. Only when exogenous pressure was argued to be present or as a part of package deals, such amendments got the support by the opposition.[5] Thus, spill-overs from cooperation routines in state-organizational issues to the field of basic rights took place, but rather rarely. However, the frequency of such spill-overs and thus, the extent of overall issues set on the federal constitutional agenda, was higher in Germany than in Canada.

The recent German federal reforms fit perfectly into that pattern (Moore and Jacoby, 2010). Although the reforms were partly negotiated in an unusual forum, the federal reform commission, the participants were mostly the same that continuously meet in day-to-day law-making by the Bundestag and Bundesrat. The actors tried out some new modes of jurisdiction but they did not give up the right to block unwanted decisions and followed the logics of interaction that had generated even those problems that shall be abolished by reform (Scharpf, 2009: 118 ff.). It is also typical that the reforms were rather quickly followed by demands for re-adjustments and further amendments. The constitution is not perceived as a document that should not be touched and it is easier to correct errors or to react to unintended effects, which become visible with practical experience.

Implicit constitutional change also takes place in Germany. As in Canada, it is especially relevant in issues where political actors are not able to solve problems with political agreements. Courts decided on the right to transfer state competences to the European Union, established a right to 'informational self-determination', the right of women to join the armed forces and others. However, there are two differences between Canada and Germany. First, in Germany more judgments that were relevant in constitutional terms later became somehow explicit in the text of the constitution by the way of formal constitutional amendment because the political actors nuanced or clarified the norms as interpreted by the judges. Second, explicit constitutional amendments are the prevalent channel of constitutional change (Hoennige et al., 2011).

Conclusion and outlook

Although a high constitutional rigidity is often hypothesized to dampen constitutional amendment activism, several federations with a high rigidity, among them Germany, frequently adopt constitutional amendments. Others, like Canada, do not. Solving this puzzle was the aim of the article. Its main theoretical idea was that the frequency of interactions, in which actors depend on other's consent, impacts on how they cope with procedural provisions as set by particular institutions. We should therefore expand the focus of analyses on constitutional politics covering a longer time-horizon and the parliamentary and federal environment. It was supposed that coalitions, a symmetry of constitutional politics and ordinary law-making, party organizational ties or other factors might foster the willingness for agreements, irrespective of a high number of veto players.

Two case studies supported the theoretical assumptions, but nuanced the picture. In Canada with its majoritarian parliamentarism and provinces lacking veto capacity in exclusive federal legislative matters, constitutional politics with its necessity to organize cross-party and cross-level consent tended to be perceived as an extraordinary field of law-making. At least some provinces insisted on maximum positions, followed a competitive interaction style and tried to add even more veto players to strengthen their position. These additional veto players (referenda, national parliaments) were not included in the framework of frequent interactions and negotiations. That made it difficult to adopt constitutional amendments, just as it is expected by institutionalist theories. Therefore, implicit constitutional change dominates, with governments and courts as key actors.

In the other case Germany, constitutional amendments were frequently adopted under varying party majorities. Here we found a more collaborative interaction style. This was explained by the successful operation of the Bundesrat as a key component of German federalism which has socialized the Länder more into federal politics in a way in which the Canadian provinces have not. Moreover, coalitions eased constitutional amendment. The actors used the existing complex practices of conflict management and often negotiated constitutional amendments as parts of 'normal' legislation. But even when the willingness to cooperate was higher in this case, it was mostly limited to issues of state organization and rarely spilled over to the more controversial rights or to adopting opposition bills.

Large-scale reforms of the federal constitution are similarly rare in both cases. Even frequent amendments tended to re-confirm institutional key decisions. This corresponds with findings of other studies: While the goal of constitutional amendments was often to re-cut some of the systemic features because they are now interpreted as "pathologies" (Colino, 2010; Broschek, 2015), the empirical evidence is mixed (Benz and Broschek, 2013).

The findings should inspire more research on how actors' strategies within the parliamentary and federal environment can neutralize the impact of particular institutional restrictions. Constitutional engineers must consider the fact that rigidity rules and other special instruments are ineffective under certain conditions. It is interesting that the study's observed practices of constitutional politics are conform with the much broader patterns of majoritarian and consensus democracies that were discovered by Lijphart (2012). Obviously it might be worth bringing such more comprehensive and more focused analyses in a deeper dialogue.

Moreover, more research is needed concerning the interdependence of explicit constitutional amendments (as prevalent in federations with more collaborative constitutional politics) and implicit constitutional change (as prevalent in other federations) because the legitimation and rationale of these forms of change vary. Finally, the quality of constitutional policies in both groups of cases should be compared in detail. The correspondence of the group characteristics with Lijphart's types of democracy does not necessarily imply that more consensus orientation really leads to kinder, gentler constitutions, as Lijphart's (2012: 274) conclusion for democracies suggests. Many observers of German constitutional politics are rather sceptical about the ability to solve constitutional problems by the observed mechanisms.

Notes

1. Burgess (2006) also analysed some federations that are not democracies according to several democracy indices. This article only considers federations which are characterised as free by Freedom House.
2. The analysis is based on a narrow understanding of constitution, following the definition by the Canadian Department of Justice (http://www.justice.gc.ca/eng/csj-sjc/just/05.html). The information was compiled from Parliament of Canada (2014, 2015); Maton (2011).
3. The nomination of Senators in Canada was reformed, but most of them are not elected.
4. The data were compiled from http://dipbt.bundestag.de/dip21.web/searchDocuments.do.
5. Examples were the introduction of the right of EU foreigners to take part in local elections (1992, caused by Maastricht treaty); the asylum right novel (1993, argued to be caused by an otherwise unstoppable migration from post-Socialist states); or the obligation of the state to promote equal rights for women and men (1994, element of a package deal).

Disclosure statement

No potential conflict of interest was reported by the author.

References

Albert, R. (2015), Constitutional amendment by stealth, *McGill Law Journal*, Vol.60, No.4, pp.673–736.

Axelrod, R. (1984), *The Evolution of Cooperation*. New York: Basic Books.

Baier, G. (2012), Canada: Federal and sub-national constitutional practices, in M. Burgess and G.A. Tarr (eds), *Constitutional Dynamics in Federal Systems*, pp.174–192. Montreal: McGill-Queen's University Press.

Banting, K.G. and Simeon, R. (eds). (1985), *Redesigning the State: The Politics of Constitutional Change*. Toronto: University of Toronto Press.

Bednar, J. (2013), Constitutional change in federations: The role of complementary institutions, in A. Benz and J. Broschek (eds), *Federal Dynamics: Continuity, Change, and the Varieties of Federalism*, pp.277–296. Oxford: Oxford University Press.

Bednar, J., Chen, Y., Liu, T.X. and Page, S.E. (2012), Behavioral spillovers and cognitive load in multiple games: An experimental study, *Games and Economic Behavior*, Vol.74, No.1, pp.12–31.

Benz, A. (2003), Konstruktive Vetospieler im Mehrebenensystem, in R. Mayntz and W. Streeck (eds), *Die Reformierbarkeit der Demokratie*, pp.205–236. Frankfurt: Campus.

Benz, A. and Broschek, J. (eds) (2013), *Federal Dynamics: Continuity, Change, and the Varieties of Federalism*. Oxford: Oxford University Press.

Broschek, J. (2015), Pathways of federal reform: Australia, Canada, Germany, and Switzerland, *Publius: The Journal of Federalism*, Vol.45, No.1, pp.51–76.

Burgess, M. (2006), *Comparative Federalism, Theory and Practice*. London: Routledge.

Cairns, A.C. (1985), The politics of constitutional renewal in Canada, in K.G. Banting and R. Simeon (eds), *The Politics of Constitutional Change in Industrial Nations*, pp.95–145. London: McMillan.

Closa, C. (2012), Constitutional rigidity and procedures for ratifying constitutional reforms in EU member states, in A. Benz and F. Knüpling (eds), *Changing Federal Constitutions*, pp.281–310. Opladen: Barbara Budrich.

Colino, C. (2010), Understanding federal change: Types of federalism and institutional evolution in the Spanish and German federal systems, in J. Erk and W. Swenden (eds), *New Directions in Federalism Studies*, pp.16–33. London: Routledge.

Elazar, D.J. (1987), *Exploring Federalism*. Tuscaloosa, AL: University of Alabama Press.

Elster, J. (2000), *Ulysses Unbound: Studies in Rationality, Precommitment, and Constraints*. Cambridge: Cambridge University Press.

Erk, J. and Swenden, W. (2010), The new wave of federalism studies, in W. Swenden and J. Erk (eds), *New Directions in Federalism Studies*, pp.1–15. London: Routledge.

Ferejohn, J. (1997), The politics of imperfection: The amendment of constitutions, *Law and Social inquiry*, Vol.22, No.2, pp.501–530.

Ferejohn, J., Rakov J. and Riley, J. (eds) (2001), *Constitutional Culture and Democratic Rule*. Cambridge: Cambridge University Press.

Filippov, M., Ordeshook, P.C. and Shvetsova, O. (2004), *Designing Federalism: A Theory of Self-sustainable Federal Institutions*. Cambridge: Cambridge University Press.

Ginsburg, T. and Melton, J. (2014), *Does the Constitutional Amendment Rule Matter at All?* University of Chicago Public Law & Legal Theory Working Paper No. 472.

Hoennige, C., Kneip, S. and Lorenz, A. (eds) (2011), *Verfassungswandel im Mehrebenensystem*. Wiesbaden: VS.

Lazar, H. and McLean, J. (2000), Non-constitutional reform and the Canadian federation: The only game in town, in R.-O. Schulze and R. Sturm (eds), *The Politics of Constitutional Reform in North America*, pp.149–175. Opladen: Leske+Budrich.

Lehmbruch, G. (2000), *Parteienwettbewerb im Bundesstaat*. Opladen: Westdeutscher Verlag.

Lijphart, A. (2012), *Patterns of Democracy: Government Forms and Performance in Thirty-six Countries*. London: Yale University Press.

Livingston, W.S. (1952), A note on the nature of federalism, *Political Science Quarterly*, Vol.67, pp.81–95.

Lorenz, A. (2005), How to measure constitutional rigidity: Four concepts and two alternatives, *Journal of Theoretical Politics*, Vol.17, No.3, pp.339–361.

Lorenz, A. (2007), *Föderalismusreform & Co. Warum ändert sich das Grundgesetz?* Berlin: Humboldt-Universität.

Lutz, D.S. (1994), Toward a theory of constitutional amendment, *American Political Science Review*, Vol.88, No.2, pp.355–370.

March, J.G. and Olsen, J.P. (1989), *Rediscovering Institutions. The Organizational Basis of Politics*. New York: Free Press.

Maton, W.F. (2011), Canadian constitutional documents. A legal history. Available at http://www.solon.org/Constitutions/Canada/English/ (accessed 20 October 2015).

Moore, C. and Jacoby, W. (eds) (2010), *German Federalism in Transition. Reforms in a Consensual State*. London: Routledge.

North, D.C. (1990), *Institutions, Institutional Change and Economic Performance*. Cambridge: Cambridge University Press.

Parliament of Canada. (2014), The constitution since patriation: chronology. Available at http://www.parl.gc.ca/parlinfo/compilations/Constitution/ConstitutionSincePatriation.aspx (accessed 20 October 2015).

Parliament of Canada. (2015), LegisInfo (data bank). Available at http://www.parl.gc.ca/LegisInfo/Search.aspx?Language=E&Mode=1 (accessed 20 October 2015).

Riker, W.H. (1964), *Federalism. Origin, Operation, Significance*. Boston: Little, Brown.

Rodden, J. (2004), Comparative federalism and decentralization. on meaning and measurement, *Comparative Politics*, Vol.36, No.4, pp.481–500.

Russell, P.H. (2004), *Constitutional Odyssey. Can Canadians Become a Sovereign People?* Toronto: University of Toronto Press.

Russell, P.H. (2010), Constitution, in J.C. Courtney and D.E. Smith (eds), *The Oxford Handbook of Canadian Politics*, pp.21–38. New York: Oxford University Press.

Scharpf, F.W. (1997), *Games Real Actors Play: Actor-centered Institutionalism in Policy Research*. Boulder, CO: Westview Press.

Scharpf, F.W. (2005), No exit from the joint decision trap? Can German federalism reform itself? *MPIfG Working Paper*, Vol.5, No.8. Available at http://cadmus.eui.eu//handle/1814/3373.

Scharpf, F.Z.W. (2009), *Föderalismusreform: Kein Ausweg aus der Politikverflechtungsfalle?* Frankfurt a.M.: Campus.

Thorlakson, L. (2009), Patterns of party integration, influence and autonomy in seven federations, *Party Politics*, Vol.15, No.2, pp.157–177.

Tsebelis, G. (2000), Veto players and institutional analysis, *Governance*, Vol.13, No.4, pp.441–474.

Index

For Product Safety Concerns and Information please contact our EU
representative GPSR@taylorandfrancis.com
Taylor & Francis Verlag GmbH, Kaufingerstraße 24, 80331 München, Germany

www.ingramcontent.com/pod-product-compliance
Ingram Content Group UK Ltd.
Pitfield, Milton Keynes, MK11 3LW, UK
UKHW021439080625
459435UK00011B/310